HONEST
WEIGHT

HONEST WEIGHT

The Story of Toledo Scale

Bob Terry

To order additional copies of this book, contact:
Xlibris Corporation
1-888-7-XLIBRIS
www.Xlibris.com
Orders@Xlibris.com

CONTENTS

Part I
Theobald

Part II
Bennett

Part III
McIntosh

Part IV
et al.

For my wife and family,
and for all past Toledo Scale people who,
over the century, played parts large and small in this story…
with a special bow to the prime entrepreneurs;
Henry Theobald, Hugh Bennett,
Harris McIntosh and Ben Dillon.

ACKNOWLEDGMENTS

Though this is a work of fact, I have taken certain storytelling liberties. All events and people named in this book are real. The dialogue in the first 15 or 20 years is based on oral history, and represents undocumented conversations the individuals had as told to, and passed on by their peers. Where the sequence or narrative strays from true nonfiction, I have tried to remain faithful to the actual events and real characters.

I'm indebted to many good people, including the late Walter Fink who left an unpublished record that detailed events during Toledo Scale's first 50 years. I extracted many facts and conversations from this record. Over his long career, Fink worked closely with company presidents Theobald, Bennett, and McIntosh. I'm also grateful to executive secretary Bessie Deain, who placed Fink's original manuscript in my care in 1976 when the company moved their headquarters to Columbus, Ohio.

Thanks also to Tom Quertinmont who arranged for me to have access to the company archives which included correspondence, photos and copies of *Toledo System* magazines from the time the company was started. I'm also grateful to Tom's father Ed Quertinmont, Ted Metcalf, Donivan Hall, Bernard Stanton, and Clarence Weinandy for the personal time and help they gave me as I gathered information for this story…and for the encouragement of countless others.

And a very special thanks to Janet Schryver for her excellent help in designing, editing, proofing and correcting the manuscript.

PROLOGUE

The Pennsylvania hills flashed by the train's dining car window, reflecting the fading sunlight. John H. Patterson gazed pensively out the window. He was probably edgy, not really seeing the moving landscape. *I wonder if I really should continue this trip?* he might have asked himself. He was traveling from Dayton to New York this cool evening in the early fall of 1900. From New York he had tickets booked on a ship to Europe where he planned to further expand his distribution network for cash registers. He brooded as he sipped coffee in the dining car.

Once I board the ocean liner I'll be away from Dayton for months, he likely mused. He was concerned about what could happen in his absence. For one thing, his aggressive young General Manager, Henry Theobald, wanted to make some manufacturing changes in the plant, and he didn't want to think about any changes until he returned. *No*, he probably thought, *Henry's got to learn to take orders. Maybe he's getting too big for his britches!*

A dining car waiter overheard Patterson mumble. He saw a rather tall, thin prosperous looking man in late middle age. After a moment he remembered seeing him on this train before. "Anything wrong, sir?" he might have asked. "No, no," Patterson might have grumbled. "Just business concerns...don't be troubled," he may have said, waving the waiter away.

Sipping his now cold coffee, Patterson pondered. He looked back 16 years to the time he and his brothers had made their living buying coal in Dayton at nearby mines, and selling it in small quantities directly to consumers. Even with plenty of cash customers they never seemed to make any money. Patterson suspected the profits were lost to petty pilferage from the cash box. He was already 40-years-old at the time. He probably told himself then, *I have to make a move soon.*

Against his brother's wishes he had installed a novel new product called a "cash register" which had recently been invented by James Ritty of Dayton. Ritty was a tavern owner. He was certain his bartenders were stealing from him and developed his cash register to stop the thefts. Within six months of acquiring his own cash register, Patterson's coal business was showing a substantial profit. He concluded the new cash registers just might have more potential for his future than the retail coal business.

Now 16 years have passed since that day in 1884 when he bought a controlling interest in the National Manufacturing Company of Dayton for $6,500…a risky new enterprise that made and sold cash registers. His purchase was so ridiculed by other Dayton businessmen, he recalled, that he lost his confidence the same day he bought control. The next day he offered the seller $2,000 to release him from the deal. The offer was refused…he owned the company.

So in December 1884 he changed the firm's name to the National Cash Register Company. He had acquired 13 employees, an old plant in a run-down section of Dayton and several cash register patents. He had serious doubts he would succeed in his new venture.

Yet in the 16 years since, Patterson had almost single-handedly created a cash register market with his National Cash Register Company. Now, at age 56, he had led his company to dominate the market he had created. His judgment had been vindicated with brains, determination, and hard work. He had started with a product nobody thought they needed and didn't know how to use.

The cash register had been vigorously opposed by those who had to use it. Patterson overcame the resistance of thousands of poorly paid clerks who had—over the years—come to consider a little pilferage to be a normal part of their compensation. He faced the resentment of any "new fangled machine". He created unique ways to demonstrate the payback, efficiency and economy of the cash register in a system he called "creative selling".

Patterson developed innovative, new advertising practices. He set up what was believed to be the first training school for salesmen where he taught that knowledge of the product was a salesman's best tool. He conducted and organized revival-style meetings in the form of sales conventions. He occasionally provided salesmen with a new wardrobe at company expense, claiming that a salesman's appearance was important if he was to be believed. At the same time, he set up a customer service operation to maintain cash registers in top condition.

Patterson was among the first to establish closed quota areas in which he guaranteed an exclusive territory for each salesman. He paid generous commissions for sales performance, and employed many new ideas within his creative selling approach. He insisted employees be loyal and efficient. At the same time he often bullied them and treated them badly. They never knew what to expect from him…one moment encouragement, the next, rage.

His mind snapped back to the present as the train approached New York. *No, I dare not go to Europe now*, he likely concluded. *I'm just going to take the next train right back to Dayton and see what's been going on. Some of those people might take advantage of my absence!*

Patterson's return train reached Dayton late at night. He quickly secured a coach and team. "Take me right to the NCR plant," he probably said gruffly, "and wait for me there. I'll just be a few minutes and then you can take me home." The driver recognized him. By now he was one of Dayton's first citizens. "Surely, Mr. Patterson," he would have replied. "Right away. We'll just leave all this baggage right in the coach then." Patterson nodded, as he impatiently climbed aboard.

The driver slapped the reins on the back of the team and they left the train station for the 20-minute trip to the plant. He was clearly agitated, looking out at everything they passed. Picking up on his passenger's mood, the driver hurried the team along.

"Wait right here," Patterson likely said as the coach arrived at the NCR gate. "I need to look around a bit." He stalked off to the security gate, surprising the sleepy guard. "Mr. Patterson! Wha-what are you doing here?" he may have asked. "I need to look around in the plant," Patterson probably barked, breezing right through to the factory floor.

He needed to look only a moment. "The damn fool!" he likely thought. It was clear the changes Henry Theobald said he wanted to make were already in progress. They involved setting up a more efficient production system, and while Patterson secretly thought the changes might work, he was determined they shouldn't be made until he returned from Europe and could watch over them personally. "I told Henry not to do this now," he would have remembered. "He went ahead anyway. I told him we'd talk about it when I got back. We'll see about this!"

Patterson hurried back out to the gate and might have asked the guard, "You know our maintenance foreman, don't you?" The guard would have nodded. "He lives just down the street. Go get him for me now," he might have said. "I'll wait right here." The guard rushed off and returned minutes later with the maintenance foreman who arrived puffing, still tucking in his shirttail. "What's up, Mr. Patterson?" he likely asked unsure.

"I want something done—completely done—before seven in the morning when people come to work," Patterson would have ordered clearly. "Get whatever help you need tonight…" The foreman probably nodded, listening carefully.

"Now, here's what I want you to do…"

PART I

Theobald

"*I am looking for an honest man.*"
Diogenes the Cynic

"*To be honest, as the world goes, is to be one man picked out of ten thousand.*"
Shakespeare: Hamlet: II, ii, 179

"*Thou art weighed in the balances, and art found wanting.*"
The Bible: Daniel: 5:25—28

CHAPTER 1

"I just got fired!"

As usual, Henry Theobald came awake all at once. He was built thin, shorter than average, but full of nervous energy. He stretched a moment, then got out of bed with even more than his usual eagerness and enthusiasm, brushing the mustache he had grown when he was 25 to make himself look older. His innate intelligence showed on his face.

It had been 15 years since he started work at NCR as John Patterson's personal stenographer, when the company was just a year old. His progress had been rapid. He rose to become Patterson's private secretary, then to secretary of the corporation and a member of its board of directors, then chairman of its executive committee. A year previously, at the age of 34, he had been named General Manager of the corporation.

His native selling ability had also been recognized. Patterson had sent him to Europe to restructure NCR's sales organization in several countries there. He knew the way cash registers were successfully sold. There was a place to keep paper money with a divided cash drawer and a convenient way to make change. A bell rang when the drawer was opened. Merchants were sold on the idea that this helped keep clerks honest. And when an optional adding attachment was sold with the cash register, the merchant could read the total of a day's receipts right on the register.

He was pleased with the way things were going this morning. Patterson had left Dayton and was expected to be in Europe for months. As general manager he was now in charge of everything. It felt good. Yet this morning was special.

Striding into the kitchen, he later told his friends that he had greeted his wife and nine-year-old son Robert with a hearty greeting. "Good morning, Mary…and Bob! And what do we have for breakfast this morning?" he asked. "My, Henry, aren't you full of pep this morning," she replied as she served his breakfast.

"I'm just eager to get to work on those changes in the plant I told you about," he said, digging into his usual breakfast of bacon and eggs. "I've already got them started. If my calculations are even close, our production costs will go down about 10% within two or three months and our employees will make a better product. John can't help but be pleased when he sees the results."

Mary cocked her head. "But I thought you said Mr. Patterson didn't go along with your ideas," she recalled. "Well, he didn't," Henry recalled. "But before he gets back I will have proved they work. When John sees the results, he'll just leave the changes in place. He'll like the results but he probably won't even say anything…they weren't his idea. That's the way he is".

She brushed his coat and led him to the door. "I just hope you don't cause any trouble, Henry," she said. "I saw Katherine Patterson with her young son and daughter a few days ago, and she said she had upset her husband when she complained he was going to Europe without them," she recalled. "He's probably cranky already." Theobald replied, "Don't worry, dear. Who can object to saving money and making better products? I'll see you tonight," he added as he left the house and began his usual brisk walk towards the plant. The sun appeared in a cloudless sky. It promised to be a beautiful, fall day.

Theobald was early. He usually arrived ahead of most employees. As he approached the plant, he saw that there was a small crowd gathered around something on the front lawn. The crowd noticed him. They began to slink away.

As he came closer, he thought he could finally see what it was. "It looks like furniture. Someone had put office furniture out on the lawn," he mused. Coming closer he recognized it. He recalled thinking, "Good Lord, it looks like *my* office furniture. My desk, my chairs, my coat rack, my bookcase, all my books and paintings…even the carpet! It's everything!"

A guard stopped him as he approached. "I'm sorry, Mr. Theobald…you're not to enter the property," he said quietly. "Mr. Patterson returned in the middle of the night."

Theobald understood. Patterson knew how to send an unmistakable message.

He turned and slowly walked back home.

Theobald picked up his pace as he approached his home. On the way he speculated on the best way to break the news to his wife. He paused a moment, then entered firmly. "Mary, where are you?" he yelled. Mary came to the front door from the kitchen wiping her hands on a towel, a concerned expression on her face. She knew that something was terribly wrong…he never returned home until evening.

Before she could speak, Theobald said, "Looks like you were more right than I was, Mary." He smiled, determined to show her that this setback couldn't get him down. "I just got fired! In a most unusual way! It was quite clever of the old man…"

"Fired!" she cried, as tears sprang to her eyes. "Oh, Henry! What are we going to do?" Theobald took her in his arms. "Now, don't worry, Mary," he soothed. "We'll be fine. Everything will work out for the best," he said. "We have a little money ahead, and…"

"Yes, but what are we going to do now? How will we live? What are *you* going to do?" he remembered her asking. "I've already got some ideas," he said. "When you settle down a bit, we'll talk about it."

"Let's talk about it right now," she replied, pulling herself together. "I'm perfectly all right. It was just such a shock. After fifteen years! And you were doing so well. I want to know what we'll say to Bob when he gets home from school. So tell me what you're thinking…you know I'll support you whatever you want to do," she said, giving him a hug.

"Well, maybe I never talked about it, but I've wanted to have a business of my own for some time now," Theobald said quietly. "Really. John Patterson showed me the way," he said. "I learned a lot from him. Not just about how to make something, but about how to sell it too. And about running a business. If he can do it, as strange as he is, I can do it too."

"But what kind of a business?" she asked. "It takes a lot of money to start a business. Where will you get the money? We don't have nearly enough…I know that."

"Well, I met a lot of people while working for NCR," he said. "And I heard from a lot of inventors with new ideas. There's a fellow over in Springfield who has a patent on a cash register that NCR didn't want to buy, even though it looks superior to any of theirs. As for the capital, there are some men I met in New Jersey, on one of my business trips there, who hinted that they might be interested in investing in any company I was involved with. I'll check them out too, to see if they meant it."

"You mean you're thinking about competing with *John Patterson?*" he remembered Mary replying. "He's the biggest! He's strong and he's tough. Why, you told me he practically owns the market. And he will not like it one bit if you get involved with cash registers and try to fight him."

"I think he just might expect it of me," Theobald answered with a smile. "After all, I learned the business at his knee," he said. "I know where he's good…and I know where he's vulnerable. I really think I can beat him at his own game."

"But that's not the only idea," he reported saying. "There's this fellow up in Toledo with a little business that makes computing scales he invented. Computing scales might be a better buy for a merchant than even a cash register. A merchant can make change out of a shoebox under the counter, and many still do. A cash register helps, but it's not vital," he admitted.

"But a computing scale tells him how much to charge for his merchandise," he said. Theobald began waving his arms with enthusiasm. "It converts any commodity in his store into money at a glance and tells him how much money to put in the shoe box. It can be even more valuable than a cash register. So I'll talk to this inventor too. Maybe we'll make 'em both. Cash registers *and* computing scales. What a story we could tell then!"

As soon as Mary settled down, Theobald went to the office he kept in his home. He sorted through some papers for addresses, sat down and wrote about a dozen letters to everyone he thought might be interested in starting a new business, or had a patent he might buy. The first, addressed to a Mr. Pfeifer in Springfield, Ohio, asked for a meeting to discuss the prospect of buying his cash register company or patents. The second, to Allen DeVilbiss, Jr. in Toledo, requested a meeting to discuss a possible purchase of his two-year-old DeVilbiss Computing Scale company.

The third he addressed to Lenox S. Rose, Madison, New Jersey. He decided to wait before mailing it, until he had worked out all his options. It took the longest to write. He had become acquainted with Rose and several of his friends on trips to the New York area while working for NCR. He knew Rose was wealthy. More important, he believed Rose was impressed with his business acumen. So he saw him as a potential source of finance for the new company he had in mind.

Theobald wanted to explain his ideas thoroughly…but first came negotiations with Pfeifer, DeVilbiss, and any others who might respond with products, patents or ideas he could use. There were dozens of possibilities. He planned to investigate them all.

Theobald heard first from Pfeifer in Springfield. His cash register patents were now owned by Mast, Foos Company who had intended to manufacture them. But second thoughts about competing with John Patterson's powerful NCR changed their minds. Since no cash registers had been manufactured yet, they were willing to talk about selling the patents. Theobald traveled to nearby Springfield, looked over the several patents and made an offer that was just barely within his means. The offer was accepted the following morning.

Theobald was in the cash register business again. He eagerly looked forward to competing with Patterson, his former mentor.

Within days he rented a small plant in Springfield, and hired Pfeifer as superintendent for $24.00 per week. Pfeifer employed a few men and began making the patterns, tools, dies and fixtures needed to produce the cash registers.

Theobald was just getting his cash register manufacturing plans organized when a letter from Allen DeVilbiss, Jr. arrived from Toledo. In it he learned that the total assets of the two-year-old DeVilbiss Computing Scale Company could be acquired for $195,000. Theobald would assume none of the liabilities. The listed assets detailed machinery tools, patterns, sample trunks, furniture, raw material and finished scales, plus a horse and wagon. It also included real property containing a new, two-story factory. This building on the Northeast corner of Albion and Bishop streets had a total floor area of 9,300 square feet.

Allen DeVilbiss, Jr. was an inventor like his father. Dr. Allen DeVilbiss, Sr. was a physician who specialized in eye, ear, nose and throat medicine. He had invented a medicinal atomizer to spray the sore throats of his patients. Dr. DeVilbiss had founded the DeVilbiss Company, a small company that built and sold his spray atomizer to other doctors, along with a line of improved surgical instruments. His shop was in the basement of his home at 13th and Jackson streets, and his two sons, Allen Jr. and Thomas worked with him.

Tom expanded on the spray technology with the invention of a perfume atomizer. Later he developed spray painting technology and also a painting apparatus. The DeVilbiss Company grew slowly, with the medicinal atomizer as its prime product. Allen Jr. inherited his father's interest in mechanics and invention. When business was slack, his father allowed him to make contracts on job work. Among other jobs he secured, Allen Jr. was hired to make a model beam scale for a man named Brough. He became interested in weighing machines and conceived the idea of an automatic computing pendulum scale. He experimented with his computing scale idea in the basement of the DeVilbiss home where the medical spray devices were assembled.

Allen Jr. studied the beam scale with its hand-operated poises. It occurred to him that scales could be made entirely automatic by means of a pendulum connected to the main lever supporting the platter. The pendulum swung outward, automatically counterbalancing the load on the platter.

By 1898 he had produced several prototypes in the basement. Allen Jr. started the DeVilbiss Computing Scale Company the next year. For capital he sold a one-third interest to Louis Rakestraw and a one-sixth interest to Chase Reed. Officers were F. M. Rakestraw, president, Allen DeVilbiss, Jr., vice president, and Louis Rakestraw, secretary. Since the company quickly needed even more capital, Allen Jr. sold more of his interest and the Rakestraw family soon acquired control.

DeVilbiss sold his first computing scale to Felker's Meat Market, a nearby butcher shop on Adams Street. Each night after the butcher shop closed, he would walk past it and peek into the window to see if the scale was still on the counter. His confidence grew every day it remained in use.

The butcher liked the scale because it computed the selling price for him quickly. Even more important, it eliminated the need to give away a little extra meat on every transaction, as he had to do up till now with his balance scale. Housewives would say, "Let me have a pound of sirloin," or "I'll take half a pound of round steak, please." The price per pound was on a little sign usually stuck into the meat. If the request was for a pound of sirloin at nine cents a pound, the butcher didn't dare exceed nine cents for the transaction.

The butcher had to place a weight, or several weights to match the requested weight, on one side of a balance and the meat on the other side. He would usually have to take the piece off and trim it closely without going under the weight requested. Then he put it back on the scale. The housewife would watch the balance with a critical eye until it moved down in her favor. She expected to get a little more than she had asked for…for free. Only then would she nod her approval.

The DeVilbiss computing scale changed all that. When the butcher first got it, he would eagerly show his customers how the scale chart was used to multiply the weight times the price to compute the selling price. "Now you won't have to worry about me making a mistake and overcharging you. The scale does the computing—not me!" he told them. It was much more price-accurate than either a balance or beam scale, he told them. His customers usually smiled their approval at the personal attention. They liked the way he looked out for them.

After using the DeVilbiss scale and educating his customers for a few weeks, he began to place a requested cut of meat on the scale, read off the computed price firmly, then look at the customer for approval. Unless the cut was significantly heavier than requested, he got an OK nod. This saved him time too…he didn't have to trim a piece nearly as often.

"It's odd," he told his friends. "Customers don't challenge us as much now as they did with the beam scale. But the best thing is that I no longer have to give away some of my meat every time. That always cost me. Still, I wonder what it amounts to in dollars and cents?"

Within weeks he came to realize the scale increased his profits much more than he would have guessed. He had happy customers. And he was making money. So he told all his butcher friends. They, in turn, began to call on Allen DeVilbiss, Jr. at his family home on Jackson Street to get a demonstration. His computing scale was catching on.

Young DeVilbiss was proud of his invention. Yet he knew he hadn't invented the first computing scale. There were others in the market before his. He discovered that a man named Phinney in Pawtucket, Rhode Island had built and sold a few cylinder-type beam computing scales as early as 1870. And that Julius E. Pitrap of Gallipolis, Ohio, was granted a patent on a beam computing scale that used a spring counterbalance in 1885. About that same time the Computing Scale Company of America in Dayton, Ohio, produced and sold scales based on the Pitrap patent.

But his DeVilbiss scale was the easiest to use. And the most consistently accurate, because his scale used his patented invention of a pendulum weighing principle that measured weight against weight. He knew a spring counterbalance changed with temperature. His scale was more accurate. It used the law of gravity. An immutable law he knew he could depend on.

DeVilbiss thought of himself as an inventor…not a businessman. He discovered that if he was going to be able to sell any significant number of scales, it would be necessary to do it on the installment plan. Usually 10% cash with the order or $5.00—whichever was greater—and at least $5.00 monthly with a maximum of ten months time. He had already traded the stock of his company to others for the money he needed to go into production.

DeVilbiss knew that a truly large market existed. As a new century approached, there were thousands of grocery stores and meat markets using non-computing even-balance and beam scales. Groceries and meat were sold in separate stores. Merchants were interested because of the computed value feature of the new scale. It took the human-computation factor, with its high potential for error, out of the merchant/customer equation, which pleased both the merchant and the customer.

Merchants knew their customers were always looking for a little extra…and usually got it. Customers believed the merchant already knew too many ways to cheat them and the balance or beam scale gave them another. Customers always looked to be sure nobody's thumb was on the scale. Merchants were not to be trusted. Yet for some reason, if the merchant had a new machine that took him out of the loop, he suddenly was trustworthy after all.

Yet without money to make a good capital investment, 29-year-old Allen DeVilbiss, Jr. simply could not afford to be in the scale business. Nor was he interested in the business side. A rather big man, young DeVilbiss already had a small paunch. He rarely exercised, preferring to spend his time tinkering in the basement of the family home on Jackson Street.

So when he learned that Henry Theobald might want to buy the company, he was eager to sell because of a profit-sharing agreement he had with the actual owners. He talked it over with them, then invited Theobald to visit. DeVilbiss wrote that he would meet him at the train station.

Henry Theobald had no trouble recognizing DeVilbiss as he stepped off the train from Dayton. "You must be Allen DeVilbiss," he recalled saying, as he shook hands and smiled. "And of course, you're Henry Theobald," DeVilbiss replied, trying to size up his smaller visitor. "My carriage is right outside. Let's get a porter for your luggage and drop it off at your hotel. That way we can go out to the shop right away, take a look at what we're doing and get right down to business."

"Splendid! I'm eager to get started," Theobald said. "Let's go."

Several days later, Theobald sat down in his Toledo hotel room to gather his thoughts before leaving for New York on the morning train. He had an appointment with Lenox Rose and several of his friends the following morning. It was the most important meeting of his life. These people offered him his best chance to find backers who would invest in his proposed new company.

Once in New York he checked into the Hotel Imperial. The meeting with Rose and his friends would take place here. He stared at the numbers again, reflecting, *It's pretty clear the building and other physical material doesn't add up to even one-third of the $195,000 he wants. So he figures his patents are worth $125,000 to $130,000. But then, I'm damned if I don't agree with him. That pendulum principle is the right one. It will let us make a scale that can lead the marketplace.*

Theobald sat down to work out his campaign to sell his ideas so they would be willing to supply the needed capital. On Hotel Imperial stationery he wrote his sales and profit forecast:

Hotel Imperial
Broadway at 32nd Street
New York, New York

Estimate of profits on sales of only 300 scales and 150 registers per month.

Cost to make 300 scales at $15 each—		$4,500
Cost to sell " " " 30 " —		9,000
	Total monthly cost	13,500

Average selling price of scales = $60

Monthly sales 300 x $60 =		18,000
	Monthly profit	4,500
	Yearly profit	$54,000

Registers—Average selling price $100. May be much larger.

Cost to make 150 registers at $25 each—		3,750
" " sell " " " 50 " —		7,500
	Monthly Cost	*11,250*

Monthly Sales 150 x $100		*15,000*
	Monthly profit	*3,750*
	Yearly "	*$45,000*

Total profits   **$99,000**

There was a knock. Theobald rose, took a deep breath, adjusted his vest and answered the door with a smile. Standing there ready to enter were Lenox Rose, Mathew Gay, and Edwin Young. These were men Theobald had met on his travels for NCR. They knew and respected Theobald from their previous dealings, but did not know him well enough to call him a friend.

Gay was president of Blanchard Bros., Lane & Co., a Newark construction management firm and Rose was treasurer and superintendent of the same company. Young was New Jersey manager for the Standard Oil Company. All three were financially successful. They had money to invest.

"Come in, gentlemen, come in! It's good to see you all again," he recalled saying. "I'm flattered you remember me so kindly...and delighted you accepted my invitation to examine this proposition. There's coffee and cigars...come in and make yourselves comfortable."

Henry Theobald was an extrovert, a charmer and a born salesman. Over his 15-year career with NCR, he learned even more about selling from John Patterson. Soon his guests were completely relaxed. The room was blue from their cigar smoke. Theobald had them hunched over his handwritten estimate of sales, discussing the numbers openly.

The men talked for several more hours. They questioned the plan. Gay asked, "How did you get the estimate to make scales at $15 each?" Theobald replied, "Because DeVilbiss is making them for about $13 right now. We need some new tooling, true, but the $15 estimate is still conservative."

Young was curious about Theobald's estimates. He asked, "Why do you say that the average selling price of your cash registers may be much higher than $100?" Theobald responded, "Because there are a number of higher priced models with popular new features and I expect they will sell the best."

The group discussed the sales estimates together again and again. They speculated with Theobald about what Patterson might do. They looked at existing competition for scales as well as cash registers. "How confident are you of these figures, Henry?" Lenox asked.

"Let me say that the estimates of sales on that paper are extremely conservative," Theobald said confidently. "I firmly believe that the results after a year will more than double my estimates." By lunchtime it appeared that Theobald's sales campaign had been persuasive.

A tentative agreement was reached. Again Theobald picked up a sheet of hotel stationery and wrote it out on the spot. Lenox Rose agreed to take it to his office that afternoon and have it formally typed up so they each could have a copy. Theobald wrote:

Hotel Imperial
Broadway at 32nd Street
New York, New York

SOME OF THE PRELIMINARY AGREEMENTS ON THE BASIS OF WHICH MESSRS. T, G, R, and Y, PROPOSE TO ORGANIZE A COMPANY

First: T proposes to give free title, patents, etc., to a cash register company and $30,000.00 in cash. G, R, and Y each propose to contribute $30,000.00 in cash, making a total of $120,000.00 in cash. They jointly propose to purchase the real estate and all the property of the scale company for $195,000.00, and pay for the same as follows:—each paying one quarter:

$25,000.00 on July 1, 1901; $10,000.00 January 1, 1902; $10,000.00 July 1, 1902; $25,000.00 in two years; $50,000.00 in five years; and $75,000.00 in ten years. These payments to be secured by first claim on the company at 5% interest.

Next : The two companies, (scale and cash register) are to be merged into a new company, of which T is to receive one-half interest, and G, R, and Y one-half interest jointly, or, one-sixth interest each. The new company to be the owner of the merged companies, and the management of the business shall principally be with Mr. T at a salary of $400.00 a month and traveling expenses.

The amount of capital stock and the final organization of the company to be arranged for, after the return of the parties who are to investigate the property, and if they deem it wise, to make payment of the $25,000.00 aforesaid on July 1st next. This $25,000.00 to be contributed in amounts of $6,250.00 by each of the parties.

Late in the afternoon, Lenox Rose returned to the hotel with four typed copies of the preliminary agreement Theobald had written out by hand…one copy for each of the four principals. Rose had made no changes. The next step, they agreed, was for Theobald to make arrangements for the three New Jersey investors to visit the DeVilbiss operation in Toledo, to inspect the property first hand. All three made the visit three weeks later. They were pleased with what they saw.

Theobald and his financial backers then offered to purchase the DeVilbiss Computing Scale Company for a total purchase price of $190,000.00. This was $5,000.00 less than the asking price. The offer was to be payable with $25,000 in cash, $155,000 in Toledo 5% 10-year bonds, and $10,000 in preferred stock.

The offer was accepted by the DeVilbiss scale company owners. Only then did Theobald discover that Allen DeVilbiss, Jr. no longer had a financial interest in the DeVilbiss Computing Scale Company. He had turned over his patent to the pendulum principle in a computing scale, for a 10% interest in the profits of the company, plus an annual salary of $1,500. He would also receive a one-time benefit of $75 for any patent issued in the future.

The real owners were the president of the DeVilbiss Computing Scale Company, F. M. Rakestraw, his brother and his two sons. They had bought out DeVilbiss. All four were also employed by the firm. DeVilbiss and the company sales manager, J. F. Pixley, had only the agreement that each was to receive 10% of the profits. F. M. Rakestraw showed that he had invested about $90,000 in the business up to the time of the sale.

This left a profit of $100,000 on the sale. The senior Rakestraw kept the $25,000 cash from the sale for himself. The inventor of the scale, Allen DeVilbiss, Jr., received only $10,000 out of the sale of the company he had founded…and none of it in cash. DeVilbiss got $8,000 in Toledo Bonds and $2,000 in Toledo Preferred. This was the 10% of profits mentioned in his agreement with Rakestraw. Yet he was pleased because Theobald offered him a position as superintendent of the new company at a higher salary than he had been earning. He was happy to still have a job...in the same building doing essentially the same thing.

On July 10, 1901 the new company was incorporated in New Jersey, the home state of the Eastern investors. As part of the agreement, Lenox Rose was listed as president, his cousin, John B. Rose as vice president and Ed Young as secretary. Even though he owned exactly half the company by himself—unlike the other investors—Henry Theobald agreed to become treasurer and general manager.

The new firm was named "Toledo Computing Scale and Cash Register Company."

CHAPTER 2

Patterson Makes an Offer

William McKinley was President of the United States in the first year of the 20th century. He had been the Governor of Ohio before being elected as president in a campaign managed by his friend Mark Hanna, a wealthy Cleveland industrialist and now a United States Senator from Ohio. Partly due to Hanna's influence, McKinley was a friend of business.

It was a time of robber barons and snake oil salesmen…of child labor and massive immigration from all the troubled nations of Europe. Patent medicines were uncontrolled. Many contained a tincture of opium called laudanum, or cocaine, or any number of other dangerous drugs. Others were worthless as medicine, largely made with alcohol, which did indeed help the user feel better for a brief while. In commerce, it was a time of dishonest weights and short measures. There were no regulations to control them. The buyer took all the risk. *Caveat emptor* ruled the land.

Many new ventures were started. Theobald moved fast with his. First, he concluded that the two-story building they acquired from the sale was too small to build both scales and cash registers. As soon as the DeVilbiss purchase was completed, he met with F. M. Rakestraw. "Mr. Rakestraw," he remembered saying, "I expect you're looking for ways to invest the funds you earned from the sale of DeVilbiss, and I have a proposition for you. Are you interested?"

"I'll certainly listen," Rakestraw replied. "What do you have in mind?"

"The thing is, the building we just bought is too small to manufacture both cash registers and scales. We need three or four times the amount of space we have. We need a new building, and I think that's an opportunity for you to invest your money at a higher return than you might otherwise expect."

Rakestraw replied, "Well, I'm interested. What are your plans?"

The two men reached a quick agreement.

Rakestraw agreed to build a three-story building on the corner of Monroe and Albion streets, just across an alley from the existing building. He agreed to accept 5% of the cost of the building as his fee for putting together the package and supervising the construction. To this total, the cost of the land was added to arrive at the total building cost. Toledo agreed to pay Rakestraw an annual rent equal to 5% of this total cost. By August 1901, only one month after the new company was founded, Rakestraw had let all the contracts for the new building.

On September 6, 1901, President McKinley was shot by anarchist Leon Czolgosz in Buffalo while visiting the Pan-American Exposition. He died eight days later on September 14. Within hours, vice-president Theodore Roosevelt was sworn in as president. Mark Hanna was crushed. He impulsively said, "Now look, that damned cowboy is President of the United States!"

Hanna knew that Roosevelt would not be as friendly to business. He was right. Roosevelt soon moved to enforce the Sherman Antitrust Act…a federal law that forbids any restraint on trade or commerce. Business practices were destined to change. Reform was in the air. It led to the breakup of Rockefeller's Standard Oil trust. Teddy Roosevelt awoke the nation's conscience.

Meanwhile, the new building was completed by the end of November. It was 130 feet long, 53 feet wide at the Monroe Street side and 47 feet wide at the alley between the two buildings. Each floor was about 6,500 square feet in size, totaling about 19,500 square feet of space.

Adding in the original building's 9,300 square feet, the company had a total of about 28,800 square feet of manufacturing space. A covered hallway was built across the alley, from the second floor of the original building to the second floor of the new three-story building.

In Springfield, plans had progressed to manufacture cash registers. The first two were shipped from Springfield in mid-November to Baker Printing Company in Newark, operated by a friend of Lenox Rose. They were broken in shipment and had to be replaced.

Since the new three-story building was finished, Theobald closed down the Springfield shop. He had all cash register parts, along with material, fixtures, tools and dies loaded on railroad cars and shipped to Toledo. He was able to start cash register production on the second floor of the new building on December 16, 1901. Since sales of computing scales were going well, scale production was expanded to include the third floor. It also continued in the original building.

The Toledo cash register had nearly one hundred variations, sizes, and styles. Prices ranged from $50 to $250. Theobald was now ready to seriously compete with his former mentor and show him how superior cash registers should be manufactured, sold and serviced.

By the end of May 1902, cash registers were selling at the rate of 100 a month. The selling organization at that time consisted of only 40 men. Each was charged with selling both scales and cash registers. Theobald's original estimate was to sell 150 cash registers a month, and he was already two-thirds of the way there in only five months. Considering the small selling force, and the fact that the cash registers were being built largely by men without experience in manufacturing them, this was a very credible showing. Both Theobald and Rose were pleased.

But Theobald's delight was short lived. NCR had been watching. John Patterson had great respect for Henry Theobald. He knew him well. And he concluded it was time to stop him.

On the 27th of May—in the first month Toledo sold 100 cash registers—a Mr. High from NCR showed up unexpectedly, asking to see Theobald. High had been friendly enough with Theobald at NCR. He counted on being able to see him without an appointment. He was quickly ushered into Theobald's office, where he was warmly greeted. In a jocular tone, High complimented Theobald's office furniture, joking about the way Patterson had let him know he had been fired. After a few moments of social talk, he passed Theobald a written message from John Patterson.

Patterson's message asked that Theobald arrange for a meeting the following Monday, between Patterson and two or three of his officers. He wanted to meet with all of Toledo's officers and directors at Toledo's corporate headquarters in Newark, New Jersey. The message said that he had an offer to make them for their cash register business…and he was sure Toledo's investors would want to give it serious consideration.

Theobald immediately wired the meeting request to Lenox Rose. Within hours, Rose wired back acceptance for himself and the other investors to meet with Patterson, and anyone he wanted to bring along to the meeting in Newark. Theobald told High the meeting was on, at the time and place requested. High left to return to Dayton.

The next morning, Theobald wrote a detailed letter to Rose, explaining his thoughts that the meeting would be a waste of time. He wrote that, after a brief social conversation, High had talked mostly about patent infringement suits that Toledo might have to defend. "I told him," Theobald wrote, "that while NCR was investigating patent infringements by Toledo, they should also carefully investigate infringements of Toledo patents by NCR!"

He indicated that Patterson's whole aim was to create an opportunity for a tirade on the difficulties and obstacles that Toledo would have to overcome…all just to get Toledo's directors frightened enough to agree to sell out at a low figure. He wrote that the meeting would be fruitless…that NCR would not make any proposition that would justify giving up the bright prospects in the cash register business.

"From a business standpoint," Theobald wrote, "I believe the meeting is unwise. However, since your money is in the business, I feel you are entitled to hear anything Patterson might have to say. I take this position because I don't want to be the subject of criticism at some future date for having approved such a meeting."

Several days later Theobald received a telegram, "Got your letter. Come Sunday at three to discuss. Regards." (signed) Lenox Rose.

When Theobald walked into the meeting room on Sunday, he saw that Gay and Young were already there along with Rose. Theobald recalled the conversation. "Come in, Henry," Rose said. "We've been talking about your letter. It seems clear you don't even want to meet them, let alone consider selling."

Theobald took off his coat and smiled. "I've been thinking about that too. Of course we should meet them and hear what they have to offer." He turned, looking at each one separately. "It's just that I know John Patterson very well. He's smooth. His argument will sound logical and sensible. And I just don't want him to be able to panic us into accepting an offer that's ridiculously low because he was able to frighten us with his patent infringement talk."

Mathew Gay turned. "Well, we do intend to meet them, Henry. It's the courteous thing to do. And we're curious. We've all heard about the legendary John Patterson, but Lenox is the only one of the three of us who has ever met him. And you're the only one who knows him well. So we're taking your concerns seriously, believe me."

Ed Young smiled at Theobald. "You know, we're pretty good businessmen too, Henry. That's why you came to us in the first place. So trust us not to do anything foolish. My guess is that he'll try to either frighten us or buy us. And we've faced both those dragons before."

"Probably a combination of both," Theobald replied. "Meanwhile, here's an idea. What do you say to this…each of us will write down on a slip of paper what we each believe to be an acceptable minimum selling figure, and just put the paper in our pocket. Right now we're thinking logically without considering any emotional argument that might come from John. Then after we hear his offer tomorrow, we can objectively say whether we thought fair or unfair."

Young removed a page from a legal tablet he carried and tore it into four parts. Each of the four wrote briefly on the slip and put it in his pocket. Theobald probably thought, *I wonder if he knows that no one can change their mind and substitute a different piece of paper. We'll just compare the torn sections if we need to. Now I'm looking forward to tomorrow!*

Theobald remembered that he, Lenox Rose and his cousin John Rose, Gay and Young were standing near a coffee service holding cups when a secretary announced, "Gentlemen, Mr. Patterson, Mr. High and Mr. Boyle of NCR are here to see you." Straightening his coat, Rose said, "Show them in, please…show them in."

Patterson was first into the room. He made straight for Theobald and put out his hand. Theobald reported the conversation and the offer to his friends later. "Henry, you've done well in a short time. I'm proud of you," he said. Theobald recalled shaking hands, grinning. "I believe you mean that, John. But if I have, I owe it all to you. You taught me everything I know. And I thank you for it."

"Perhaps I taught you too well, eh, Henry?" Patterson said, glancing around and moving to the seat at the head of the conference table. "Gentlemen, I won't keep you long. Let me introduce my associates. Mr. High works for me in Dayton. And James Boyle here is a member of my law firm here in New York." The Toledo executives from Newark recognized the name of the law firm…one of the most prestigious in New York. They glanced at each other.

Theobald saw that by mentioning the law firm's name and assuming the president's usual seat, Patterson automatically had become the dominant person in the meeting. Theobald vaguely recalled having seen him do this before. He pondered a moment. "It's good to see you operating from the chairman's seat again, John," he said grinning, "even though you don't own a thing in this room yet. And may not ever. But from that seat we can all keep a better eye on you."

Everyone relaxed a little. Patterson's eyes twinkled. His dominance gambit had been exposed by his protégé, which somehow made it more acceptable. He chuckled along with the others, but quickly got down to business again.

"As I said gentlemen, I won't keep you long. Jim Boyle here is a patent attorney. He tells me that we would probably win a patent infringement suit against you. You probably have attorneys that tell you that you will likely win. That's legal marketing, in my opinion. Three out of four interests in any lawsuit are winners...the winner, the winner's law firm, and the loser's law firm are all winners. These three get paid. There's just one loser, who pays them all. Well, I don't want either of us to be a loser just to make more money for the lawyers.

So I'm giving you this offer. It expires at the end of business today. Boyle has the formal written offer, which details NCR's purchase of your complete interests in cash registers. He'll give each of you a copy. But let me summarize in the interest of time."

Patterson had everyone's attention now. "My financial people advise me that your cash register patents and property are probably worth altogether somewhere between 60 and 70 thousand dollars. But I'm going to offer you more than that. For one thing, the lawyers would cost me a lot of money. They're good, but they're expensive. They're expensive because they're good. But as I said, let's not give them any more money just yet. I'd rather give it to you."

Patterson looked at the Toledo directors in turn, with his eyes settling finally on Theobald. "The offer is conditional on one legal stipulation," Patterson said firmly. "The condition is this...it must include a binding agreement from Henry Theobald that he will not engage in any form of the cash register business for a period of no less than ten years. That's essential. No agreement, no sale. But with this agreement, I offer you the sum of $115,000 for your complete cash register interests. In cash." He sat back, relaxed, and looked at each Toledo director in turn again.

Theobald, who had worried that the others might panic, appeared to be in a state of panic himself. "That's unacceptable! That's not fair, John. It's too serious a decision to make before the end of the day! Please..."

Patterson spoke quietly. "I need you out of my hair, Henry. You've become a lot of trouble and expense. It's clear to me that if we go on the way we are, we'll just spend a lot of time scrapping with each other. Unproductive time." He looked right into Theobald's eyes. "I'm really doing you a favor. You'll be able to devote your time and attention exclusively to the scale business. I expect that's what your partners want anyway. Ask them."

"Now I know you're going to want to talk this over among yourselves," he said, rising out of his chair. "So we'll get out of here and let you gentlemen do that. About 4:30, Mr. High will return for your answer. Please try to have it by then. His instructions are to leave by 5 p.m. whether he has your answer or not. If he doesn't have your verbal agreement by then, we assume you have turned us down. Then you will be hearing from Mr. Boyle's firm before the end of the week. Good day, gentlemen. Thank you for seeing me…and for your hospitality."

Patterson rose and shook hands all around, leaving Theobald for the last. "It won't be so bad, Henry. If I know you, you'll become totally immersed in the scale business very soon. You could be a real pioneer. And I truly would not enjoy fighting you. You see, I really am proud of you." At the door he turned and said, "My best to Mary and young Robert!" as he led the other two out.

Nothing was said for the first few moments after they had left. It was as if a cyclone had left the room and each of them needed time to catch a breath. The first to speak was Mathew Gay. "Wow!" he exclaimed.

"I thought he would be more like John D. Rockefeller," Young said. "I know Rockefeller a little since I work for him. But this guy is not at all like Rockefeller. Old John D. would never offer more than a company is worth. Always less. Always less."

"Henry was right about his charm," Lenox Rose exclaimed. "I had met him several times before but never in a situation like this. He did make several points that impressed me too." Rose continued, turning to Gay. "Mat, you once said you were worried about

Henry's health, carrying the load he's carrying trying to get the company under way."

"Right, I did." Gay replied. "He's spread too thin as it is. We're all betting our money on Henry Theobald and we don't want an unhealthy general manager."

"I don't want him distracted from the scale job trying to compete with the mighty NCR," Young said. "Patterson made a good point there. And I sure don't want to take him on in the courts either. He left no doubt that's where we're headed..."

Theobald remembered interrupting. "Wait a minute. I've spent so many years in the cash register business that it would be really difficult for me to consent to give it up. That is a serious proposition for me! The truth is, I really want to continue in the cash register business. I want to compete with Patterson, head on. We can do it! We can take him on and win! As for the patents..."

"Henry," Rose said quietly. "It looks like you may be outnumbered. But wait a minute. We forgot to look at our own estimates...the ones you asked us to put in our pockets, Henry." He reached in his pocket. "Here's mine...," he started to say.

Theobald interrupted, waving his slip . . . . "My estimate is right here. Read it...it says $200,000. He offered about half that..."

Rose spoke louder, "My estimate was a range. $70,000 to $80,000. What was yours, Mat?" Gay replied, "I put down $50,000. What about you?" he asked, turning to Young. "I wrote $55,000 on my slip," Young said. "Henry, even though you know a lot more about the business than we do, you're way out of the park on your estimate. Patterson made us an offer that was more than fair."

Gay added, "And we'd like you to take better care of yourself, Henry. Concentrate your incredible energies on scales. That alone should help you from spreading yourself too thin. I'm sorry you disagree, but I'm voting my shares to accept the offer."

"So am I," Young added. "It's a fair offer. And it's worth it if for no other reason than to give you more capital and the time to build the scale business, Henry. There's no NCR in the scale business."

"Well, it's clear what these two partners want, Henry," Rose said. "I'm very much inclined to agree with them. $115,000 cash will go a long way in giving the company a faster start. But I don't want a corporate crisis…even with my vote, the three of us represent only half the stock. You own the other half, Henry. A tie would be disastrous. What are you going to do?"

Theobald had badly miscalculated. He was devastated that it was his idea that each of them should write down their guess of what the offer would be. His voice choked. "I hate the idea of selling. I've lived cash registers for most of my life. It will be hard to change my focus. But you three are my partners. I trust you. I came to you in the first place because I respect you and value your judgment. If all of you want to sell, I'll go along even if I don't want to."

Rose strolled to the cupboard. He returned with whiskey and four glasses…

The deal went through rapidly. After only eleven months of business, in June 1902, the Toledo Computing Scale and Cash Register Company sold the cash register patents, inventory, parts, machines, jigs, dies, fixtures, patterns, and tools to Patterson's NCR. Theobald was out of the cash register business for good.

And since cash registers were no longer part of the business, the corporate name had to be changed. Theobald suggested Toledo Scale Company. His sales people argued that the word "computing" was too valuable to give up.

So in 1902 the name became Toledo Computing Scale Company.

CHAPTER 3

Down Weight

As Patterson predicted, Theobald quickly put his mind and energy to work in the scale business. He had learned how cash registers were sold, and began to adapt many of the same techniques to selling scales. He knew he had to prove beyond any doubt that a Toledo scale actually increased a merchant's profit. He also had to prove that it would pay for itself quickly. Beyond this, he had to provide a means for the merchant to pay for the scale with time payments out of his increased profits.

A cash register had a drawer with divided space to keep the money in denominations, which gave the merchant a fast, convenient way to make change. A bell rang every time the drawer was opened which called the merchant's attention to the fact that a clerk had opened it. This kept the clerks honest, it was believed. And when an adding attachment was sold with the register, the merchant could read the total of the day's receipts…if no one made a mistake in ringing the register and always made the right change.

Theobald quickly came to believe that the scale was far more important to a merchant than the cash register. The merchant could make change out of a drawer or even a shoebox under the counter. Many of them still did, resisting the blandishments of cash register salesmen. But the scale told him how much to charge for his merchandise. Theobald became convinced that the scale was the most important piece of equipment in the store. It converted a commodity directly into money, telling him how much to put in the shoebox. Without a scale, the store could not operate.

His customers were two distinct food stores; a grocery store and a meat market. In the grocery, food was sold in bulk out of barrels or bins…dried beans, peas, prunes, peaches, apples, salt, pepper, coffee, cookies, and of course crackers out of a cracker barrel. Most food stores used an even balance scale. Only a very few used a spring counterbalance cylinder scale or the DeVilbiss fan scale. These were both still new and relatively rare. And with the even balance scale, "down weight" was a practical necessity.

A customer would ask for, say, a pound-and-a-quarter of dried beans. The merchant would place a one-pound weight and a quarter-pound weight on the weight platter side of the balance, then put a paper bag on the commodity platter side. Then he would dip into the bin or barrel with a small scoop and start filling the paper bag. The customer's eyes were drawn to the beam. This is where the action was.

She soon learned that her side of the scale must go "down" if she was to get full weight. The merchant didn't dare remove a few beans to get an even balance…the customer would think him stingy and take her trade to another store. So "down weight" was the custom.

The same was true if a beam scale was used. A poise was moved on the beam to the desired weight. When the desired weight was greater than the capacity of the beam, a weight was added to the end of the beam. The merchant poured the beans into the bag but couldn't easily predict when the beam was in the exact center of the trig-loop. Again "down weight" was his only solution.

Theobald understood this problem. He realized that his automatic indication computing scale largely solved the problem of "down weight." The merchant could now charge for the overweight almost every time. "Ma'am, it's slightly over, the price calculation is 28 cents…is that all right?" No problem. As a result, both his sales volume and profits increased.

The real problem, Theobald knew, was convincing the merchant that replacing his $8 to $10 balance scale with a Toledo

Computing Scale at $35 to $50—four to five times the price—was a good business decision. Time and labor were not important and merchants were always short of cash. An effective selling demonstration was needed to get over this hurdle.

He then developed a dramatic demonstration using tea. This kind of demonstration lasted for years...changed only by refinement. Tea was sold by weight in small quantities. Since tea was imported from the Far East, it was relatively expensive. He gathered his sales managers in Toledo and conducted a role-playing demonstration personally. He had one of the sales managers act as the merchant. His demonstration used a cloth bag that contained exactly two ounces of tea.

He set up a sample store with a few commodities and both an even balance scale and a beam scale. Acting as the salesman, he would say, "Please give me two ounces of tea," watching closely to be sure it was weighted 'down weight.' He would then produce his two-ounce bag of tea. "Let's compare," he would say, placing his order on one side of the balance and his pre weighed bag on the other. Then he would remove tea a little at a time from the bag he had purchased, pile it up carefully and weigh the excess.

"Look what you gave me," he would exclaim acting surprised. "Let's figure out what this costs you." Together they would calculate the daily and weekly giveaway with pencil and paper. "Here's the point," he enthused. "With this system, you can prove that a new Toledo Scale will pay for itself in a very brief time...sometimes in just a few weeks."

The sales managers were enthusiastic. At the end of his presentation, Theobald would give each of them enough preweighed bags of tea for each of their salesman. They, in turn, were instructed to show each of the salesmen in their territory how to use it.

"Be sure to explain that you have to watch the merchant closely when he's weighing the tea," Theobald said. "Most merchants know that men don't look for 'down weights' as carefully as women do. So let him know you're watching. Then he'll be concerned enough to automatically give you a little extra so you won't complain. The more 'down weight' he gives you, the shorter the pay back time."

The two ounces of tea gave way to a finely polished nickel-plated one-pound "button" weight in a specially built jewelry box, together with a signed, sealed certificate from the Bureau of Standards, Washington, D.C. that certified the weight was exactly accurate.

The salesman would open the fine walnut jewelry box, carefully remove a chamois bag, delicately remove the weight, blow off some imaginary dust and present the Bureau of Standards Certificate for the merchant to inspect. He would then test the accuracy and readability of the merchant's scale with the certified weight.

Theobald called this a "scale audit." The salesman would write down the actual results as he weighed various commodities on the Toledo demonstration scale he hoped to sell and the merchant's existing scale. These scale audits were so effective that often the results had to be played down as they were quite unbelievable even though completely honest.

Several factors lent themselves to this. The demonstration scale was new and in perfect working order. It was generally of a lower capacity, often with one-cent graduations. It was being compared to a scale that had been in use for some time with critical parts that were worn. It soon became clear that a scale with worn parts always was off in favor of the customer…never the merchant. And it was often compared to an inherently inaccurate spring counter-balance scale.

Salesmen soon recognized that the scale audit was their best tool. It was kept alive by one of Toledo's best salesman, Frank Ditzler, who later became the company's first sales manager. Like many other Toledo employees, he was an alumnus of NCR, trained by John Patterson. Before joining Toledo, Ditzler was NCR's general sales manager.

He wrote Theobald of his conviction that it was the best tool they could have. Ditzler expanded on the scale audit. He created a scale audit form, one column for the readings from the merchant's scale and a second column for the readings from the Toledo scale. A space at the bottom showed the total of the merchant's own figures which detailed the savings he would realize with a Toledo Scale.

Theobald passed on Ditzler's remarks and a quantity of scale audit forms in a kit was sent to each salesman. It contained a tube of 30 carefully polished one-pound test weights plus an assortment of one-ounce and fractional-ounce weights. Salesmen treasured the kits.

Before long, many of the most successful salesmen reported that when they used a piece of the merchant's own brown butcher paper or paper bag it was more effective than the specially printed audit form with carbon copies. An unsophisticated merchant was suspicious of the special form. He trusted his own butcher paper or bag...he added on it every day. So butcher paper together with a large pencil with thick, soft lead became the best way to record the results of a scale audit.

After a few years in Toledo, Ditzler transferred to San Francisco as a regional sales manager, where he built the company's best performing regional sales group.

Soon Theobald passed on what he had heard about the most effective demonstration of all. He wrote to the field, "Convince the merchant to reweigh baskets of food on a Toledo Scale that are ready for delivery to his customers. Let the merchant himself, along with his own clerks, do the reweighing. He'll come up with positive proof himself that he'll realize large savings with a Toledo Scale. He'll see for himself the amount of money he was entitled to and didn't get. He'll see what he could have charged. All you need to do is watch. He'll convince himself!"

He continued, "Always try to make sure all the store clerks are part of the audit. They hate it when a customer challenges their readings. So they'll be on your side. They'll want the new scale. It's easy for them because it's not their money that needs to be spent. Use them."

Theobald urged his sales force to sell a "system of weighing", not just one scale. He insisted they travel with eight sample trunks so they could demonstrate every scale in the line. A Toledo salesman covered his territory by train. The trunks traveled with him as baggage. When the train arrived at a new town, his first stop was at a livery stable where he hired a horse and buggy or buckboard. He then drove the buggy back to the train station to pick up his trunks.

Then he canvassed the town for prospective purchasers, called PP for short in all correspondence. Roads were unpaved. A horse and buggy or buckboard provided a bumpy ride over dirt roads or cobblestones. To protect the scale samples Theobald had the factory develop a special scale trunk. Since the trunk was expensive, they were serial numbered and charged to the salesman on memorandum and had to be accounted for in periodic audits.

The two-ounce tea bag, the shiny, certified test weight with demonstrations and a scale audit proved effective. The sales force expanded and sales continued to increase for the new company. Early in 1902, Toledo had a salesman in Canada. Later that year a large order was received from Canada. Theobald made a manufacturing arrangement first with the Hamilton Brass Company, then later with the Gurney Scale Company. Later scales were exported to Canada from Toledo until an assembly operation was started in Windsor, Ontario.

Competitive scale companies quickly began to react to the growing Toledo presence. Toledo's main competitor was the Computing Scale Company of America located in Dayton, Ohio. Starting in 1891, Dayton manufactured and sold scales using a spring counterbalance. Dayton evolved from a computing scale patent issued in 1885 to Julius Pitrap of Gallipolis, Ohio. It was for a multiple beam scale with a capacity of 100 lb. Pitrap sold his patent rights in 1888 to R. E. Hull.

Within three years, Dayton businessmen O. Osias and Edward Canby became interested and bought out Hull. They incorporated the Computing Scale Company of America in March 1891. They organized the Moneyweight Scale Company in Chicago as the selling arm for their scales. For a time, Dayton scales were identified and sold as Moneyweight scales. Later the company name was changed to Dayton Scale Company. It was well financed and had a ten-year head start over Toledo. By the time Toledo Scale was founded, Dayton had established a national sales organization. They claimed to have about 30,000 spring scales in use by 1901.

In August 1902, Dayton Scale Company sent four salesmen and a manager with four horses and wagons to St. Louis to seek business. Theobald happened to be in St. Louis and heard about the Dayton team. He wrote home, "On Friday night, August 15th, the whole gang, bag and baggage, went back to Chicago, horses, wagons, men, all except one salesman who tarried long enough to see me, and I employed him. Then I went to Chicago too and employed three more of their salesmen. The only two remaining with the Dayton company have practically promised to come with me too, so it was quite a killing for one trip."

In September 1903, Theobald put a field sales operation in effect. He located men in Atlanta, Boston, Buffalo, Chicago, Dallas, Denver, Minneapolis, New York, Omaha, Philadelphia, Pittsburgh, San Francisco, Seattle, St. Louis, and Toledo. Young, the company secretary, urged Theobald to open an office in Newark, his hometown. Theobald promised to do so just as soon as he could locate a good man.

He wrote Young, "The great difficulty is to get the salesman. In the first place, a good horse and rig costs somewhere in the neighborhood of $150 to $175 and even more. Then the expenses of a man traveling in that manner are $18 or $20 per week."

Theobald sent his salesman in New York try to sell scales to the Great Atlantic & Pacific Tea Company. The salesman spent several weeks calling on John Hartford, the "head of the house." Hartford finally agreed. It was the beginning of a long relationship. During A & P's great expansion period in the 1920's, Toledo sold them more than 10,000 cylinder scales.

The Toledo Computing Scale Company was only two-years-old when Dayton Scale threatened suit under a recently purchased MacPhelps patent of Red Oak, Iowa for a spring scale. The threat immediately caused Theobald to write a pamphlet, which he mailed to butchers all across the country with the headline, "Timely Warning!" The copy read, "If you have any idea about buying a spring balance computing scale, you had better consider the matter carefully before investing." It continued by explaining the inherent inaccuracy of spring scales and of the charts used with them.

The *Toledo Times* wrote an article: "Get What You Pay For." Theobald sent the article to other newspapers across the country, hoping they would print it to warn their subscribers against dishonest spring scales.

In response, Dayton Scale published a circular showing a Dayton scale and a Toledo scale side by side. Under the Dayton scale was printed the word "Genuine." Under the Toledo scale, "The Imitation." Theobald saw at once that Dayton had never manufactured a scale such as they showed in the circular. He wrote his own circular calling the Dayton scale "Fake! A bold-faced impudent lie." Both Dayton and Toledo salesmen knew the Dayton scale shown in the circular didn't exist.

The battle against "dishonest scales" was joined.

Theobald defined dishonest scales as all spring scales no matter who manufactured them. He took them all on. Other scale companies who manufactures and sold spring computing scales included Anderson, Angldine, Strubler, Stimpson, and Standard. Spring scales were simpler. More important from a competitive point of view, they were much less expensive to manufacture. Since Toledo Scales were more expensive to make, they had to sell at a higher price.

At the same time, spring scales were also considerably less accurate than a pendulum scale which measured gravity against gravity. Spring scales were sensitive to temperature changes. Accuracy changed constantly throughout the day as the temperature increased or decreased in the merchant's store. The merchant soon learned how to take advantage of this to make his scale more "profitable." He regularly used his scale to maintain his advantage.

In Newark, Young became concerned about the threatened lawsuit and Theobald's aggressive reaction. As the New Jersey manager for Standard Oil, Young was living through the legal troubles of Standard Oil prompted by President Theodore Roosevelt who was successfully breaking up Standard Oil's monopoly. He was sensitive to legal troubles.

On April 1, 1903, Young wrote Theobald about his concern. "Suppose Dayton wins out," he wrote. "What have we gained by goading them into an action against us? It seems to me nothing but trouble. On the other hand, if we should win, what damages could we gain as a benefit to us? Is there any danger of the circulars you are sending out regarding the Dayton Company acting as boomerangs? Have you secured legal opinions so that no danger of libel, etc., is liable to occur?"

Theobald answered Young immediately. "I drop everything to answer your letter because I am very anxious for you to know that my aggressiveness in the campaign against the Dayton Company is positively necessary. We started in the business in a very mild and meek-mannered way. Did not say a word about Dayton. Were even so polite that we did not publish testimonials containing their name. I mean testimonials of merchants who had used their scales and discarded them and are now using ours."

"OH! I could go on indefinitely and tell you the reasons for our aggressiveness," he continued. "I cannot fight on the defensive. Suppose you had a company, larger, with more prestige, with more experience and an established reputation, attacking you every time you tried to sell a barrel of oil. I wonder if your tactics would not be somewhat different from your present ones. You are the 'upper dog,' we are the 'under dog.' However, as stated above, I could go on indefinitely and string this letter out, giving many excellent reasons for all our printed matter, but I will reserve that.

The principal object of the tone of my circulars is to keep our salesmen encouraged and enthused. To keep them filled with their fighting nerve so they will not be cowed by our competitor's agents. I think so far I have been able to detect by careful thought and study of the situation, and by counsel with others in the business and questioning of agents, that our method is reasonably successful."

Reluctantly, Young dropped his objection. Dayton dropped their patent suit. But the fight went on.

Fights over scale accuracy were inevitable because there were no established standards anywhere in the nation. Many jurisdictions had weights and measures officials but there were no legal standards they could use requiring that a scale meet any accuracy standard. Spring scales were not illegal, inaccurate as they were. Yet many weights and measures officials tried to establish accuracy standards on their own.

When they did, Dayton brought suit against them in a number of places. Weights and measures officials in Omaha, Grand Rapids, Detroit, Pittsburgh, McKeesport, and several in Massachusetts were among the first to be sued by Dayton. The first trial was in Omaha.

Theobald traveled to Omaha to be a witness at the trial, which was held before a judge. He noticed several newspaper reporters present. When it was his turn to testify, he remembered explaining the difference between a spring scale and a pendulum scale, and the differences in the chart that each used.

Then he turned to the judge and said, "Your Honor, I have a better way to convince you that the Dayton scale is dishonest. On the way to court this morning, I purchased eight food packages over a Dayton scale. I have them with me. I also have a Dayton scale and a Toledo scale here. The best way for you to understand just how dishonest the Dayton scale is, is to weigh the packages yourself. If you would come down here, I'll show you."

Theobald was very persuasive. Reluctantly, the judge left the bench and approached the scale. "Now sir, just weigh each package yourself on this Dayton scale and write down on a piece of paper the value it shows at 28 cents per pound; the actual amount I paid this morning."

The judge carefully weighed each package, read the computing chart and wrote down an amount. After weighing them all he added up the total for the eight packages. Theobald publicly agreed with each reading the judge got. "Yes sir, that's the amount I read too. Now let's weigh them again on the Toledo Scale." The judge again weighed each package, read the computing chart and wrote down an amount for each. He added his eight new values from the Toledo Scale.

"You see, Your Honor, the total you got from the Dayton scale is 16 cents more. The scale stole two cents a package on the average. That's about—what?—seven percent! This scale is a thief! And you can't blame the merchant…he did nothing illegal. It's in his self interest to use a dishonest scale. He'll continue until your state legislature passes laws against crooked scales like this one."

The judge nodded. He scowled as he again examined each scale.

"But, for heavens sake, don't blame your weights and measures officials either," Theobald continued. "Their job is to protect the public and they were just doing their job in the best way they knew how. Here in Omaha they were doing it too well to suit the Dayton Scale Company! No, blame them; the Dayton Scale Company for deliberately making a dishonest device, designed, built and sold to rob the innocent consumer!"

The judge resumed his bench and threw the case out of court.

Later, Dayton dropped the suits in all the other cities.

CHAPTER 4

"The public is being robbed…"

It was just the beginning of Theobald's fight against dishonest scales. On July 4, 1903, the *New York Tribune* wrote a story about spring scales titled: "Short Weight Fraud." Theobald obtained copies and mailed them to every salesman. He wrote his directors: "I think within another year everybody in the United States will know that these barrel-shaped spring balance computing scales are thieves. I am going to pursue such a campaign that every time the grocer or butcher goes out his door, he will feel as though he has a card on his back labeled 'thief.'"

Theobald had an instinct for publicity. At his instigation, more stories about dishonest scales were printed in newspapers all over the nation. He hassled state legislatures to pass weights and measures laws. When they were slow to respond, he intensified his campaign.

While Theobald was spending time fighting dishonest scales, troubles emerged back at the plant. It became clear that Allen DeVilbiss was the wrong choice to be plant superintendent. His personality clashed with the workers. He could tell he wasn't getting along with them. As a result, he did little supervising. He thought of himself as an inventor and spent most of his time tinkering. He was soon replaced as plant superintendent and was given the title "Head of the Inventions Department."

O. C. Reeves became the new plant superintendent. Like several other Toledo executives, Theobald had recruited him from NCR. Theobald commented to several friends, "If Patterson won't let me make cash registers, at least I can hire some of his best people away from him." He also wooed W. A. Zolg away from NCR where he was a senior accountant. Zolg was named company treasurer, replacing Theobald, to free up Theobald's time for a second job he took on.

The sales manager of the DeVilbiss company was J. F. Pixley, who assumed the same job with Toledo. Theobald soon concluded that Pixley was not able to recruit good salesmen...critical to growth. Pixley was fired and Theobald took on the duties of sales manager as well, until he appointed Frank Ditzler to the position. Ditzler was as successful at this as at everything else he had tried. By the end of 1905 he had 97 salesmen on his list, scattered all over the nation. Between 1903 and 1905, they had sold more than 30,000 scales.

Zolg, the new treasurer, had to deal with the rapid growth of the company. Because of the way the scales had to be sold, increased sales regularly required more working capital, and there was constant shortage. In effect, the buyer had to be financed by Toledo for up to ten months. Terms were 10% cash with the order—or $5.00—whichever was greater, a minimum $5 monthly payment, and a maximum term of ten months. The salesman would usually keep the down payment as part of his commission. So cash was always in short supply.

Theobald made another major decision in 1905. To service his growing line of products, he established a national service organization staffed with factory-trained mechanics. In announcing it he wrote, "We are not obligated to sell one more scale but we are morally bound to service those scales we have sold." It was the beginning of the largest, best-trained and most professional scale service organization in the industry.

He created one of the first house organs in the nation to communicate with an ever-expanding sales force. Calling it the *Toledo System*, it was issued monthly and carried information on successful system selling techniques from one salesman to all the others. It conveyed individual sales performances to generate competition. And of course it reported on the latest regarding dishonest scales, along with methods to compete with them successfully.

Progress in the U.S. seemed to be made everywhere. New inventions excited the nation, enriching the lives of everyone: King

Gillette's safety razor, the mechanical pencil, the subway, long distance telephone calling, inside plumbing, the Victor Talking Machine, and the Kinetoscope that projected moving pictures on a screen. Feature films with a plot were beginning to catch on, promising a whole new field of diversion for everyone.

The automobile was claimed to be more reliable. The whole nation cheered the two men who successfully completed the first coast-to-coast auto trip. *Popular Mechanics* magazine wrote, "One stretch made the autoists think they had certainly strolled beyond the domains of human aggression. An indefatigable perseverance and determination, however, successfully steered them out of this unearthly region." The writer was referring to Utah.

The next year thousands of autos headed in the opposite direction, aimed for the great Louisiana Purchase Exposition in St. Louis, Missouri…better known as the St. Louis World's Fair. "Meet me in St. Louis, Louis" was the song of the day. A new process of "house cleaning done by pneumatic process without removing the carpets" was demonstrated, and came to be known as the vacuum cleaner. But what was remembered the longest was the huge Ferris Wheel that rose 250 feet above the ground.

President Theodore Roosevelt successfully sold his Pure Foods & Meat Inspection Act to Congress in 1906. It became the first of many acts designed to protect consumers.

And news about the airplane finally began to appear, which oddly enough generated little interest among the public. Most people believed it would never have any commercial value. Theobald read about the successful flights of the Wright Brother's Power-Flyer. He recalled visiting their simple bicycle shop to have his son's bike repaired when he lived in Dayton. It was hard for him to believe that these two shy, simple brothers had designed and built the first successful airplane.

Toledo's inventions department was busy throughout this period too. In 1906, the company added a cylinder scale to the line. It was a great improvement. The new cylinder scale had one-cent graduations with a chart computing capacity up to 30 lb—compared to the Toledo fan scale with a 10 lb computing chart. The fan scale required two 10 lb beams to reach a 30 lb capacity.

It included more than twice as many calculations as previously offered. With the cylinder scale, the computing capacity was the total capacity of the scale. No beams were required. It still used a pendulum to measure gravity against gravity. Next, a new candy scale was introduced.

When the new cylinder scale was introduced, Toledo initiated a trade-in policy for the first time. Toledo fan scales could be traded in and the value of the trade-in used to reduce the cost of the new cylinder scale. Because Toledo allowed real dollars for the exchanged machine, it had to be resold to recover its cost. Newly trained servicemen refurbished most of them. With the one-cent graduations and increased number of calculations, Theobald intensified the fight against spring scales.

Large signs that read "We protect our customers by using Toledo Scales—NO SPRINGS—HONEST WEIGHT GUARANTEED" were shipped with every scale. Merchants were proud to hang the sign in a conspicuous place near the Toledo scale. A bit later the word "guaranteed" was removed and the wording changed to "Our Weighing Service is Rendered by Toledo Scales 'No Springs—Honest Weight.'" Housewives learned to look for Toledo scales in every butcher shop and grocery where they did their shopping to be sure they weren't being cheated.

Throughout the years, certain scales sold in bulk quantity to large customers were given a special designation to justify a lower price. The Kroger Company bought many hundreds of Toledo cylinder scales finished in gold with a special model number for Kroger, K581. Actually it was the model 581 with a rich gold finish.

In Northern New York State, the Mohican Company bought many hundreds of Toledo cylinder scales painted "Mohican Blue." Each of their stores was supplied with two framed signs reading, "We Protect Our Customers—No Springs—Honest Weight." Each was also supplied with an enameled iron sign for outside the store reading, "Toledo Scales Used Here."

When a Toledo salesman was not successful in replacing a competitive spring scale, the merchant received a sign that read "WE USE SPRING SCALES" to be placed in his front window. Just a few were made because not a single merchant was willing to display it.

Dayton Scale, under their selling organization, the Moneyweight Scale Company ran an ad that became infamous for its dishonesty throughout the industry.

The Moneyweight advertisement read:

Can you do this?
on your scale

Buy 20 lbs of pork loin at nine cents a pound,
retail them to your trade at the same price
and get your money back ? ? ? ? ?

We Can
on our scale and make you
3% profit besides

If your business amounts to **$10.00** a day,
sales **can earn you 30 cents in fractions**
you don't get now.

30 cents a day means you buy the scale every 180 days.
How many have you bought in that time? Think of it.

One scale lost every six months.
Let our man prove this

Moneyweight Scale Co.
47 State Street
CHICAGO, ILL.

"How's that?" Theobald bellowed when he saw it, "Buy pork loins for 9 cents a pound, sell the same pork loins for the same 9 cents a pound, and make a 3% profit besides? By God, they've even got the gall to *advertise* that their scales are crooked!"

Toledo System ran a Photostat of the ad under a large cartoon showing a Dayton Moneyweight scale with a hand reaching into a customer's market basket. Under it Theobald wrote, "Did you ever see anything so brazen and shameless? How long will the public tolerate such scales?"

On September 10, 1908, the Dayton Scale Company sent to Lenox Rose, president; John B. Rose, vice president; Edwin Young, secretary; Jerome Taylor, director; and Eugene Unger, director, an official "warning." The last paragraph of the warning read. "You, and each of you to whom this notice is addressed, are hereby warned that unless all libelous publications by the Toledo Computing Scale Company are discontinued at once, you, and each of you, will be held individually and personally responsible." For some reason Theobald did not receive a "warning".

In the warning specific things were documented. A photograph showed an exhibit in front of a Toledo sales office. Eight Dayton cylinder scales were shown with a hatchet driven into the cylinder of each. Above the display was a placard reading: "These Moneyweight spring scales are thieving devices. See how we treat them."

Another photo showed more than a dozen Dayton scales with a large sign above them. The sign read: "The public is being systematically robbed by purchasing over Dayton Moneyweight spring scales of the type shown here. (Dayton models 61 and 63.) The following is a copy of a circular sent out by the makers of these scales advertising the 'special advantages' to be gained by using a certain type of their scales. Did you ever see anything so shameless and brazen? How long will you stand for this?"

Left of the scale display was a placard of a man dressed in convict garb including a ball and chain. Above was a balloon showing him saying, "I robbed a safe at night—got caught, got 12 years, but safe robbing is more respectable than robbing widows of half pennies in broad daylight under the guise of 'commercial honesty.'" At the right of the scale display was another shackled convict with another balloon which showed him saying, "I stole $500.00 from a rich firm and got 10 years but it hurts my pride to mix with these penny snatchers who claim to be 'commercially honest.'"

In front of the scale display was a live, uniformed guard who paraded up and down in front of the exhibit. Each scale had a disparaging placard. A typical one read, "Ho Ho! Ha Ha! I tell de boss dat three is de half of five, four is de half of seven, five is de half of nine. He believes me so I help him get dat '3% profit besides' he ain't entitled to."

Dayton had taken three photos of this exhibit and enclosed a copy for each of Toledo's officers and directors. All that is, except Henry Theobald…even though he was Toledo's general manager and a director of the company.

Previously Dayton had filed a suit trying for an injunction to stop this exhibit. Again Theobald attended the hearing and, in his characteristic way, succeeded in getting the judge to come down from his bench and weigh a product on both a Toledo and a Dayton Moneyweight scale. Of course, the Moneyweight scale showed incorrect computations and the injunction was denied. Again Theobald had won his point. He told the court, "With the assistance of the honest merchants of this country, we propose to expose any company which may resort to trickery or fraud in the sale and the use of its scales."

CHAPTER 5

NO SPRINGS—HONEST WEIGHT

The fight against spring scales began to pay off. On October 1, 1907, the General Court of the State of Massachusetts enacted a Weights and Measures law. The law was titled, "An act to provide for the testing and sealing of weights, measures and balances having a device for indicating the price as well as the weight of commodities offered for sale."

Massachusetts thus became the first state in the nation to enact a weights and measures law. State Sealers wasted no time in condemning Dayton scales. In one town alone over 200 Dayton scales were confiscated. Dayton Scale Company quickly sought an injunction against the Sealers. The injunction was rejected. Next, they filed a claim that the law was unconstitutional.

One year later the Supreme Court of Massachusetts handed down its decision in favor of the Sealers. They ruled the Act within the Constitution of the State.

Theobald was ecstatic. He wrote his directors: "The Supreme Court of the State of Massachusetts (seven learned judges) handed down its unanimous opinion in the scale cases. It is the most wonderful opinion that has ever been rendered. It explodes every theory and every argument that has ever been advanced by the Dayton Company in support of its fake scales. The language in which this great court denounces these machines and the makers and the attorneys is certainly a work of art. It is the most valuable document existing in the scale literature.

This magnificent decree should remove from our minds once and for all any concern as to the truth of the statements we have made towards Dayton scales, and as to the ultimate result of the fight. I cannot sit still while I am writing this letter, this opinion was so exceedingly gratifying to me. It shows that we have been right from the very beginning on every single claim and statement we ever made about Dayton scales. It is perfectly beautiful to note how this great Court takes up each of the Dayton Company arguments and punctures it. In three particular parts of the decree they have gone so far as to direct attention to the fact that not only the Dayton Company officers, but also its attorneys, have indulged in misrepresentation to the Court."

The Court's Justice Loring was delegated to write the verdict ruling that charts showing money values must be arithmetically correct. The part of the language Theobald was most fond of in the court ruling, calling it "a work of art", was this:

"The several numbers given in alignment with every two ounces are confessedly correct values where an article is sold by weight. The Plaintiff contends that they are correct within the meaning of St. 1907, c.535. The Defendant contends, the values indicated by the odd ounces are in many cases not even commercially correct. What is meant by these two contentions is best shown by an example. Suppose a customer asks for half a pound of cheese at 11 cents a pound. A piece is cut off a cheese and placed upon a scale and the indicator in the center shows that it weighs 9 ounces.

The same indicator will be exactly half way between two lines, one in alignment with 8 ounces and the other in alignment with 10 ounces. In the case put, it will be between the figures 6 and 7. The price indicated on the chart is halfway between 6 and 7 cents, that is to say, 6-1/2 cents. The half cent cannot be paid in addition to the 6 cents nor returned if the customer pays 7 cents.

Under the commercial system, which is the Plaintiff's sole justification for the figure 6 on the chart now in question and for similar figures placed upon it, the dealer takes the half cent and charges the customer 7 cents for his cheese.

In point of fact, the value of the cheese in the case put is 6-3/16 cents, and under the commercial custom the fraction being less than half cent belonged to the customer, not to the dealer. The amount legally due for the cheese in question is 6 cents.

The reason why the chart gives 13/16 of a cent to the dealer in place of giving 3/16 of a cent to the customer, is that the fraction of a cent in favor of the dealer is included in the figure 6 opposite 8 ounces. Eight ounces at 11 cents a pound is 5-1/2 cents. The chart gives the dealer the benefit of the half cent and calls 8 ounces 6 cents. Therefore when the dealer taking the mean between 6 and 7 cents for 9 ounces finds the price is 6-1/2 cents, and takes to himself the half cent, *he gets the fraction twice.*"

The decision was printed in the reports of every law library in the country. Reprints were sent to every state legislature in the hope they would pass similar legislation. Theobald saw to it that the Massachusetts ruling received national publicity.

He was helped by a story that appeared soon after the ruling in the *Boston Post.* It read: "Deputy Sealer Conners discovered that many scales of the Dayton Scale Company favored the dealer against the purchaser about three times out of four. When the purchaser called for five or ten cents worth of meat, particularly, the dealer was apt to get one or two ounces of advantage, so the poor people suffered by the short weight." About 120 Dayton scales were condemned in Boston soon after the story appeared. Then more were condemned throughout Massachusetts.

"NO SPRINGS—HONEST WEIGHT" soon became a well-known trademark all over the country. Merchants who had been using spring scales from any manufacturer began buying Toledo's so they wouldn't get blamed for cheating their customers. Sales increases continued. Yet not everyone was interested in honest weights, judging by a story that Frank Ditzler reportedly told Theobald.

Ditzler said, "Henry, you've done a fabulous job selling honest weight. But you haven't sold everybody...did you hear the story going around about the two brothers out West?"

"No, who's not sold…what story?"

"Well, it's about two brothers who are running a store in a small Western town. They do a large trade in wool on barter, according to the story. One day one of the brothers became converted at a revival meeting when it came to town. He urged the other to follow. 'You ought to join, Jake,' said the converted brother. 'You don't know how helpful and comforting it is to be a member of the church.' His brother answered, 'I know, Bill, an' I would like to join but I don't see how I can.' Bill persisted. 'Why not? What's to prevent you?' 'Well, it's jes this way, Bill,' Jake replied. 'There's got to be somebody in the firm to weigh the wool.'"

Theobald didn't see the joke. "We'll get him sooner or later, Frank," he shouted. "Don't worry, we've converted hundreds of merchants with a crooked, medieval attitude like that. We'll get him!"

Toledo's corporate secretary, Edwin Young, became increasingly concerned about Theobald's aggressiveness and sold his interest in 1909. The occasion was chosen to reorganize management of the company. Frederick Geddes, a senior partner in a large Toledo law firm, was named a director. He had been the company's legal counsel from its inception. Lenox Rose moved to chairman of the board. And for the first time, Henry Theobald became president of the Toledo Computing Scale Company…eight years after he founded it.

Theobald continued his aggressive fight against dishonest scales. He wrote in the *Toledo System*:

The Honest Weight Movement is Gaining Strength and New
Advocates Every Day

"One would naturally think that all scale manufacturers would be on the side of honest weight, but on the contrary, when this business began business it found other scale manufacturers not only making and selling scales designed to short-weight the consuming public, but brazenly exploiting them as having been designed for that very purpose. The use of these dishonest scales was causing an annual loss of millions of dollars. We exposed them. We informed the merchants and the public and warned them against the evil. We have spent thousands but with good results. Newspapers in all parts of the country have been aroused to the situation, and are devoting their columns to furthering the cause.

Thousands of merchants have written us and assured us of their support. Cities and states have passed laws to suppress the evil. High courts have condemned the crooked computing scale and have supported us in our contentions against them. The whole country is awakening. The movement for Honest Weight is becoming more and more effective."

He supported a resolution adopted at the National Conference of Weights and Measures on December 18, 1908, which read, "Resolved, that a committee be appointed to confer with prominent citizens and at least twelve national commercial organizations with the objective of setting up a 'National Full Weight and Measures Association,' whose membership shall be unlimited and to which anyone in favor of honest weights and measures shall be eligible."

The committee, made up of state and university officials and a member from the Bureau of Standards in Washington, became another effective tool in the fight.

Meanwhile, the Theobalds had purchased a home at 422 West Woodruff in the estate section of Toledo. Mary Theobald was delighted with the large home and spacious grounds and hated to leave it for any length of time. Still, Henry was able to convince her to accompany him on a trip to Europe. Their son, Bob, was away at boarding school.

Henry and Mary Theobald sailed for Europe in March of 1909. Before boarding the ship in New York, he wrote a letter home from the Waldorf-Astoria Hotel for the *Toledo System*. He wrote, "I am writing this letter on the eve of my departure. Accompanied by Mrs. Theobald, I will sail tomorrow morning for Italy on the North German Lloyd Steamship 'Barbarosa'.

We expect to arrive in Naples on April 8th. We will visit a few of the leading cities in Italy, France, Switzerland, Belgium, Hol-

land, England and possibly Germany. I am making this trip for
the purpose of investigating the conditions existing in the scale
industry in Europe, the needs of the merchants, and government
restrictions pertaining to scales."

Before leaving, he appointed an Executive Committee to act
in his absence. Allen DeVilbiss, Jr. was named chairman. The plant
superintendent, Reeves, was a member, as well as Sales Manager
Frank Ditzler, Assistant Treasurer W. P. Kiser, and Assistant Secretary M. L. Thompson, who represented other arms of the business
on the committee.

After Theobald returned home, his first response came from
England. The Managing Director of W & T Avery, Ltd. wrote
him, "After months of painstaking research, Avery came to the
conclusion that the Toledo Computing scale was the only reliable
and honest computing scale for retail use." This was good
news…Avery was the largest scale company in the world. Like much
of industry in England, Avery was several hundred years old and
was respected throughout Europe.

Theobald reached a licensing agreement with Avery to manufacture Toledo's patented weighing instruments under the Avery
label for sale in Great Britain. A Toledo engineer, L. G. Wetzel, was
sent to England to help Avery get started in the manufacturing of
Avery-brand Toledo scales for retail use. He remained for about
nine months until he was satisfied that Avery could do a good job.

Theobald was endowed with a true sense of the dramatic. His
constant fight for Honest Weight resulted in much favorable publicity. Honest Weight was something the public understood…something
the housewife was truly interested in. It also made good newspaper
copy. When there was no news, he made news. In the summer of
1909 shortly after he returned home from Europe, he arranged a
dramatic scale delivery by "Aerial Craft" in Dayton, home of the Wright
brothers…and of the Dayton Scale Company.

Theobald had Toledo's agent in Dayton, E. R. Lines, prepare a
large helium balloon. Printed on the side of the tethered balloon
were large letters spelling out "Toledo Scales Above All." Theobald

announced to the gathered press that the balloon would be used, "To deliver a Toledo scale by aerial craft, the first such scale delivery in the history of the world. It would be delivered to a specific customer, Mr. A. A. Case in Camden, Ohio."

He had prepared circulars with reprints of stories about short weight for the press. He recalled telling reporters, "Think about it…the scale is the only fixture in a store in which the customer has a financial interest. The customer and the storekeeper have a fifty-fifty interest in its operation. When the scale is deliberately made to read in favor of the merchant, it's fraudulent! And gentlemen," he said, "Right here in Dayton is where the fraud begins.

The Dayton Scale factory here produces more crooks every day than the rest of the entire state of Ohio! It's your wives and sweethearts they cheat with their spring scales. They must be stopped! We need laws to protect the public. It's your money they're stealing. Our legislature must act!"

When the wind was from a direction that looked like it would blow the balloon towards Camden, it was released to much applause. It came down well before Camden of course, and the scale made its final journey by truck. But the crowd who witnessed its ascension didn't know that. The "Aerial Craft" balloon ascension created a sensation in Dayton. The story also was printed in newspapers all over the nation.

Later that same year, a chariot race was held in New York City. Toledo sponsored one of the chariots and had "Toledo Scales—No Springs—Honest Weight" hand painted on the side of the chariot. The publicity generated by the chariot race was so successful that, several years later Theobald knew that the public still remembered the "Great Chariot Race" and the companies that sponsored it.

The next year a great electric display featuring "The Leaders of the World" began a long run above Herald Square in New York City. Toledo's sign read, "Toledo Scales Contain No Springs—Give Honest Weight. This electric sign was on top of the Hotel Normandie at 38th and Broadway, facing Herald Square. The sign lit up every nine minutes from dusk until a half hour after midnight. Over 200,000 people saw the sign every night.

Thirty-two of the nation's leading companies were represented among "The Leaders of the World" on the great sign. A contest was held to generate publicity for the great display and the companies shown on it. All people in the world were invited to write advertising slogans for each company. A total of $15,000 in cash prizes was to be awarded to those who submitted slogans that were accepted. First prize was $2,000 and a silver trophy. Even a Russian Princess submitted a slogan. In all, over a quarter of a million slogans were submitted.

Toledo received more than 10,000 slogans from over 6,000 people, and 34 were accepted. For every slogan accepted, a dollar was awarded along with a beautiful diploma that certified the author had his slogan accepted.

A bit later Theobald concluded that he should take the fight against dishonest scales directly to the consumer. Acting as his own advertising manager and agency he created a series of full page ads railing against spring scales. He placed these ads in the most popular consumer magazines, including *Argosy* and—the largest consumer magazine available—*The Saturday Evening Post*. Creating advertising was a task he very much enjoyed. Toledo continued to advertise directly to consumers for the next 18 years.

One of the early ads had a line drawing of Blind Justice above one of a pensive man sitting under a tree with an apple falling above him—along with a sign given to customers. The headline was:

"The Significance of a Sign backed by Nature's Unchanging Law."

The ad read, *"In England one day, the story goes, a falling apple led young Isaac Newton to the discovery of the Law of Gravity. Two hundred and thirty-three years later other scientists developed the Toledo Pendulum Principle, and by building the first successful pendulum computing scale applied Newton's law to automatic weighing.*

Newton's discovery spread knowledge of a great truth—the Toledo invention spread the practical, direct application of that truth to the weighing of the world's commodities. Instead of measuring gravity with springs, which vary with changes of temperature and alter with use, the Toledo Pendulum Principle relies solely upon Nature's unchanging law. Toledo Scales—No Springs—Honest Weight, *measure gravity with gravity itself.*

Because Toledo has come to stand in the public mind for constant accuracy in weighing, thousands of grocers and butchers display the sign illustrated above, "We Protect Our Customers By Using Toledo Scales, No Springs—Honest Weight."

The scale is the only fixture in a store, in which the merchant and the customer have an equal interest."

The message was taken all over the world. For many years Toledo gave their foreign distributors 2.5% of their annual purchases as an advertising allowance. The distributor only had to submit proof of having spent at least that amount on advertising Toledo scales in his own country.

Theobald was convinced it worked. As evidence, he saved a letter he received from Brazil. A prospect for Toledo equipment in Brazil cut out a picture of the Toledo plant on Monroe Street, pasted it to an envelope with the words "Ohio—Estados Unitos." Addressed in Portuguese, the letter was safely delivered to the company in Toledo, Ohio.

More than anything else, these ad campaigns contributed towards making the public weight and value conscious. They made NO SPRINGS—HONEST WEIGHT TOLEDO SCALES world famous.

CHAPTER 6

The 100% Club

Theobald made it a practice to have lunch in the company dining room at a long table reserved for department heads. It was his custom to discuss company problems with this group, and the lunch period was often extended.

At one of these regular meetings in late 1910, sales manager Frank Ditzler observed, "I've been thinking about what might be done to afford some special recognition to those field salesmen who consistently make their sales quotas. Some of those men are as regular as clockwork...making quota month after month. They're special."

"What do you have in mind?" Theobald asked.

Reeves jumped in. "I remember at NCR, Patterson had annual sales meetings. Invitations were based on performance. He was convinced that it was worthwhile."

Kisser said, "Sounds expensive. What are we going to get out of it?"

"I think what Frank has in mind," Thompson said, "is some kind of organization that promotes harmony and good fellowship...a kind of fraternity of men whose daily interest is closely linked."

"That's it," Ditzler said. "If we bring together the recognized leaders of the sales force, they would surely discuss their successful sales methods based on their actual experience. We'd learn a lot."

"Let's do it!" Theobald declared.

This lunch discussion resulted in the company forming what they titled "the 100% Club." Company salesmen automatically became members when they achieved 100% of their annual quota. The first ten salesmen who reached their quota were to be declared Club Directors. Among the Directors, the salesman who attained the highest percentage over quota was Club President. The Club Vice President, Secretary, Treasurer and Historian were those who ranked second, third, fourth and fifth.

All salesmen who had reached their quota were members and invited to a 100% Club convention in Toledo as honored guests of the company. The "quota year" was from July to the next June so conventions could be held in the summer.

The first 100% Club convention began on July 25, 1911 and ran for four days. Twenty five salesmen reached quota and attended. William Horstman was the first president.

At the end of the convention Horstman told Theobald, "This was great, Mr. Theobald. I was talking to Jim Early and some of the others…they all said they're going home much better equipped for their work. We all learned from each other and everyone in the plant. It really generated a lot of enthusiasm!"

The success of the first 100% Club convention assured there would be one every year. At both the 1911 and 1912 100% Club conventions, the membership was welcomed to Toledo by Mayor Brand Whitlock, who was nationally known for his care of the city's poor.

Meanwhile Theobald had expanded the Inventions Department. A number of other engineers with an inventive bent were hired, reporting to Allen DeVilbiss, Jr. DeVilbiss was enthusiastic about the expansion of his department. Then tragedy struck on April 22, 1911.

Reeves heard first from the DeVilbiss family. He walked into Theobald's office with a stricken look on his face. "Henry," he said, "I have some very bad news. You know that Allen went home sick a few days ago. I just got word from his brother…he died early this morning."

Allen DeVilbiss, Jr., the inventor of the pendulum scale upon which the company was founded, was only 39-years-old at his death. Though not universally popular, he was universally mourned in the company. Without him, all their lives would have taken a different course.

The Inventions Department continued to function with the new engineers. Theobald believed in a competitive spirit between his engineers. Each had his own small room where he worked on his own projects, more or less secret from the other engineers. Earlier, DeVilbiss had attempted to invent a weight printer. His project failed without anyone being aware of his lack of success.

Unknowingly two men might be working on the same general idea. Cooperation among the members of the department was not encouraged. Yet, Theobald was convinced that he got the most out of the dollars spent in engineering by this method. In just a few years it paid off.

One day in 1911 Clarence Hapgood, an engineer in the Inventions Department, demonstrated his latest idea at one of the regular noonday lunch meetings of the company officials. Often a new scale or an improvement was displayed, with the engineer who designed it demonstrating it to the group.

Hapgood's invention was for a double pendulum mechanism mounted in a large dial on a platform scale. The double pendulum made it possible for the scale to be out-of-level, at least in one direction, and still weigh accurately. Most floors in industrial plants were wood and not at all level.

Everyone at the table was excited. "Clarence," Theobald remarked sharply, "I think you've really got something here. If this works out like you've demonstrated, you just might have put us in the industrial scale business. We could compete with Fairbanks-Morse, Howe, and Kron...the dial makes it much more useful."

Reeves, the plant superintendent, asked, "What do you mean, Henry...more useful?"

"Think about it," Theobald replied. "Those others use a beam to read the weight. With this dial, anyone filling a drum or bucket can easily see when he's approaching the desired weight of the product they're filling. He slows down and is able to hit the weight he wants right on the money."

"That's right," Ditzler added. "I've been in a lot of plants and watched how they fill on a Fairbanks or Howe scale. They just keep pouring it in until the beam goes up in the trig-loop. There's no way they can see that they're getting near the weight they want, so they overfill. They've got to be giving away a lot of their product that way. Just like retail scales until we came along."

"Think of the time it could save too," Hapgood said. "No need to nudge a poise back and forth until the beam centers in the trig-loop. No need, either, to add a weight at the end of the beam. When the weight exceeds the capacity of the beam…the dial can indicate the full capacity of the scale. Just put what you want to weigh on the platform and read the weight directly on the dial."

They agreed they should produce a double pendulum platform scale line aimed at industry. Early in 1912 the industrial line was introduced. At the beginning, only one model of a portable scale was available. It was announced to all salesmen and they all were privileged to sell it.

Toledo manufactured only the head mechanism at the beginning. The base, levers and column were purchased from competing industrial beam scale manufacturers…largely from Strait Manufacturing Company of Kansas City, Missouri. H. O. Hem was Strait's Superintendent and Chief Engineer. During his 26 years with Strait, Hem had designed their Monarch line of heavy duty scales ranging from a 600 lb portable to a 200 ton railroad track scale. He also designed barrel-making machinery, the Monarch-Corliss Steam Engine, and a modern type of the 1000 horsepower gas engine.

Hem became a consultant to Toledo. As such, he often attended the lunch meetings where an engineer presented a new scale design. On one occasion, one of Toledo's engineers proudly demonstrated a new fan scale he had designed. Theobald asked Hem's opinion.

"It won't work," he said.

The engineer was defensive. "What do you mean…why won't it work?" Hem replied, "Let me show you." He then showed the group that the tare and capacity beams were not properly mounted. "Fix those," he said to the engineer, "and it will work."

Here was a proven inventor. Theobald began to seriously recruit Hem. Within a short time Hem became Toledo's Chief Engineer. With Hem on board, Toledo began manufacturing industrial scale understructures and the industrial line became a true Toledo product.

The industrial scale line was an immediate hit. The double pendulum mechanism was a real breakthrough. More manufacturing capacity was needed. Toledo added a fourth floor to the Rakestraw building at its own expense and continued to pay the same rent. This added 6,500 square feet to the building. A Convention Room was included in the fourth floor plan and the District Manager's Convention of 1912 was held here. It became the company dining room.

The building was not solidly built. It was not designed to take a fourth floor. Most of the time when a train passed or stopped at the Milburn Wagon Works Station across the street from the factory on the other side of Albion, it shook the building enough that the retail scale balancers would have to stop work until the train passed. This happened regularly all day. It was a busy station.

The Wagon Works Station was named after Milburn Wagon Works, located across Monroe Street from the Toledo factory on Milburn Avenue near where it ended at Monroe. Milburn Wagon Works manufactured horse-drawn buggies and wagons until the automobile made them obsolete. Then they manufactured the Milburn Electric Auto until a devastating fire drove them out of business.

Auto manufacturers were among the first to use the industrial dial scale. Cars were getting better. Just two years previously Charles F. Kettering had invented the self starter, which greatly increased auto sales.

Early in 1912, Theobald hosted seven executives of Toledo Scale's neighbor, the Willys Overland Company, for a plant tour and a luncheon in the new company dining room. The guests included John North Willys, founder of the company, and his general manager George Bennett, the guiding genius in the company's early days. Willys often stated that much of his success was due to Bennett's guidance. George Bennett's two sons, Hubert and Geoffrey, would later play major roles at Toledo Scale.

It was time to change the company name again. Industrial scales did not compute. With the rapid growth of the industrial line, the company needed a new name. On February 18, 1913, the word "Computing" was dropped and the company name became simply "Toledo Scale Company."

And, by the end of the year, Theobald's campaign to the various state legislatures urging them to enact weights and measures laws had begun to pay off. Now Montana, Ohio, Utah, New York, Nevada, New Jersey, Indiana, Vermont, Michigan, Wisconsin, Minnesota and the state of Washington had passed laws similar to the first such laws in Massachusetts.

Theobald began to aggressively sell the industrial line. He firmly believed in aggressiveness. He reprinted an excerpt from an article written by W. H. Cunningham, president of the Sherwin-Williams Company in the *Toledo System* magazine headed:

AGGRESSIVENESS

"Aggressiveness you should always have. The fighting spirit should be the dominating spirit in the sales department. Pride in the institution, in its products, in its management, and in its customers is what makes aggressive, enthusiastic and successful fighters."

Theobald added, "This aggressive spirit, this fighting spirit, is the spirit we desire to engender and foster in the sales organization. If every member of our organization, be he inside or outside, in the sales or service department, a clerk, a mechanic, or a salesman, will develop a true spirit of aggressiveness, pride in the institution, its products, its managers, its selling force and its customers, and will use it for the best interests of the company, then our progress will keep pace with our ambitions."

His approach was ideal for the new industrial line. The new dial's design had the weight increments on the outside circle. Another circle inside the increments had TOLEDO reversed out of black on top and Toledo's already famous trademark, "No Springs—Honest Weight" reversed out of black on the bottom. Demand for heavy capacity scales grew by leaps and bounds. Toledo had something new, the only automatic indicating industrial scale. Many special purpose industrial scales were designed using the double pendulum mechanism during the first World War.

The Toledo mechanical dial scale soon became a familiar sight in virtually every manufacturing plant in the nation and throughout many parts of the world. All over the globe, the city of Toledo became known for scales. They proved to be remarkably reliable, some in regular use decade after decade. The dial remained essentially unchanged throughout the entire mechanical scale era. Even though mechanical scales, with their large dials, were largely replaced by electronic scales, tens of thousands remain in use even in the last decade of the 20th century. Thousands are expected to remain in use throughout industry for simple weighing tasks well into the 21st century.

About the same time Hapgood demonstrated his double pendulum mechanism, the Dayton Scale Company changed ownership. Bill Zolg, who came to Toledo as company treasurer from Dayton first heard about it from relatives. He broke the news to Theobald. "Henry, there's some news about Dayton Scale…it's been sold."

Theobald perked up. "Oh, really. Who bought it?"

"The word is that Charles R. Flint put together a holding company that acquired three other companies," Zolg explained. "One of them was Dayton Scale Company. The other two were the International Time Recording Company, and the Tabulating Machine Company of Washington, D.C. They incorporated the holding company in Endicott, New York as the Computing-Tabulating-Recording Company…C.T.R. for short."

"You mean Flint, the old buccaneer? The one who was a famous gunrunner? I heard he stuck his nose in some South American revolutions, even acting as a spy…a double agent."

"That's the one. But don't forget, he also was one of the organizers of the U.S. Rubber Company. He's getting respectable."

"I hope the shake-up means that Dayton will be less troublesome," Theobald said. "Did you hear who's going to run the company?"

"No. They're looking for someone, I understand."

C.T.R. drifted for several years. Then in 1914 the board employed Thomas J. Watson to head it.

When Watson became president of C.T.R. the company was in poor financial shape. He had to secure a $40,000 loan on his own account to keep it going. It started with less than 4,000 employees who made and sold spring scales, tabulating equipment and time recording devices. Later Watson had the name changed to International Business Machines, soon to be known as IBM.

Watson began his business career in 1891 as a bookkeeper in a small town food market. Becoming bored with that, he took a job peddling organs and sewing machines. Later he peddled phony building stocks, although he was not aware they were phony.

Desperate after the stock swindle was exposed, Watson went to the Buffalo office of NCR seeking a job. At first the manager put him off, but he was persistent. After several months of regular calls upon the office manager, he was hired as a cash register salesman.

Within a couple of years, Watson became the top salesman in the Buffalo office. In 1899, Patterson named him a branch agent in Rochester, New York, where he did well. In fact, he did so well, Patterson brought him to Dayton in 1903. He was given a staff with the charge to eliminate competition in the second-hand cash register business.

He set up a dummy company with the announced purpose of competing with NCR. In reality, under Patterson's orders, Watson's purpose was to undercut competitor's prices and eliminate anyone who stood in the way of NCR's drive for a monopoly.

This was illegal of course, although it's not clear that Watson was aware of it. Still, in 1912, Watson, Patterson and 28 others were indicted and convicted of the scheme. An appeals court later ordered a new trial but it was never held.

Patterson had successfully used Watson, then calmly fired him in 1913. Watson felt abandoned even though Patterson gave him a final settlement of $50,000. His great opportunity came a few months later when he was named to head C.T.R., located near his old hometown of Elmira, New York.

Theobald and Watson knew each other at NCR, though not very well. Watson was still in Rochester when Theobald was fired so they never became friends. He knew he now had an especially tough competitor, trained in business as he was by the current master, John Patterson.

Theobald was right. Later, the relationship resulted in serious trouble for both Toledo and Theobald personally.

Meanwhile, business was picking up in Canada where a manufacturing plant was started in 1911. It increased everywhere overseas as well. Theobald sailed again for Europe in September 1913, to further develop Toledo's foreign business. He spent eight months studying the markets in various European countries and helping distributors. In England, he worked with the W & T Avery company to expand their Toledo cylinder scale business.

When he returned home, he continued work to develop world markets. In December, he appointed a distributor in Japan with headquarters in Tokyo and sub-office in Yokohama. And the following month he named John Mitchell a company sales manager for all of Central and South America. Mitchell had served several years as district sales manager in Montreal, Canada. Next he appointed O. Preetzmann-Aggerholm sales manager for the Scandinavian countries.

Toledo scales became well known through much of the world. The slogan No Springs—Honest Weight was applied to export scales in more than a dozen different languages even before the start of the first World War...which was rapidly approaching.

CHAPTER 7

Two Pounds of Gold

In 1914, Henry Ford astounded the business world by announcing that he would give his employees a minimum wage of $5 a day and would share with them $10 million in last year's profits. Even the boys who swept the floors would be paid at least $5 a day. Another part of the plan stated that no person would be fired except for proven unfaithfulness or inefficiency. Anyone doing poor work in one department would be given the chance to make good in another part of the plant. In announcing the plan, a Ford spokesman said, "It is our belief that social justice begins at home."

Theobald was also concerned about his employees. A recent death in the shop revealed the man had no life insurance. The company helped the widow but he wanted a better solution. On July 1, 1916, the company gave its home office employees a life insurance program through Aetna.

It was one of very few companies in the nation to provide free life insurance to employees, paying the entire premium. The Aetna Life Insurance Certificate was numbered 122; Toledo was the 122nd company in the U.S. to voluntarily adopt Aetna's group insurance policy for its employees. A few years later, this insurance was extended to members of the 100% Club and finally to all field employees.

By the time of the 1915 100% Club Convention, Frank Ditzler had transferred to San Francisco. Frederick Geddes was made an honorary member at this convention. Geddes was the company attorney as well as a company director. At the 1916 convention,

Theobald announced the insurance plan for home office employees. This meeting cost the company $25,000.

Toledo developed a public relations approach for their salesmen to use, to help merchants identify themselves with honest weight. When a new store was scheduled to open, they sold the merchant on holding an Honest Weight and Pure Food Opening. These openings often attracted thousands. The Toledo salesman handled the details for his customer. The merchant set special, attractive prices and included other promotions for opening day. Through circulars he invited people from miles around. The Toledo salesman demonstrated his scale time after time to the visitors.

A new salesman in North Carolina, F. E. Tipton, was quoted in the *Toledo System* magazine. He said, "On February 29, 1916, I conducted my first Honest Weight opening in the meat market of Z. B. Bullock, Rocky Mount, North Carolina. More than eight thousand people thronged the place. I became endowed with new enthusiasm. Other merchants were attracted to see it from as far away as fifty miles. Since then I've conducted many Honest Weight openings. Let me relate another opening in Elizabeth City.

I learned that a progressive merchant, D. R. Morgan, was about to open a fancy new grocery store. Mr. Morgan had been in business a number of years. He had been using several different types of computing scales, none of which was a Toledo. When I called on him he said he didn't need any more scales. When I tried to show him the real merits of the Toledo, he waved his hand and said, 'I've heard all of that little spiel. No, young man, you can't sell me a Toledo scale.'

Right then I started with the proposition of a pure food and honest weight opening…the *strongest selling ammunition* ever produced. In spite of all he had said, he became very much enthused. When I had talked over the Honest Weight opening idea with him thoroughly, had shown him all the great advantages and advertising he would derive from having so large an attendance on an occasion of this kind, and had assured him that it meant new customers as well as binding him to the old ones, he seemed to have lost sight of the fact that he was buying scales. He signed the order as freely as a young man signs a marriage certificate!"

Several of his customers sent letters to Toledo praising Tipton and the experience. Mr. Bullock in Rocky Mount wrote, "Our Honest Weight Opening conducted by your Mr. Tipton was a huge success. It greatly exceeded my fondest hopes. Eight thousand people attended. Hurrah for Toledo scales and Tipton."

The head of Mutual Stores in Goldsboro, North Carolina wrote, "At the suggestion of your Mr. Tipton we had an opening reception, the finest display of this sort ever seen in Goldsboro."

As a result of success stories like these, Honest Weight openings swept the country.

The *Toledo System* magazine was the vehicle for Toledo salesmen all over the country to tell others of their successful approaches. Later that year *Toledo System* published "A New Eye Opener" from a salesman who used this way to dramatically point out how profits are lost when a merchant uses even-balance scales or inaccurate spring scales. He wrote:

"Here's a new way of making the average merchant realize how great his losses are from inaccurate scales. You know how often a merchant turns up his nose when you talk about his losses in overweight, how he takes the attitude that it's only a trifle and not worth bothering about. They're usually using old-fashioned even-balance scales, or sometimes spring scales. Here's a thought that will usually give them a jolt. It's a way of looking at it in a way they've never been shown before.

Approach them somewhat in this manner: 'Mr. Old Notion, what percent of net profit do you make? Probably not over 10% is it?'

It's quite likely he'll evade an answer, so you must say:

'Oh, well, I know you don't make an awful lot over 10% after everything is decided, and I think you're smart enough not to make very much under that. So assuming you do make 10%, have you any idea what percent of your profits you lose on a transaction of one pound, when you only give a half ounce of overweight?'

Merchant: 'Oh, I don't know. I don't suppose very much.'

Salesman: 'No, that's just it. You don't suppose very much so you keep on giving it. Well, sir, every time you give a half ounce of overweight on a transaction of a pound, you just throw away over 30% of your profit.'

Merchant: 'Oh, that's preposterous.'

Salesman: 'Well, I'll prove it to you.'

Merchant: 'Well, prove it.'

Salesman: 'Just for easy figuring take an arbitrary value like $1.00 a pound. You sell a pound and the price is $1.00. Your profit is ten cents; you give a half ounce of overweight; that half ounce is worth one-thirty-second of a dollar, isn't it, or about three cents. Well, that three cents has to come out of your profit. There's no place else for it to come out. And since your profit is ten cents, that three cents is 30% of your profit. And if the transaction happens to be for half a pound, why then you just gave away over 60% of your profit. If it's a quarter pound transaction, well, I hate to say what you're doing then but it amounts to this…all of your profit is thrown away and you take a 25% loss besides.'

Merchant: 'I guess I never thought of it that way.'

Salesman: 'Don't forget, this holds true whether your product is worth $1.00 a pound or five cents a pound. And remember, there are a lot more half and quarter pound sales in these days of high prices. Your half pound and quarter pound sales are usually on the high priced goods and the pound and five pound sales are on the low priced goods with short profits. You know all these things.

Now, I've shown you in black and white what a big proportion of your profits goes walking out the door when you just give a tiny pinch of overweight. Your average clerk doesn't think it amounts to a hill of beans.'

Now this is a new way of putting the thing up to the merchant who doesn't think the overweight amounts to much. Try it a few times and see if it doesn't reach your hard prospect."

New weapons like these in the fight for Honest Weight and accuracy developed constantly.

And once again plant capacity had to be expanded to keep up with an ever growing demand for industrial scales. A new plant was built in 1916 on the southwest corner of Monroe and Smead, about a block from the original plant. Additions were soon added which raised its capacity to 40,000 square feet. By this time, the United States had entered the first World War.

The 1917 100% Club Convention was announced in 1916 before the U.S. entered the great war. By the time it was to be held, our nation had entered the conflict. The largest number of salesmen ever had qualified for membership and the company was eager to hold the convention. Rather than cancel it, the management team decided to hold it with a patriotic theme to show support.

It was a spectacle. The 1917 meeting of the 100% Club broke all records. 86 Toledo salesmen against 44 the previous year made quota to become the 1917 100% Club members. This group also broke all records in the average amount of business produced in the year. The pageantry was especially impressive, exceeding anything ever seen before in Toledo.

The group was housed in Toledo's Hotel Secor. The hotel was decorated with large "HOWDY" signs. A Toledo Person Weigher was displayed in the lobby, particularly interesting to those who had never seen one. A large display of counter scales on gold pedestals made everyone feel at home. After traveling for days, the men gathered in the lobby on the convention's first day. It was a noisy gathering. They greeted old friends from past conventions or shook hands for the first time with men they had learned to regard highly only through correspondence.

Promptly at eleven o'clock, the word was passed that the formal opening of the week's activities was about to occur. Men from the home office gathered the club together and moved them outside in a double line to board special cars for a ride to the Toledo Art Museum several miles down the street. They were met by the carefully trained Toledo Scale Company Drill Squad, standing at attention in front of the museum. It was a beautiful summer day.

Next, the men were formed into a parade on the steps of the museum. Led by the Drill Squad, the parade marched down Monroe Street to the plant about a mile away. The city had closed Monroe Street to traffic for the parade. A large, noisy crowd of onlookers cheered the group on its way. Upon reaching the plant they were welcomed home by the office staff. They cheered when they saw that every window in both factory buildings was hung with patriotic bunting.

A band played as they raised the flag. From that moment, the entire plant was in possession of the 100% Club. The convention was on.

The first event was held on the fourth floor where the lunch room had been specially decorated and turned over to the 100% Club. Theobald heartily welcomed them. After they were served lunch, home office people escorted them in small groups through the plant.

As soon as the men had completed a rapid trip through the factory, they were picked up by a train of automobiles and taken to a 25-acre site on the corner of Bennett Road and Sylvania Avenue. The land had recently been purchased as a "new plant" site. A large sign displayed on the site showed a ground plan and plant layout for the proposed new building. Standing before the sign, Theobald told the Club of his plans for the new factory as he stood on the spot where the building was to rise. The 100% Club members then took part in a groundbreaking ceremony at the site.

Reeves, the plant manager, spoke of the need for a new plant. "Since last year, our output of heavy capacity scales has greatly increased. Just last week we not only had the largest output that department ever attained, we also had the largest output in the counter scale department. So we gave the company a 100% week as far as output was concerned. But we've had to operate a double shift to do it. We believe that we've reached the limit our present plant can produce."

When the ceremonies at the new plant site were over, the men boarded the train of automobiles and traveled to the Theobald home on West Woodruff. They were greeted by Mary Theobald, who charmed the group. She said, "It's a real pleasure to welcome the members of the 100% Club, many of whom I now look upon as old friends." On her own, she presented two sales awards she had herself created for May-June sales achievements. Enjoying refreshments, the club members had their first chance to informally talk among themselves and get better acquainted.

That evening, there was a banquet at the Country Club on River Road where the company attorney Fred Geddes spoke. He told the story of an Alaskan miner. "James Stevens was one of four prospectors in the Klondike who struck it rich," he said. "They divided up their gold and started for San Francisco. But just before leaving, Stevens got in a faro game and lost everything he had.

Winter was coming and he would starve unless something was done for him. So the other three decided to pay his way home to San Francisco and give him a fee to guard their gold on the ship. They each had their share of dust and nuggets accurately weighed and placed in a strong box. Stevens' job was to watch the box by day and sleep by it every night until the ship reached San Francisco. There was exactly 600 lb of gold, sworn to by a regular weigher."

Geddes had their attention now. This was going to be a scale story.

"Well, everything went along smoothly until the ship came into port. The box was officially reweighed. This time it weighed just a bit over 598 lb. They weighed it again. Again a bit over 598 lb. It appeared that Stevens had stolen about two pounds of gold from his partners. Convinced of his guilt, the partners swore out a warrant for Stevens' arrest. He was indicted, arrested, thrown in jail and held for trial. Not able to account for the loss, he gave up all hope of being acquitted."

Everyone was leaning forward, listening carefully.

"Since Stevens didn't have any money, the court appointed a young lawyer to defend him," Geddes continued. "When the case was called, Stevens' lawyer, Thaddeus Wayne, didn't even bother to question the witnesses. The prosecution rested. Now it was Wayne's turn. With few clients and plenty of time, he had done some research.

Opening his defense, Wayne called Sam Johnson as an expert witness. Johnson taught physics in a local high school. The judge didn't see any relationship between physics and the theft but decided to humor the young lawyer and accept the witness. Wayne began to question Johnson.

'With what does physics deal?'

'With natural phenomena, or the changes in the state or condition of matter.'

'Does the weight of an object or person change as he changes his location on earth?'

'Yes.'

'Just how does this happen and how much does the weight change?'

'The weight of any body is greatest at the poles of the earth, as they are the nearest points to the center of the earth. It gets less and less the farther we travel toward the equator. The weight of any substance would be less here in San Francisco than in Nome, Alaska."

'About what fractions of its weight would a body lose in going from Cape Nome, Alaska, to San Francisco?'

'I should say about one in three hundred.'

'Then gold weighing 600 pounds on the scale used in Nome could not possibly weigh much over 598 pounds on the scale used here, could it?'

'It could not. They were both spring scales, I understand.'

The men applauded vigorously. "But wait," Geddes warned. "There's more. The judge was quite interested by now. He questioned Johnson from the bench. 'Well then, how does the government weigh bullion when they send it from Washington to the New Orleans mint. New Orleans is at sea level…a lower altitude. Don't they have the same problem?'

'No, Your Honor, I understand the government uses special scales that show true weights on any different part of the earth.'

'Special scales…what's special about them?'

'The government uses pendulum scales that measure gravity against gravity. They weigh the same everywhere on earth at any altitude…and at any temperature for that matter.'"

Geddes paused, then spoke quietly. "Stevens was acquitted," he concluded.

The 100% Club rose and cheered.

Secretary Dan Kelly then read 25 telegrams from those who were unable to attend. Among them were telegrams from former president Theodore Roosevelt, John North Willys of the Willys-Overland Company in Toledo, and finally from Bob Theobald, now a commissioned Ensign at Annapolis. Yet Geddes was clearly the hit of the banquet.

The next morning the group was transported to the Toledo Coliseum. There, the largest scale exhibit the company ever had was set up. The huge room was lined with scales. A large built-in type of scale was centered in the room…the first of its kind the members had ever seen. The Inventions Department had its own display. Engineers in the department went into detail about the new devices they hoped to perfect soon.

After lunch, the men boarded special interurban cars and traveled to Cedar Point, a resort area near Sandusky. When they arrived, they were again greeted by the Company Guard of Honor Drill Squad who escorted them on their half mile march from the promenade of the Breakers Hotel to a cafe reserved for them where they were served dinner. After dinner they marched to the Auditorium for a patriotic rally.

The company invited people from Cedar Point and Sandusky to attend the rally. Attendance was over 3,000 people. The hall was filled to capacity. Names of Toledo Scale employees who were serving in the armed forces were read to much applause.

The speaker was Lieutenant Eugene Roberts, formerly of the British Expeditionary Force who was sent abroad in 1914. He was introduced by Dr. W. O. Thompson, president of both Ohio State University and Aetna Mutual Life Insurance Company. Enthusiasm, applause and patriotic fever ran high as Roberts spoke about his own experiences in France. To conclude his talk, he said. "Take the news back to your part of the country that America must wake up if we are to do our part in this great conflict."

The next morning a business session was held. After lunch everyone adjourned to the lake. It was hot; a great day to enjoy Lake Erie and the beach at Cedar Point. The men appeared on the beach donned in the tops and bottoms of their wool swim suits. Softball games, wrestling matches, sand fights and water sport lasted until the sun went behind a cloud late in the afternoon. A cooling, refreshing rain made it possible to enjoy a late dinner at the cafe...almost as if it were planned.

The group returned to Hotel Secor for a wrap-up. In saying good-bye, Theobald said, "I thank you for your patience, your attention and your manners. It enables us to stand up before our community and be proud of the way traveling salesmen from a hundred to several thousand miles away from home have conducted themselves. When we walk up to each other and meet face to face, and look into each other's eyes, there is something that makes words unnecessary. We expect to have you all here next year. Good night."

The July 1917 100% Club was the largest, most successful and popular convention ever. Theobald hoped that the July 1918 100% Club convention would be even better, but it was not to be. The 1918 convention was canceled when the U.S. entered the war in April 1917. By the end of the war when an armistice was signed by the Germans on November 11, 1918, Toledo Scale displayed one Gold Star and 225 Blue Stars on its service flag, a large percentage of the 700 employees at the time.

CHAPTER 8

"There's a submarine on our port bow!"

Meanwhile, Henry Theobald's son Bob had grown up. On summer vacations from Andover, then Yale University, he had always worked at the plant. He knew it from the ground up. He was attending Yale when the war broke out, then transferred to the Naval Academy at Annapolis. After graduating with honors, he was immediately sent to the Mediterranean. Rapidly promoted, he commanded the submarine destroyer Decatur with the rank of lieutenant commander.

He wrote his father about one adventure: "I must tell you of our latest encounter with Fritz. It happened on November 9th, and that day will live in my mind as one of the greatest in my life for on that day I saw the most awe-inspiring, magnificent and yet pitiful sight I can ever imagine; the torpedoing and sinking of a great battleship."

His destroyer was assigned to the waters surrounding the British Isles. In November, his ship was assigned to escort into port the H.M.S. Britannia, a British battleship. They joined up with a British submarine for the escort. His letter continued, "To begin with, at 7:14 a.m. the Britannia was torpedoed. Two torpedoes were fired, the first just missing our stern and crossing the Britannia's bow, and the second catching her just forward of her after turret. We rushed to take off the crew before she sank. They were near shore and many British patrol boats also rushed to rescue the crew."

When they were alongside, the captain of the Britannia yelled down to young Theobald, "Never mind us...there's a submarine on our port bow. Go get it!" Theobald wrote, "We tore loose and started at full speed towards the submarine. My ship and a British destroyer reached it at the same time. We both dropped four depth charges, which tore up the ocean and threw debris and wreckage high into the air. We couldn't see what damage we had done as there was too much water flying through the air. When we got back to the sinking battleship we were told by the cheering crew that we got the sub. After survivors had been picked up, we circled the battleship until she sank with a loss of over 100 lives...men who couldn't get off."

Henry Theobald had released his son's letter to the newspaper who printed it in its entirety. When the war ended, Bob Theobald returned home a minor celebrity, and went to work for his father as a supervisor in the sales department and coordinator of inventions, scale construction and production.

During the war, labor shortages, higher labor costs and the demand for more industrial production caused a further increase in the rapidly accelerating demand from industry for automatic dial indicating scales. Toledo made special scales for the war effort, including force measurement devices and shell loading scales. This started the development of a wide variety of unique scales for special applications; all of which led Toledo to create a wholly owned subsidiary named Toledo Precision Devices, a forerunner of Toledo Systems.

American industry recognized and valued Toledo precision. Cadillac Motor Car Company ran an advertisement in the *Saturday Evening Post*. It pointed out the accuracy and care used by Cadillac to insure accuracy in all of their processes...and featured a Toledo scale in the illustration for the ad.

Cadillac used a Toledo fan scale to weigh its piston rod assembly, to make sure that each one of the eight piston rods used in its engines weighed exactly the same. A slight variation in weight made the engine run rough and set up a vibration that was unpleasant to the driver and bad for the life of the engine. The message was that the Toledo scale was used to improve the quality of their car.

The war was not quite over when Toledo faced serious legal and financial problems. Dayton had filed a suit against Toledo in 1910 in the Federal District Court, Chicago, claiming that Toledo's 1906 cylinder computing scale had infringed on one of their patents. The suit was for infringement of Smith Reissue patent No. 11,536 covering "an indicator drum for a weighing mechanism consisting of a spindle provided with a plurality of skeleton frames of light material and secured to said spindle, and having secured to their peripheries a sheet of paper forming a cylinder."

The company's legal counsel, Frederick Geddes, fought the suit for years. It was one of many suits between the two companies.

Though this suit was filed before IBM owned Dayton, Watson pursued it vigorously along with several other lawsuits. Then in May of 1918, Geddes stopped by to see Theobald. "Bad news, Henry. I just got the ruling on the Dayton lawsuit from the Federal District Court in Chicago. It ruled against Toledo."

"Damn! What did they rule?"

Geddes hesitated. "Well, the court ordered Toledo to pay all profits realized on the sale of cylinder scales covered by the patent, plus accrued interest and the cost of attorney fees. That's all profits on our cylinder scale from its beginning in 1906. And if we want to appeal to the Supreme Court, we have to post a bond."

"Well, we have to appeal," Theobald replied. "That's going to add up to a fortune. It could wipe us out. It's just plain wrong! Dayton's patent wasn't for the first cylinder computing scale...Phinney's was. If we only could find a Phinney scale. We've got to try harder!"

Theobald asked Geddes to explain the suit to the management group at lunch. "This lawsuit is a strange one," Geddes said. "Dayton claims that their cylinder computing scale patent was infringed beginning in 1906 by our first cylinder scale. Watson knows that Dayton's patent wasn't the first. In 1870 a man named Phinney in Pawtucket, Rhode Island had the first patent issued on a cylinder-type computing scale...many years before Dayton's patent."

Bill Zolg asked, "Then why wasn't the Dayton patent declared invalid?"

"It was never challenged," Geddes said. "Phinney's business didn't last long, and he was dead by the time Dayton's patent was issued."

"But I understand we have a Photostat of the actual Phinney patent," Zolg said. "Doesn't that prove our case?"

"Not under the law," Geddes replied. "It's not enough to prove Phinney received a patent. We have to prove he actually produced and sold some cylinder scales based on his patent. We know he did make and sell a few in 1870, but we can't find any to prove it. We've been looking for one of them for eight years now. If we could have got our hands on one we would have won easily."

"We've had the entire field trying to find one," Theobald remarked. "But don't forget, Phinney made his few scales about 48 years ago. We've been looking for a needle in a haystack that's almost half a century old."

Toledo didn't know that in 1908 Dayton had first started the same infringement suit against the Standard Computing Scale Company of Detroit. And unknown to Toledo, the Standard Scale Company in Detroit owned one of the original 1870 Phinney scales. When Standard introduced the Phinney scale as evidence, Dayton withdrew its claim.

Dayton then began an intensive search for Phinney scales. They believed that only seven scales were still in existence. When they had located and bought six of them, they knew that the only one left belonged to Standard. They were sure that Standard would not tell Toledo about the one Phinney scale in their possession because they knew that the Standard and Toledo owners didn't like each other. Standard made spring scales. The president of the Standard Scale Company, Thomas Commerford, deeply resented Theobald's spring scale attacks.

Toledo couldn't produce any evidence that the Phinney scale was ever manufactured, which was required to win the suit. So even knowing that they didn't hold the first legal patent, Dayton filed the 1910 suit against Toledo. When Watson took over IBM, he pursued it until the end.

Toledo didn't have to lose this patent suit. The Phinney scale predated the Smith Reissue Patent by years. Personal animosity between the principals of Toledo and Standard caused Standard's president to keep the Phinney scale to himself until it was too late.

Theobald hired accountant Walter Fink and told him to comply with the court order. His job was to determine the amount to be paid under the court judgment if the appeal to the Supreme Court failed. Since the accounting had to go back to the beginning of Toledo's manufacture of their first cylinder scale in 1906, Fink learned about the early history of the company. He worked closely with Theobald who soon became Fink's mentor. The two became friends. Theobald told Fink of many early company experiences and Fink began recording them in a journal.

By December, Fink determined the profit amount was in excess of $440,000, a huge sum. Toledo's treasurer was authorized to set up a reserve account in this amount out of surplus and undivided profits. Shortly, the manager of the accounting department resigned and Fink was appointed to the job. Along with his close relationship with Theobald, this gave him an even wider knowledge of the business and its early problems.

After the 1918 ruling against Toledo by the Federal District Court in Chicago, Standard's president Commerford concluded he would be sued next by Dayton since Toledo had lost their case. To avoid that, he finally decided it was in his own best interest to write Theobald and tell him that he had the missing Phinney scale. It was time to put his dislike for Toledo aside for the moment. After some bickering back and forth, he delivered it to Toledo. Finally, Toledo had a Phinney scale.

Theobald immediately applied to the Federal District Court for Northwestern Ohio for a rehearing on the basis of new evidence. The rehearing was granted. In the new hearing, the Court ruled that Dayton's patent was no good. Toledo won.

TERR

Theobald breathed a sigh of relief even though things were still in a state of legal flux. Now, if Toledo paid Dayton Scale as required by the Chicago Federal Court, it would be in contempt of the Toledo Federal Court...if Toledo did not pay, it would be in contempt of the Chicago court.

Toledo filed notice of their intention to apply to the Supreme Court of the United States to secure a stay of mandate to the previous finding in favor of the Dayton Scale Company. With the Phinney scale in hand, along with a copy of its original patent, Toledo had proof they didn't infringe on a valid patent. So Toledo went back to marketing their scales and attacking other problems.

Several years previously, Theobald had begun holding weekly educational meetings with employees. He wanted them to know the complete line forwards and backwards in order to be more efficient in "rendering the best possible service to Toledo customers." By 1918, regular night classes were conducted for employees in the Sales and Service School on Smead Avenue.

Employees were taught the entire line...model numbers, capacities, prices, allowances, different chart and beam combinations, and more. Most employees took the voluntary course. They learned to visualize an individual scale at the mention of the model number. A number of them chose to become a Toledo salesman as a result of what they had learned.

At the same time, seeds were planted in Europe that would lead to the next World War. On March 3, 1919, Vladimir Lenin formed the Comintern in Moscow, an international communist organization with the goal of fostering world revolution. Lenin argued that the security of the Russian regime depended upon its sparking a revolution throughout Europe.

Then, later that month on March 23, Benito Mussolini organized a new movement in Italy. His Fascist party was claimed to be the answer for Italy's postwar problems of strikes, social unrest and parliamentary disorganization. He vowed to fight liberal and communist influences through aggressive nationalism and rigid military discipline.

CHAPTER 9

"As a friend, you were loved."

On January 16, 1920, Prohibition took effect in the United States. Beer, wine and liquor were officially banned by the 18th Amendment. Enforced by the National Prohibition or Volstead Act, it was nothing new to the 25 states that had already passed their own Prohibition laws. New York's Alderman LaGuardia was skeptical about the law, saying that it would take 250,000 police to enforce it in that city alone, and nearly as many more to police the police.

Later that year on August 26, a proclamation was signed giving American women the right to vote. No women were present when Secretary of State Bainbridge Colby signed the papers certifying ratification of the 19th Amendment. This ended an 81-year-old struggle that began when Lecretia Mott was denied a seat at a conference.

However, it was many years later before Susan B. Anthony managed to persuade a member of Congress to introduce a proposed constitutional amendment for suffrage. Blocked for years, the amendment was finally approved by Congress and sent to the states. Some states had allowed women to vote within their borders for years. Wyoming, with its tradition of strong pioneer women, was the first state in the nation to do so, in 1869.

Theobald once again sailed for Europe. Before leaving, Bob Theobald was named a vice-president by the board of directors. While he was gone the company was officially managed by an executive committee. Bob Theobald was appointed permanent chairman of the executive committee. Reeves was vice chairman and other members were L. G. Christman, company secretary, Tom Goodbody, comptroller, and Zolg, the treasurer. Bob Theobald was to replace Henry Theobald as chairman of the committee even when his father was in Toledo. He was clearly "heir apparent."

In Europe, Theobald arranged for Toledo scales to be manufactured in Nuremberg, Germany, and for marketing in Holland, Belgium, France, Luxembourg and Denmark through the Toledo-Berkel Company of Holland. Toledo-Berkel was a new selling company organized by Toledo Scale Company and the Van Berkel Company. Van Berkel had one of the largest manufacturing and selling organizations in Europe. W. F. Van Berkel was the inventor of a popular meat slicer sold in the United States under the name "U S Slicer." Theobald now had a large, European marketing group working with him.

As a result of his trip to England, Gilbert Vyle, the managing director of the Avery Company, along with their general sales manager, a company director and two technical engineers, visited Toledo to explore the possibility of manufacturing the industrial line of scales under license. Avery had been manufacturing and selling Toledo retail scales since Theobald's 1909 agreement with them. An agreement was reached. Avery began making and selling Toledo industrial scales.

He next appointed Aubrey Houston the Toledo distributor for New Zealand. Houston had offices in Wellington, Christchurch, and Dunedin. Scales for New Zealand were to be built in Canada. Houston gave the Canadian company a $40,000 order to be paid in Canadian currency. Houston had experience as a scale salesman with a competing company before becoming the New Zealand Toledo distributor. He immediately sent his chief serviceman to the Toledo Service School, who spent a year in the school.

An existing Australian company, A. Woodhead Pty. Ltd., was appointed Toledo distributor for Australia. Their headquarters was in Melbourne and they had a sub-office in Sydney. This meant that Toledo scales now had distribution and sales capabilities in every major world market.

Bob Theobald made a trip through the Western states and returned home firmly believing that Toledo needed a lower priced line of scales to compete successfully. Toledo created a lower priced line by painting Class B scales in maroon. This line had a solid pendulum and chart end scrolls. Merchants said that maroon was the wrong color for both meat and grocery sales.

The line was quickly discontinued. The few maroon models that were sold were traded back. Toledo tried to repaint them in white lacquer but no matter how well the castings were stripped, the maroon bled through. There was no way to salvage them. It was a costly effort.

Henry Theobald continued to promote the value of service. He wrote "Service should be practiced as well as preached. It goes without saying that service is our first duty to our users. It's an obligation we assume when we accept an order. Too many men talk about service and fail to render it after they get the order. These are the men who care nothing about the future of our industry. The policy of the company is at all times to give service precedence over sales."

He said, "Selling is one thing. Service is another. The two should always be in close accord but never combined in one man. Let it be understood that the salesman's work is not finished when he gets the order. His next duty is to cooperate with the service man in seeing that the scale is properly installed and adjusted to the last nut and bolt and that the purchaser is completely satisfied. At intervals of 60 to 90 days reports should be obtained as to the condition of the scale with the sales manager, the salesman and service man cooperating to accomplish this result. This is service."

During the early 1920s chain stores rapidly expanded. This had a double effect on the scale industry. First, chain stores installed meat departments for one-stop shopping convenience. Many independent meat markets disappeared as a result. Secondly, food that had traditionally been sold in bulk by grocery stores was now sold in packages in which the product had been weighed and packaged at the producing company. The popular "cracker barrel" disappeared...along with bulk coffee, tea, beans, peas, prunes and a great many other food items.

Sales of Toledo's retail scale line had long ago been overtaken by the industrial line…and now the sale of retail scales dropped even more. About the same time a new firm, The Sanitary Scale Company, was incorporated in Belvidere, Illinois that caused retail scales sales to fall seriously.

Toledo management had heard it coming. One of the founders was Samuel Hastings who had been treasurer at the Dayton Scale Company. All the men who founded it had been in the retail scale field so they knew it would be for retail store use. Toledo assumed the scale would have a spring counterbalance so they weren't too worried. Toledo knew how to compete with spring scales. However, they quickly became concerned when they heard from their Chicago office.

Reeves received a letter from Toledo's Chicago office that reported on the new Sanitary scale. He took it in to Theobald, "Chicago is worried, Henry. They tell me the new Sanitary was introduced with a porcelain enamel finish. It looks really good and the merchants like what they see. They asked me if we could finish our scales in porcelain."

"Let's ask Chicago to buy one through one of their customers," Theobald said. "We need to look it over…see how it's made and what it looks like."

When the scale was examined by Toledo engineers, they concluded that it had been designed on the drawing board for a porcelain finish. It was indeed a spring counterbalance scale…with a split chart so the rack and pinion chart drive was in the center of the chart. Since only a spring connected the lever to the chart rack and pinion, the column between the scale base and the chart housing was small in diameter. The scale was not well built and would not wear well in use, the engineers claimed, and was not the most accurate competitive weighing device they had seen. The cost to manufacture it should be low however.

Sanitary made no attempt to develop a direct selling force. They chose to sell their new scale through store fixture houses, and through sales representatives who handled other lines of merchandise for retail stores. Using this method of selling, there was no such thing as a standard selling price even though it carried a low list price. Each sales outlet set their own price, often in combination with a store fixture package or other product.

The Sanitary scale proved to be formidable competition. It was something new, it was attractive and easy to clean with its porcelain finish, and it sold at a low price. Toledo tried to react quickly. As a stop gap, they began using a cylinder housing made out of sheet steel finished in white lacquer with the rest of the scale finished in porcelain enamel. They soon discovered this solution wouldn't last. After the scales were in use for a few months the cylinder housing changed to a light amber color. Customers complained.

The Toledo community was proud of the company that carried the city's name all over the world. Stories regularly appeared in local newspapers. In the early 20s, a full page story reviewed many accomplishments. In part it said:

"*Under a picture of Henry Theobald, president of the Toledo Scale Company, published in the Roycroft magazine, this inscription appeared: 'The man who made it disgraceful to manufacture, sell or use a dishonest scale in America. His fearless fight for honest weight does credit to the integrity of modern American business methods.'*

To Mr. Theobald goes the credit of having established as a matter of law the principle that the retailer's computations or selling price are the concern of the customer. In a word, there must be a square deal on both sides of the counter. And to the fearless fighting spirit with which that principle was battled for, is due the substantial success of the Toledo Scale Company."

Theobald was already looked upon as the father of our nation's weights and measures laws. Yet all was not well.

A postwar economic depression struck the nation in 1921, lasting for two years. The depression was severe. Sales suffered. Everyone scrambled to recover lost sales. At the same time, Toledo had to invest in the redesign of its entire line of retail scales. They needed to compete with the porcelain finish that Sanitary Scale Company had introduced. It was rapidly eating into their market share.

Word got around the company that Jack Dee, a young new Chicago salesman, satisfied his customers with a rather creative explanation. He told them that the housing was "supposed to mellow with age, just like a fine meerschaum pipe mellows to a beautiful amber color with use." Dee was destined to become a company legend with a long, successful career. Meanwhile, research on porcelain continued.

The economy had just begun to recover when early in 1922 Toledo and its vigorous, energetic president were hit with the most serious economic problem they had yet faced. Theobald felt he was personally dealt a terrible, unfair blow…one that could prove fatal and destroy the company. Destroy everything he had worked for, for more than 20 years.

On January 9 the Supreme Court of the United States announced their refusal to interfere with the decree of the lower court. Chief Justice William Howard Taft wrote the opinion. It stated that on the grounds of "Res judicata pro veritate accipitur" the Chicago court was upheld. It held in substance that Judge Killets of the Federal Court in Toledo had no jurisdiction to go into the matter the second time and his decision was therefore void.

Toledo Scale was immediately ordered to pay the Dayton Scale Company $420,883.44 plus interest and attorney fees. The total came to $650,883.44. To pay this huge sum and try to survive, Toledo had to increase their bank borrowing…not an easy task. The total amounted to over $990,000. The banks required Toledo to pledge every account and notes receivable, to the banks. Walter Fink was appointed Trustee. He had to prepare a monthly statement of the pledged assets to the banks.

Bob Theobald said the ruling "took the starch out of my father." Henry Theobald began to experience health problems. His enormous enthusiasm diminished. From that point on, he seemed to be running the company by instinct, simply going through the motions.

Bob Theobald then made a move that cheered his father up considerably…in March he married a girl he had courted seriously for the past five years. He was already 31 years old when he married Mary-Meloy Rankin. The bride had the same first name as his mother. She was the daughter of the Rev. and Mrs. James Rankin of New York and the marriage service was performed by the bride's father in the home of her uncle in Chicago. Henry and Mary Theobald were elated…they had almost given up hope of having grandchildren.

During their long courtship Mary-Meloy Rankin had often teased Bob, he told his friends. She had discovered that he became almost instantly aroused when she softly ran her fingers through the short hairs at the nape of his neck. Bob would caress her lightly. He could tell she was aroused too. But it did him no good. She held him off.

In spite of the teasing, Mary-Meloy was an innocent. Bob Theobald was possibly more experienced . . . his friends thought that he had enjoyed a few of the ladies of France and England during his Navy service in Europe. After all, he was a sailor. Still, he held the usual notions about the daughter of a minister. He rather expected his bride would be a bit repressed. He told his friends that he was wrong. She took to loving her new husband with enthusiasm. Bob was surprised and delighted at his bride's unexpected ardor.

The newlyweds booked a Pullman room to make a tour of the West. During daylight hours the room was made up with coach seats. On the train she often casually laid her arm over his shoulder and played with the back of his neck. Bob exaggerated a yawn. They decided then that they needed a nap.

In hotels they made love, took naps together in their private world, playfully bathed together, engaged in bawdy comedies over soap and shared towels—a playtime so alien to what he had expected that he felt he had become an entirely different person. He was surprised at how remarkably good he felt. He wanted to hit his head with a hammer for having deprived himself so long of this kind of arrogant smugness he had never known existed.

When they finally rested, Bob might have scowled and said, "I didn't know you were such a wanton." "Yes," she usually replied looking down demurely, "I'm so ashamed." Then she would look up at him and they would smile at each other. They were very much in love.

The trip combined a honeymoon with visits to Western Toledo Scale offices. They planned to visit New Orleans, Houston, San Antonio, El Paso, Phoenix, Los Angeles, San Francisco, Seattle, Portland, Spokane, Butte, Salt Lake City, Denver and Omaha. The new Mrs. Theobald, now part of the Toledo "family," was introduced to others in the family on the trip. She charmed them in the same way as the senior Mary Theobald had at every previous 100% Club convention.

She continued to tease him, Bob said. Even during an office visit she would put her arm behind his shoulder and play with the hair on the back of his neck. He discovered that his marriage brought him all the anticipated joys. On top of those expected pleasures, he found it was simply great fun to be married to Mary.

The result was quick and inevitable. The bride became pregnant early in the trip. They returned home earlier than planned. Traveling made her morning sickness worse. On January 3, 1923, not long after settling into their home, a baby girl, Mary Meloy Theobald, was born.

The parents and grandparents rejoiced...but their joy was short lived.

The new mother had a troubled delivery. Her health steadily failed. Bob hovered over her. She would look up at him and smile wanly. "I'm sorry, I'm sorry," she would say as tears came to her eyes. Greatly worried about his wife, Bob took little joy in his new daughter.

Six weeks after their daughter was born, it was clear a crisis had been reached. Her doctor had been with her for several hours when he came out of her room. "I'm sorry, Bob," he said, "she's gone." Bob and Mary had been married only eleven months when Mary-Meloy Theobald died.

Gloom overtook the Theobald family.

Bob Theobald was in a daze, overcome by grief. He was often found staring off into space. His work suffered. He became passive in meetings. Though he reported to work every day, almost a year passed before he appeared to have recovered. Concerned for him, his father gave him special assignments he thought would interest him in an attempt to get him involved and excited again.

At the same time, Henry Theobald had slowed down himself…his own health was failing. On June 5, 1924, he took a turn for the worse. His doctor convinced him he needed to stay home and rest his heart. Even then he insisted on keeping in touch with the business through daily reports. He appeared to be more weary than ill. With his wife, Mary, he planned a vacation, which they thought would restore him to full health.

Saturday morning, July 12, he was feeling as well as he had for some time. Then about 10:30 he suddenly felt much worse. "Mary, better get the doctor," he said quietly. "Something's wrong." Mary could see he had turned pale. She rushed to call the doctor. He arrived quickly. "I think it's a heart attack, Mary…there isn't much I can do," he said. "The next 24 hours are critical…let's hope for the best." With his family gathered at his bedside, he steadily grew worse.

At 4:30 that afternoon, Henry Theobald died. He was 56 years old.

Tributes poured in. Many state officials wrote the company, calling Henry Theobald the "father" of their weights and measures laws. The funeral was held in the Theobald home at 422 West Woodruff Avenue. By the time of the funeral on Tuesday, July 15, friends and members of Toledo's field organization had arrived from Atlanta, Montreal, New York, Texas, Minneapolis, South Carolina…from as far as it was possible to travel in the available time.

Theobald's old friend and associate, Frank Ditzler, wrote a eulogy, which read in part, "You were respected and trusted as a man; you were admired as a great builder; you were appreciated as an unusual and most successful teacher; but as a friend you were loved."

Surrounded by the graves of many pioneer Toledo families, Henry Theobald was buried in Toledo's Woodlawn Cemetery.

After Henry Theobald's death, the Executive Committee he had formed three years previously took on the complete management of the company. Still headed by vice president Bob Theobald as chairman, the committee was made up of seven members who represented various divisions of the business. Production was represented by O. C. Reeves, finance by Bill Zolg, legal matters and foreign sales by L. G. Christman, auditing and accounts by W. W. Winn, engineering and patents by C. O. Marshall, purchasing by Earle Smith, while Bob Theobald chaired the committee and supervised sales.

Bob Theobald had lost two of the people he loved the most, within 16 months of each other. His marriage of slightly less than a year had given him the greatest joy of his life. The death of his wife Mary-Meloy left a huge void and the death of his father struck another enormous blow. He had loved and respected him not only as a father but also as a mentor and friend.

Yet he seemed to take to his new duties, taking charge of the company in the name of the executive committee. Within two months of his father's death, he called all of the district managers to Toledo for a meeting of all sales managers.

In his opening remarks he spoke to them about, "Our Platform and Program." He said, "This is the first meeting of the district managers in a body since 1921. At that time my father was away in Europe. Now the responsibility of management has been wholly passed on to us."

He paused. "Of my loss as a son, I am constrained not to speak. As to my loss as a member of the Toledo Scale organization I realize, in common with all other members of the organization, the need for harder work and closer application in order to offset the taking away of our leader."

He continued more firmly. "Communications from the field should be directed to those department heads to whom you would normally send them to. Whenever a matter affects company policy, or if a general decision is required, the matter will be referred to the Committee by the department head."

He said, "Each member of the Committee and each department head is responsible for the operation of his division or department. Likewise, each district manager is individually responsible for the operation of his division. We must understand each other's viewpoint. With this outlook and with the new porcelain finish line, the company is prepared to embark on a program of progress in which we invite the enthusiastic cooperation of every member of the organization."

The porcelain problem had been troublesome to solve. The most common method of obtaining a porcelain finish was known as the "dry" method in which a casting was heated cherry red and powdered frit sifted over it. This didn't work well for Toledo. With this method the porcelain didn't fuse uniformly, due to varying thicknesses of the same casting. Some chipping resulted.

Toledo chose a "wet" process not in general use. The liquid frit was sprayed on a cold casting, then the casting was placed in an oven heated to about 1340° F which fused the porcelain to the metal evenly on both the thick and thin sections of the casting. Special ovens and handling equipment were designed and installed in a new Porcelain Enamel Department. Toledo now had a superior porcelain finish. The new line of porcelain-finished cylinder scales was introduced in January 1925.

Porcelain is made much the same as glass. Since it's fused to the surface of the metal, it doesn't have the brittleness of glass. The finish is hard and glistening and has a permanent luster. It's durable and easy to clean. Since it doesn't discolor, it eliminates much of the cost of refinishing. As a result, the resale value of the scale increased. This helped preserve the buyer's investment. Toledo's porcelain problem was solved. The line was a hit. Sales increased immediately.

1925 was a good year for sales. Chairman Lenox Rose informally canvassed other members of the board. They were in agreement that Bob Theobald was soon slated to be named president to replace his father, since he seemed to be doing well leading the company through the executive committee.

They weren't aware of his depressed emotional state. The people he had treasured most in his life were gone.

At work he appeared normal, though he refused to occupy his father's office. He handled all of his duties well. He was warm and friendly to everyone. He appeared to have as many ideas for strengthening the company as ever. Yet he kept his feelings inside himself so no one knew of his growing depression. There seemed to be no joy left in living.

Immediately after his wife's death he had hired Miss Nina Flinn as a full time, live-in nurse for his baby daughter. As the year drew to a close, he became even more deeply depressed.

On Friday evening, December 17, 1925, at about 10:00 p.m. he came to his 717 West Bancroft Street home and went right to his room. At 8:30 on Saturday morning the baby's nurse knocked on his door to wake him. He usually answered quickly but she couldn't get a response. She opened the door…and screamed.

Sometime during the night, 34-year-old Robert R. Theobald had stood before a mirror in his bedroom, put an automatic pistol to his temple and blown his brains out.

The Theobald era was over.

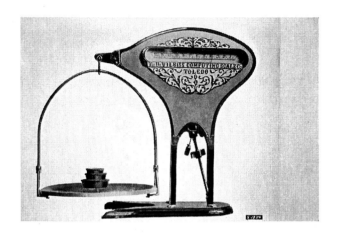

1. Original DeVilbiss computing scale.
2. DeVilbiss company employees with inventor Allen DeVilbiss, Jr. circled.

Original plant was at Albion and Bishop Streets in 2-story building at right. The three-story structure in foreground at Monroe and Albion was added; then an addition along Bishop Street. A fourth floor added later to main building.

3. Henry Theobald, founder of Toledo Scale.
4. First Toledo Scale plant (original DeVilbiss plant on right).

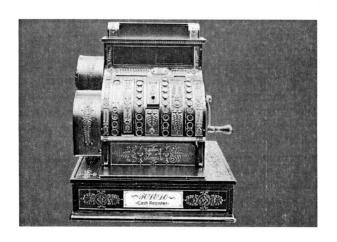

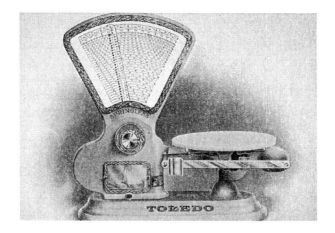

5. Toledo Cash Register.
6. Early Toledo Computing Fan Scale.

7. Toledo Cylinder Scale introduced in 1906.
8. Crowd at early Honest Weight opening.

9. Phinney Scale…the first computing scale.
10. Dayton Moneyweight ad claims merchant can both buy and
    sell at 9¢ per lb. and make 3% profit besides.

11. Toledo Scale delivery by balloon lifts off across from Dayton
    scale factory
12. Early industrial scale.

13. Hugh Bennett, second president.
14. Rattlesnake Island lodge.

15. Interior of Rattlesnake Island lodge.
16. 100% Club dinner at Rattlesnake Island, 1931.

17. Norman Bel Geddes' designs for new plant campus (airstrip on the left).
18. Closer look at Bel Geddes' new Toledo Scale plant designs.

19. Large "Guess Your Weight" scale dial.
20. First scale housed in Plaskon.

21. Weighing B-24 Liberator at Willow Run factory during WWII.
22. Original DeVilbiss employee Chase Reed, third president Harris McIntosh and Walter Fink look at Theobald portrait.

23. Hugh Ditzler, San Francisco region manager, receiving President's Cup from Harris McIntosh.
24. Tony DiVincenzo and Jack Dee look at new digital retail scale.

PART II

Bennett

"In creating, the only hard thing's to begin;
A grass-blade's no easier to make than an oak."
James Russell Lowell, 1848

"You have created a new thrill."
Victor Hugo, 1854

CHAPTER 10

A New Owner

After the death of her husband, Mary Theobald moved to New York but frequently returned to Toledo to visit her son, granddaughter and friends. Now with her son's suicide only 16 months after the death of her husband, she wanted no more to do with the company that had consumed their lives.

The Toledo Trust Company was the administrator of her husband's estate and she quickly let them know that her interests in the company were for sale.

A buyer was found immediately. Less than a month after Bob Theobald's suicide, Toledo Trust asked the probate judge for permission to dispose of the 1760 shares of common and 1049 shares of preferred stock of the Toledo Scale Company they were holding in trust for Mary Theobald.

The common was valued at $200 per share and the preferred at $90 per share. In January 1926, they were sold to Hubert D. Bennett of Toledo. Total purchase price was $446,410.

On January 19, 1926, Hugh Bennett was elected a company director and president of Toledo Scale Company. Lenox Rose remained chairman of the board. Bennett immediately assumed control. One of his first acts was to bring his younger brother Geoffrey Bennett into the company as his assistant.

Only 31 years old when he became president, Hugh Bennett was a vital, handsome and adventurous young man. After graduating from Williams College and before the United States entered the First World War, he joined the French army where he served as an ambulance driver and made some long-term French friends…one of whom was fellow ambulance driver Pierre Pasquier.

Some time after the war, he had helped Pasquier come to the United States. He became a teacher at Thomas A. DeVilbiss High School…a school named after the brother of the man who invented the first Toledo Scale. Pasquier taught French and history at DeVilbiss for decades.

Bennett was decorated by the French government after he was gassed while picking up wounded French soldiers. When the U.S. entered the war, he became a pilot in the U.S. Navy flying service. His Navy experience prompted a life-long love of flying.

After the war, he joined Willys-Overland in Toledo. His father, the late George Bennett, had been one of the most notable figures in automotive circles and a close friend of company founder John North Willys. The senior Bennett had counted Henry Theobald among his friends since first meeting him when visiting the Toledo Scale plant in 1912. The huge Willys-Overland factory was less than a mile away from the small Toledo Scale operation.

At the time of his death, George Bennett was general manager of Willys-Overland, then the second largest car manufacturing company in America, behind only Ford. He had been the driving force for putting together the first insurance-covered health plan at Willys Overland.

It was rumored that the insurance company, as a gift in appreciation of George Bennett's help in putting together the health plan, paid the premium on a million-dollar life insurance policy good for one year…and he died within the year the policy was in force. In any case, Hugh Bennett's inheritance was large.

After several years at Willys-Overland, working in the shops and on various departmental assignments, Hugh Bennett joined Studebaker in South Bend as assistant advertising manager. He next worked in field sales in Boston for Studebaker and was soon promoted to assistant sales vice president.

Yet Bennett wanted to run his own company. He had learned a bit about Toledo Scale from his father. So he put his inheritance to work by buying the stock interests from Theobald's widow.

He immediately announced to the field that all January 1926 sales were complimentary to Mary Theobald. The sales force turned in an increase of 25% over the same month the previous year.

Bennett moved fast to reorganize the company's capital structure. Theobald had resorted to bank financing rather than sell any common stock. He had wanted to keep effective voting control of the company. Because of the huge bank debt acquired after losing the Supreme Court appeal, Toledo had not met its accounts payable obligations on time or earned any cash discounts for years.

Theobald had even sold a number of his salesmen on the idea of building no-interest credit balances rather than take commissions. Financial conditions were strained when Bennett took charge.

He quickly arranged to bring new local stockholders into the company. Among these were Henry L. Thompson, John T. Rohr, Rathbun Fuller and W. W. Knight, Sr., all elected to the Toledo Scale board. The additional capital allowed him to pay off all the bank loans. And for the first time in years, Toledo was discounting its accounts payable.

All bills were now paid before the books closed at the end of the month. On those statements not showing a cash discount, Bennett introduced an innovation. He took an "anticipatory" cash discount based on a rate of 6% annually. Vendors regularly allowed the discount. Protests were rare.

Bennett made another important move right away. The company had a number of patent infringement suits pending against the Dayton Scale Company…and Dayton had a number pending against Toledo.

He called Thomas Watson, Sr., the president of IBM who owned Dayton Scale Company and asked for an appointment to see him in his New York office. Watson agreed to see him. He told Walter Fink about the meeting.

When he entered Watson's office he found the IBM president alone. Bennett said, "Thanks for seeing me, Mr. Watson, I've been looking forward to meeting you."

"Nice to meet you too, Mr. Bennett," Watson replied. "I've been told that you've already made some worthwhile changes at Toledo Scale. You're a fast-paced young man, it seems. Now then, what did you want to see me about?"

"About all these lawsuits, Mr. Watson. The first thing I discovered is that Toledo has many patent infringement lawsuits against your Dayton Scale subsidiary and you have many against us. Since I'm new to the scale industry I have no reason to have ill feelings against anyone. Mr. Theobald is gone now. All these patent suits cost us both a lot of time and money. They take our attention off managing our companies and it seems neither of us really gains anything by them. So I came with a proposition for you. It's this...let's both agree to cancel all actual or threatened litigation between our two companies and go on from here. I think we'll both be better off."

"You mean if I cancel all our lawsuits against you, you will cancel all yours against us? We both just stop suing each other?" Watson is said to have asked. "Is that what you propose?"

"That's exactly what I propose," Bennett replied. "Cancel all those now in the courts and all that have even been threatened in those legal terms lawyers use in their letters. Start with a clean slate."

Watson paused. "That's a rather appealing idea." The two men discussed it thoroughly. Abruptly Watson slapped his hand on the desk and said, "Agreed!" He leaned back in his chair. "Our lawyers are going to complain, but I like the idea of a fresh start. Now, since it appears we have concluded our business to our mutual satisfaction, it would be my pleasure if you would join me for lunch."

When Bennett returned to Toledo, he called long-time director and company attorney Fred Geddes to tell him about the agreement he had reached with Watson. Somewhat to Bennett's surprise, Geddes appeared pleased. "Why do you think he agreed, Hugh?" he asked.

"Well, first it made sound business sense," Bennett replied. "Then too, I think he recalled the infringement suit he won a few years ago that he knows he probably should have lost...the one where Theobald couldn't turn up a Phinney scale for evidence in time for the trial and it cost Toledo over half a million dollars. He knows that's the thing about trials...you win some you should have lost and you lose some you should have won. I think he figured he should quit while he was ahead."

"Well, I'm pleased...now maybe I can spend a bit more time with my law firm," Geddes said.

By March, Bennett had completed plans for better sales control. He announced a uniform field operations plan at a zone managers conference in Toledo at the end of the month. W. C. Gookin, recently named sales vice president, was given responsibility for the sales division. The ten zone managers now reported directly to him.

Bennett next turned his attention to manufacturing. O. C. Reeves had been plant superintendent since 1905 when Theobald recruited him from NCR. Now named first vice president, Reeves was given full responsibility for all manufacturing operations. Bennett shared Theobald's absolute confidence in him. When Reeves delivered reports to Bennett and the board they were usually considered final.

Because of the ongoing financial problems, manufacturing methods and tools were largely obsolete. Machine tools were old, slow, and needed constant maintenance. The entire plant was operated by an old-fashioned overhead belt system. Tooling was inadequate...the rule had been "file and fit." Reeves was told to develop plans for a new factory...which had been long anticipated.

Reeves appointed W. R. Emig production manager to give him more time to work on plans for a new plant. Emig began modernizing the machine tools. Every machine was individually motorized. Tools, jigs, dies, and fixtures were updated. Many new machines and tools had to be purchased to complete the huge task.

Bennett next implemented a new consignment control plan, which included ways to dispose of excess consignment stock. He established a warehouse in Toledo to speed up delivery of standard scales. At the same time, Reeves made plans to eliminate the excess inventory of raw materials, and finished and unfinished factory stock parts.

Dead inventory was a problem. Bennett discussed it with his brother. Geoff said, "Why don't you require that all purchase requisitions be referred to you? That will help to make it clear how serious this problem is." Hugh Bennett agreed. He questioned most requisitions and disapproved many.

Employees who had become comfortable with the lack of firm controls during the time the executive committee managed the company soon realized the need for close control of inventory and purchasing.

Factory employees, the department heads and members of the executive committee themselves had all become lax about getting to work on time. Executives had set a bad example. Many employees drifted in late for work as a result. Bennett set a visible new example. He was in his office no later than 7:30 every morning. He kept his window wide open whatever the weather. Since most employees rode to work on streetcars, they had to pass his window. Workers quickly got the point.

To make the same point with management people, Bennett began phoning department heads promptly at 7:55 every morning. When they were not at their desks he left word that he had called. Soon everyone in the company was ready for business by 8 a.m. every day.

In May, Bennett reorganized Canadian operations to match the new Toledo structure. He appointed Roy Keeley the new general manager, and two district managers—one for Eastern Canada and one for Western Canada. In the home office he named a new export and European sales manager.

Then in July, Bennett arranged a special celebration for the company's Silver Anniversary. He invited all employees and their families to an Ox Roast in Vollmar Park on the Maumee River near Grand Rapids, Ohio. Vollmar Park was an amusement park with a large picnic area.

The company rented the entire park, including a small steam locomotive that pulled a miniature train. It was a beautiful summer day. All the amusements, including the train, were used to capacity by children and adults alike. More than 2,500 people joined in celebrating Toledo Scale's Silver Anniversary.

An Ox Roast was a fascinating innovation…something never seen before. The food was superb. The crowd enjoyed socializing in family groups. The day was off to a fine start. Formalities began with short talks by three executives. Gookin spoke briefly about sales plans. Zolg reported on the company's now strong financial position. Emig's talk on the manufacturing program was short and to the point.

Then it was Hugh Bennett's turn. Many employees and their wives were still apprehensive about their handsome 31-year-old leader. He had been at the helm only about six months and had already made many changes. He quickly allayed their fears.

Hugh Bennett was an outstanding public speaker. With his wavy blond hair caressed by a light breeze and speaking without notes, he introduced a service emblem plan for the first time. With personal remarks directed to them, Bennett passed out awards to those with 20 years, and even a few with 25 years of service…the entire life of the company. Lapel pins were given to 562 employees having 5, 10, and 15 years of service.

Bennett next told the crowd about his vision for the company's future…which was their future. His style was informal, friendly and sincere. He said, "I've told you of the research we plan…we're going to create new things. But I want to tell you of something else too. In the next few years we're going to realize Henry Theobald's dream of a new plant. We need it badly. Now our efforts are scattered in four plants all over the city. And I wanted you to know that plans are under way."

The entire group cheered at the end of his brief talk. He had won the respect and loyalty of every employee. Perhaps more important, he won the respect of their wives and families as well. Everyone felt reassured that the future under Hugh Bennett's leadership was bright. The Silver Jubilee was a huge success. It marked the beginning of a new era for Toledo Scale.

CHAPTER 11

New Inventions—New Companies

In the spring of 1927, 25-year-old Charles Lindbergh made his solo flight in The Spirit of St. Louis from New York to Paris, landing at Le Bourget. In the fall, Babe Ruth hit home run number 60 in Yankee Stadium. The first talking motion picture, *The Jazz Singer*, starring Al Jolson opened. And Henry Ford introduced the Model A with an instant backlog of 50,000 orders.

About this time, Geoff Bennett, Gookin and Reeves stopped in to see Bennett. "We've had several inquiries from other companies asking if we would like to bid on custom porcelain work," Gookin said. "These requests came from firms outside the scale industry…one from as far away as Omaha. I checked with Reeves here to see if we could handle it and he said we could."

Reeves nodded his agreement. "It might be a good thing," Reeves exclaimed. "We're really using only about half of our porcelain capacity on our scales. The people doing it have to do other kinds of work to fill their time."

"We could do the kind of custom work they're asking us to bid on with little trouble," Geoff added. "It would take very little additional investment to double our output."

Hugh Bennett had learned that Toledo's wet process used to apply a porcelain finish to scales was significantly superior to any other method then in use. It fused the porcelain to metal evenly on both thick and thin sections of a casting.

"Well, if you all agree, let's try it," Bennett said. "Bring some in and we'll see how it goes."

Outside custom porcelain work proved to be profitable right away. It made the department more efficient. Within a short time, Bennett realized that he could expand by setting up a separate corporation to exploit the superior porcelain finish Toledo had developed.

He discussed the idea with a number of company employees. Most proved to be enthusiastic. Several asked Bennett if they could invest in the new company as minority stockholders. Because he realized they would take a larger interest in seeing to the company's success, he chose men to lead the new company from the group who wanted to buy shares.

On September 1, 1928, Bennett arranged to incorporate The Toledo Porcelain Enamel Products Company with a common capital of $100,000. For business reasons the announcement stated that the company was organized by Earle S. Smith, a minority owner. Smith, who was Toledo's purchasing agent, was named president. Later Earle Smith's son, Carleton Smith, would have a long successful career with Toledo Scale culminating as a region manager in Minneapolis.

Toledo's assistant accounting department manager, S. F. Chappius, was named secretary and assistant treasurer of Toledo Porcelain. Ed Adams, Toledo's retail sales manager was named as sales manager of the new company, and the foreman of Toledo's porcelain enamel department, Leo Figmaka, was named superintendent.

Over 87% of the common stock was owned by Toledo Scale. Ten percent was owned by Earle Smith, and the balance by other Toledo employees who moved to Toledo Porcelain. The new company purchased Toledo's separate porcelain enamel plant and equipment on Smead Avenue just south of Monroe Street. This plant already contained all of the equipment used in the process.

Because of the deliberate way in which the company was established, it was not generally known that Toledo Scale owned the Toledo Porcelain Enamel Products Company. Soon, two of Toledo Scale's competitors shipped castings—including those for new models—to Toledo Porcelain to apply the superior porcelain finish. Toledo Porcelain quickly established a good reputation over a wide area and was immediately successful. It earned a profit even during deep depression years.

Bennett had no more than launched Toledo Porcelain, when he set up another new subsidiary. He had discovered that many industrial scales were built during World War I…for counting, batching, force measurement, shell loading, and many special purposes. Yet no special effort was made to sell these unique scales.

He had a major interest in them. They were, after all, new inventions. He concluded the best way to develop this business was to set it apart. So in October 1928 he incorporated Toledo Precision Devices, Inc. as another wholly owned subsidiary. C. O. Marshall, Sr. was transferred and named vice president and general manager. A group of the best engineers were also transferred to Toledo Precision Devices, led by the brilliant H. O. Hem.

Bennett and Marshall next established a group of specialists to train the sales force on how to sell this special line of equipment. Toledo's industrial salesmen were not engineers. They didn't understand this special line of equipment. So Toledo Precision named seven sales engineers who were experienced in selling custom scales. They were assigned to Boston, New York, Philadelphia, Detroit, Cleveland, Chicago and Toledo…the most promising field locations. It was the beginning of Toledo Systems.

Bennett next turned his attention to Europe. He had previously appointed W. A. LeBrun as European Sales Manager. LeBrun had spent six months in Toledo learning Toledo products, policies and export plans for the future. He established his headquarters in Antwerp, Belgium.

Late in 1928, Bennett transferred Paul Greene from Toledo's export department to Antwerp as assistant to LeBrun. A company was organized in Belgium as a subsidiary to Toledo Scale. Greene helped LeBrun start an assembly plant in Antwerp. The plant was about two blocks from the docks where scale parts from Toledo were unloaded.

Greene made an arrangement with Belgium custom officials to make the area in which the plant was located into a "free port." This permitted Toledo to bring in parts "in bond" so the company had to pay duty only on those scales assembled and sold in Belgium. A Belgian customs officer was put on the company payroll. The customs officer's only duty was to unlock the door to the assembly area in the morning and lock it up again in the evening.

The Antwerp plant assembled about 600 scales before it was closed in 1931, due to the world wide depression. Paul Greene returned to Toledo as assistant export manager.

Meanwhile, Bennett became concerned because sales of the porcelain scale line were not what he thought they should be. He made a trip throughout the country to find out what might be wrong. The finish and the scale were clearly the best. There had to be another answer. After visiting dozens of field locations, he was sure he had found the problem. Of all things, the reason was weight.

As one field salesman told him, "I always have to take the scale into the store and demonstrate it to show the grocer how quickly it will pay for itself. And I can't demonstrate it often enough 'cause I can't lift it anymore…already I got a rupture." Porcelain scales weighed up to 165 pounds. They were simply too heavy for most salesmen to haul into stores for demonstrations.

When the salesman conducted a "scale audit" which compared the demonstration scale with the actual scale the merchant was using, he usually could prove a savings to the merchant of at least two cents on every weighing. Most merchants claimed they used their scale about 300 times a day. A saving of $6.00 a day times 25 working days a month equaled $150.00 per month; half the price of the scale.

A demonstration was the only way to get an order. Bennett returned home convinced he had to find a way to drastically reduce the scale's weight. He called a meeting of his staff to discuss the problem.

"I came away from this trip with a lot more respect and sympathy for our retail salesmen," he reportedly said. "That porcelain scale is way too heavy for them to handle."

Emig spoke up. "But it's the best scale in the industry. It seems a shame to change anything."

"The thing is," Bennett replied, "the salesmen know that they have to demonstrate it to sell it. Without being exposed to a complete demonstration, there's little chance that the grocer will buy it. So they have to haul a 165-pound scale in and out of stores all day. They have to lift it onto the counter for the demonstration. And it's too goddam heavy!"

"I understand that most salesmen try to talk the grocer into helping bring the scale into the store, then help lift it onto a counter," Gookin said.

"Yeah, they do try," Bennett responded. "But that doesn't work very well. The grocers don't really want a new scale in the first place. They make all kinds of excuses not to help. So the salesman drags it in and lifts it. Almost all of the best salesmen already have hernias! Their doctors tell them not to lift. If they keep on doing it, they'll hurt themselves a lot more seriously. Many already need a hernia operation…and they can't work for a long time after that. We can't go on asking our salesmen to haul and lift a 165-pound scale many times every day. We have to lower the weight."

The group talked for hours. Engineers discussed many options. Nothing was resolved. Bennett was proud of the many inventions developed by Toledo Scale. Yet it was clear that it would be a long time before this problem would be solved. "Maybe we should get some outside help," Geoff Bennett said.

"Yes, we're gonna do that," Hugh replied. "We need research help." He began immediately.

He established and funded three research programs. The first was to study current production problems, the second to find new uses for existing products and technologies, and the third for long-term research, which included the charge to find a way to reduce the weight of retail scales.

Bennett retained four outside research consultants. He established a Toledo Fellowship at the Mellon Institute of Industrial Research in Pittsburgh, who awarded the fellowship to Dr. A. M.

Howald, a chemical research expert. Another fellowship was established at the University of Michigan to study production problems. He retained Van Doren and Associates as design consultants, and Dr. A. E. Marshall as a chemical engineering consultant. He was eager and impatient to create new products.

Part of the reason for his enthusiasm for research was because several new breakthrough products had been recently developed inside the company. Toledo engineers announced they had successfully developed a remote weight indicating device.

Even more important, they announced that a weight printer for industrial scales had been successfully developed...the first in the scale industry. Toledo had tried to invent a weight printer for decades...starting with Allen DeVilbiss, Jr. who kept trying up to the time of his death.

While both the new products were well received, the weight printer caused the most excitement. For the first time customers could have a printed record of the weight information shown on the dial. It solved problems in reading, remembering and recording weight readings correctly.

To develop pride in the job, Bennett commissioned a number of large paintings from artist George La Chance. Each painting featured a long-time employee at his job. The series was called "Paintings of Master Craftsmen." La Chance completed the series by May 1, 1929. They were routed and exhibited in 22 large cities throughout the country, then hung in office areas of the main plant.

The dozen or so craftsmen were flattered and pleased to be featured in the paintings. Job pride increased in the work force. When the Telegraph Road plant was completed, they were hung along the walls of the executive floor. They remained there until the company moved to Worthington in 1976 where many were hung in the new headquarters building.

Bennett then turned his attention to a new plant to replace the five separate rented plants scattered around the city and bring together the subsidiary companies. Business had been good for several years now. It was time to build. The 25 acres of land that

Theobald had bought on Bennett Road was sold for $100,000. Later, Spicer Manufacturing Company built a factory on that site.

In April 1929, Bennett announced that Toledo Scale had purchased an 80-acre tract for $100,000 on Telegraph Road just north of Laskey…the same amount of money received for the Bennett Road property. The land had a frontage of half a mile on Telegraph Road. Construction would start by early summer. They hoped to move in by January 1, 1930.

When he learned Bennett had bought the land, Toledo Scale director and company attorney Fred Geddes spoke to Bennett. "I've got a suggestion for someone to design your building for you, Hugh. I know you want something modern and beautiful…something that doesn't look like a typical factory. And while he's not an architect in the strict sense of the word, I believe that my nephew Norman Bel Geddes is just the kind of designer to give you what you want. He's incredibly talented…and I'm not saying that just because he's my nephew."

"Well, he's certainly widely known for his creative work, Fred. I saw the play, *The Miracle*, in New York . . . I know he designed the stage settings for that. And a lot of other notable work too. I like your idea. Call him and see if he's interested in talking to us about it."

Norman Bel Geddes was a futurist. Born in nearby Adrian, Michigan in 1893, he added Bel to his name when he married Toledoan Helen Belle "Bel" Schneider in 1916. He was immediately eager to design the plant. He went right to work, soon submitting more than 50 design suggestions.

Bennett and his people sifted through them. They approved a set of designs that were far more radical than typical plant designs of the day…or any day. The engineering to meet Bel Geddes' designs would be accomplished by A. Bentley & Sons Company of Toledo.

The plans were revolutionary. Bel Geddes had designed a campus-like arrangement of separate buildings for each major operation…each with a unique design. The first unit to be built would be Toledo Scale's new plant. It was to be 640 feet long and

340 feet deep. The nearby administration building would be 14 stories high in the center, graduating to four stories at each angle in keeping with the remainder of the plan. Yet each building would cost no more than ordinary types.

Geddes had determined that a square building wouldn't work well for Precision Devices, so he designed a circular building in the form of a precision device itself. Another plant on the campus was designed in the shape of a race track for Toledo Porcelain Products.

The plans included a landing field for airplanes that would meet government requirements. This was of special interest to pilot Hugh Bennett…he'd be able to hanger his new Sikorsky biplane right at the factory.

Landscaping was designed to give the entire development a setting that would make this industrial development the most unusual and beautiful in the country. The grounds and every building in the group were designed with their appearance from the air in mind, in keeping with the nation's increasing interest in air travel caused by Lindbergh's solo flight to Paris the previous year.

Norman Bel Geddes' plans represented a radical departure from an ordinary industrial complex. Nothing existed that was anything like it. His drawings received much favorable national publicity when they were made public. They liked his futuristic imagination.

However, the entire plan for the new plant was dependent on the state highway department consolidating Telegraph Road and Dixie Highway near Laskey Road. The state was slow in consolidating the roads. Construction had to be delayed for months.

Then came "Black Thursday." The stock market crashed October 25, 1929 marking the beginning of the Great Depression. The entertainment newspaper *Variety* carried the headline, "Wall Street Lays An Egg." For months, everyone was convinced the economy would recover soon. Bennett had the loan approved for the new construction and planned to proceed with it.

Still, new products proliferated. In February 1930, the first red traffic lights were installed in Manhattan. Bennett had some exciting new products to sell. In 1930 the company introduced an

Electric Eye cutoff and interlocking device that permitted containers to be filled automatically.

Next standardized parts for heavy duty scales were developed, which greatly reduced manufacturing costs. Previously each part had to be made one at a time. Several special force measuring devices followed. Many new models came out of research...Guardian and Sentinel cylinder scales, SpeedWeigh, Gravitygram, electrically controlled batching and proportioning scales, and more.

Yet sales kept dropping. The economic depression kept gaining momentum. Reluctantly, Bennett put construction of the revolutionary new plants on hold.

The year also saw Toledo's familiar trademark introduced...an even arm balance superimposed on a capital T inside a circle. Informally called the "T-balance" logo, it appeared on all products and in advertisements for decades and soon became widely recognized. It's still seen on the many Toledo mechanical scales that remain in use all over the world.

Meanwhile Bennett heard from Dr. Howald at the Mellon Institute. Howald had been awarded the Toledo Fellowship to research a new, lightweight plastic for retail scales. In a very short time he had developed a plastic material far superior to anything then known...and at a cost under $50,000.

It was a urea-formaldehyde molding compound with characteristics that were far superior to any known plastic. The new compound produced a beautiful, tough translucent material that could be molded into delicate pastel shades. Bennett was wowed. He had the vision to see far-reaching potential in the new material many decades before Dustin Hoffman had the magic word "plastics" whispered in his ear in *The Graduate*.

Bennett saw applications for plastics far beyond those for his scales. But the Great Depression was deepening. And Toledo Scale was operating deeply in the red.

Once again he saw the need for a new company and new capital. Toledo Scale directors who were not company employees were conservative...not given to venture into unknown fields even in the best of times. There was no way they would pour more money into any new venture as the Depression deepened. Bennett looked for other investors to share his vision.

The new material had to be fabricated in hot steel dies under great pressure. Bennett arranged to have a small steel die made, from which a number of two-ounce whiskey jiggers were molded in various shades. He then invited a group of potential investors to an informal meeting on the mezzanine floor of the Toledo Trust building at Madison and Superior in downtown Toledo.

When the group had gathered, he took several of the sample jiggers in various colors from his pocket and passed them around. "Notice the beautiful translucent colors," he said. "This material can be molded into just about any color you want…all as attractive as these samples. Bakelite is limited to dark brown or black like this small radio I brought from home. And notice…the Bakelite cover on the radio already has a crack in it. I don't know how it happened. But Bakelite breaks easily."

He motioned them to the rail overlooking the first floor. "Now watch this." Bennett had arranged for his brother Geoff to keep bank customers away from the drop site. He yelled down, "All clear?" Geoff nodded, and Bennett dropped the jiggers one at a time over the railing. They fell more than 20 feet to the first floor and bounced around.

Geoff gathered them up and returned them to the mezzanine. The group checked them. None had broken nor were damaged in any way.

To show the material's potential, Bennett then had Geoff explain how the material would be used in many thousands of retail scales to reduce their weight…and why it was needed. Straining mightily, he dramatically attempted to lift an imaginary 165 lb scale…and failed, falling to the floor.

Chuckling, Bennett regained their attention. "Think about it," he said. "Scales are just a drop in the bucket. This plastic has enormous potential. The color goes all the way through. And it's really tough. It will be used for radios, like the one I brought along. For all kinds of other appliances where a rugged finish in

TERR

subtle colors helps sales. Stoves. Refrigerators. And I'm most excited about the potential for use in automobiles. There are thousands of parts in a car that will be better made of a rugged, attractive plastic like this. The potential is endless!"

In spite of themselves, the potential investors were enthused.
In less than an hour they agreed with Bennett to incorporate Toledo Synthetic Products, Inc. funding it with a common capital of
$125,000. The company was structured to be wholly owned by
Toledo Scale. The material had not yet been named when the company was organized, but was soon named Plaskon. Later, the company name was also changed to Plaskon.

A pilot operation was started in a corner of the Toledo Scale warehouse and box making plant at Fitchland and Sylvan, a few blocks
south of the main plant. As the new company grew it took over the
entire building. Since the manufacturing process required a large
amount of water, a deep well was drilled on the Fitchland property.

Soon many small items were being manufactured out of this
plastic. It was easy to sell it for electrical products, containers,
tableware, utensils, cups and tumblers, and hundreds of other uses.

Hugh Bennett thought in terms of larger items. He still believed that a scale housing could be molded out of Plaskon in spite
of its larger size. Then an important policy decision was
made…rather than going into the molding business itself, the company would make the material available to all plastic molders and
ship it in dry granular form.

To do this, a new plant was planned for Plaskon within the Toledo Scale campus at the south end of the Telegraph Road property. A
750-foot deep well was drilled on the property in anticipation of
Plaskon moving there with the rest of the company operations.

Plaskon was growing fast, yet nothing beyond drilling the well
was done. Construction of a Plaskon plant was delayed. Plans were
to build it when the rest of the Toledo Scale campus was built. The
Depression deepened. Once again, all construction was put on
indefinite hold.

Plant employees had their hours cut so the available work could be spread to more people. During the first three years of the Depression, Toledo's industrial sales volume dropped off 70% and retail scale sales about 50% from their 1929 levels. Service sales increased…scales were being maintained rather than replaced and service remained the only profitable operation.

In October 1931, the greatest inventor of our time, Thomas Edison, died at the age of 84. Born in nearby Milan, Ohio, "The Wizard of Menlo Park" gave us the electric light, the phonograph, the motion picture and hundreds of other inventions. Over 1,300 inventions came out of his laboratory in Menlo Park, New Jersey.

Perhaps inspired by Edison, the Toledo Scale inventions department kept coming up with new products. In 1932 alone, Toledo introduced aluminum charts for cylinder scales along with the Duplex optical indication, which allowed the scale to contain twice as many price calculations.

The ingenious "duplex lens" was developed by Bausch and Lomb research, working with Toledo senior engineer L. S. Williams. Wind tunnel scales were introduced for aircraft, and a scale was developed to determine the moisture content in concrete.

During the 1930's penny-operated person weigher scales became very popular. They were profitable to both the owner of the scale and the location owner. Toledo's plan was to sell its penny scales to "operators."

The Toledo salesman would sell location owners—drug stores, department stores, banks, etc.—on the idea that he would be rendering a service to his customers by making a Toledo penny scale available. On top of this, he would get 30% of the monthly receipts; a real incentive during the Depression. The "operator" would maintain the scale and keep 70% of the receipts.

Next, the salesman would find an "operator." This was anyone who was willing to make an investment of $3,250 to take over ten Toledo model 8300 penny scales on proven locations. Each scale would already have a record of monthly gross receipts of $250 to $400.

Many "operators" were sold. They would continue to find more locations and buy more scales. But credit experience was bad with this group. Many penny scales had to be repossessed. Toledo finally required 50% cash up front for the scale, with no more than ten monthly installments.

Toledo's long-time agent in Cincinnati, T. P. Keefe, bought 20 penny scales for his personal account. This saved him 25%, which was his sales commission, another 10% agency commission, and since he paid cash, he received the usual 5% cash discount. He bought the scales for only 60% of the selling price...or $195 each.

He placed most of his penny scales in Cincinnati banks, selling them on the idea that they were rendering a service to their bank customers by providing an accurate, regularly serviced scale for their convenience.

Keefe got 100% of the receipts. He operated them for years, then sold them to an operator for $4,000...$200 each, which was $5 more than he had paid for them years before. Keefe said, "Those 20 penny scales paid the cost of sending my five daughters to college."

It wasn't long, however, before penny scales began to cause trouble for Toledo. Many were located in J. C. Penney stores across the country. And it didn't take long before kids discovered that a bit of chewing gum or wadded paper inserted in the coin slot just far enough to let a penny be inserted could stop the coin. The kids would retrieve it later with a bent paper clip after the customer left.

Meanwhile the scales didn't work. Eventually a disgusted customer would notify the store manager who would put an "out of order" sign on the scale...not good publicity for Toledo.

Kids also discovered the scale was mounted on casters. This made it an ideal scooter. Since the scale was usually outside the store, kids would scoot them in the evening, often causing damage. To stop this, Toledo developed a bracket, which crossed the scale base and then bolted to the sidewalk. The scale could no longer be used as a scooter.

And when the scales were located near a high school or college, young athletes would run and jump on the platform, driving down with their feet. The scales were built strong enough to take weights well beyond the capacity of the scale, but wouldn't support a 220-pound football player jumping on the platform from a running start, where his downward force would momentarily be many times his actual weight. There were broken levers in penny scales all across the country.

Sometimes the penny scales were stolen, broken open for the pennies in the coin box. They would later be found destroyed by police in fields or at the bottom of quarries. One scale was retrieved from Lake Ponchartrain near New Orleans, Louisiana.

As time passed, more and more competitive coin-operated scales were placed on the streets. Income from Toledo's penny scales continued to drop. The company finally discontinued making the tombstone-style coin-operated penny scales at the end of the decade.

Still, Toledo continued to manufacture dial style person weighers without coin slots for years. They were sold as goodwill ambassadors to banks and food markets. Even today, Publix Markets, a Florida-based supermarket chain, continues to use them in many of their stores, and they still are found in many banks.

CHAPTER 12

Rattlesnake Island

In the deepening Depression, much thought was given to dropping the 100% Club convention to save the thousands of dollars it cost. Finally Bennett concluded they needed to continue holding the meetings. It helped get orders. The meetings were a real incentive that actually produced increases in sales. And greater sales were needed now more than anything else.

To reduce costs, Bennett decided to use his private Lake Erie island, Rattlesnake Island, as the site for the 1932 100% Club convention. Since it was scheduled for a full week, Toledo Scale would save outside lodging and other costs by hosting the meeting on his island…and Bennett could expense the costs.

Rattlesnake is an island of 47 acres in Western Lake Erie just to the west of popular South Bass Island which contains the village of Put-In-Bay and the Perry Monument. He had used his island for some time as a family retreat, and to entertain personal and business guests.

The island already contained a main cabin, a guest cabin and a large farmhouse. He had built a small landing strip to land his Sikorsky biplane. By adding a tent-covered dining hall and kitchen, and a "tea house" for hospitality, he had a large enough facility for the 100% Club convention.

In 1932 the Depression had reduced the number of those who qualified from the field to 35 men. Zone managers and home office executives raised the total attending to about 50.

100% Club members who earned the trip were given first consideration. The five highest club officers occupied the main cabin with Hugh Bennett. The guest cabin was the second most desirable and the next 12 men in sales volume slept here. The balance of the members were bunked in the nearby farmhouse. Sales manager Lloyd Colenback, other home office executives and zone managers were bunked on Middle Bass Island, a short boat trip away.

Bennett arranged for culinary artists from Toledo's University Club to prepare a wide variety of foods...classical breakfasts of bacon, ham, eggs, potatoes, French toast and coffee. Upon request, pork and lamb chops were included for breakfast fare. At noon, buffet luncheons from a long table were served.

Prohibition was still the law of the land, so everyone was invited to an English four o'clock tea hour in the Tea House where various brands of imported "teas" kept the clubmen in good spirits. It proved so popular that the dinner hour was extended by unanimous consent. Finally, a full gourmet dinner was served every evening. Evening dinner entrees varied...chicken and fish, steak, and roast duck were served, capped by a traditional New England shore dinner on the final evening.

The Tea House was also the home of the Rattlesnake Broadcasting Company...really a public address system run by the members themselves. It reached everywhere on the small island. The members broadcast a wake-up every morning, calling for everyone to go outside and do handsprings and somersaults.

They built a "jail" and conducted mock trials...then invented passwords to get out of jail, and of even greater interest, a password to get service in the Tea House. And they commented on all the sporting events.

Activities included bass fishing tournaments, dice games with millions in script given to everyone, boat cruises around the islands, tennis, volleyball, horseshoes, and golf on the mainland at the nearby Catawba Cliffs club. And, for an adventurous few, a ride over the islands in the Sikorsky biplane with company president Hugh Bennett at the controls.

It wasn't often that convention business interfered with convention fun at Rattlesnake. But this was an ideal place for the salesmen to exchange selling ideas. On the second morning a general meeting was held. The new Duplex drew the most attention due to the quick, gratifying response of the market to the new scale. Many valuable selling ideas were exchanged.

The Duplex had twice as many graduations as previous scales. The scale was named Duplex because it allowed two sets of graduations to be seen simply by sliding the magnifying reading lens back and forth. A cardboard selling tool in the shape of a rather large balloon had been developed to show how big a scale would have to be to show all the graduations on a single chart. The balloon was so large that it had to be folded for shipping and then unfolded to see it all.

Jack Dee, Division Sales Manager in Chicago, told his peers how he used the balloon to sell Duplex scales. Dee was already very well known throughout the company for his selling skills and his many creative approaches. In Chicago, merchants called him "Mr. Toledo."

In his theatrical style and deep, rich voice, Dee said, "Here's what I do…I walk into the store with the balloon closed but obvious to see. I keep it closed for a while to arouse curiosity." He had a balloon with him and opened it dramatically.

"Then I open it and hold it next to each scale in the store. I ask the merchant, 'How would you like to have a scale with a chart as large as this with its one cent graduations, more prices per pound, and with no reading errors caused by tall or short clerks?'

The merchant says 'It's too big.' I say you only think it's big because you're used to smaller ones. I ask the merchant to think about the advantages. I repeat them, emphasizing each one separately. He's interested but he says 'Yeah, but it's too big.'" Dee shrugs as if he gives up. "Then I act as if I just remembered something. I say, 'Listen, I've got something in my car you should see. You never saw anything like it before—never! I just want a minute to show you.

I take him out to the car and show him the Duplex right there. I tell him, 'Everything you saw on the balloon is in this scale…every graduation, every price per pound, magnified so they're easy to read, tall or short. And it's not any bigger than the scale you've got!' Pretty soon he's willing to call a couple of his young clerks to help carry the scale into the store for a demonstration. This way I don't have to carry it myself 'cause it's way too heavy." At this, he glanced at Bennett and paused a moment.

Then he continues. "Once it's in the store, I don't let 'em take it out again…I'll tell you that! I get all the clerks, tall and short, to read it. They read it the same way. I get them to move the Duplex lens back and forth. I get them to talk among themselves about the one cent graduations and the many prices per pound.

Clerks always like this scale 'cause they don't know how to act when a customer challenges them on the price when they hesitate trying to get a good reading. It'll help them do their job better…and it's not their money I'm after. So use the clerks. They can really help. And finally, no matter how long it takes, I walk out with the order!"

The men cheered. Marion Klapp from Davenport raised his hand. "That's great, Jack," he said. "Now here's one for you…I've had good luck emphasizing the many exclusive Duplex features…I show him patent numbers on the spider under the scale platter. There's 31 patent numbers engraved there. These patents represent 31 exclusive Toledo features. It's proof!"

Western zone manager Frank Ditzler was next. "Here's what we do out west," he said. "We go in as if we're doing research. We ask the merchant, 'If you were making up specifications for a scale to be built to your order with every feature you wanted, what would it include?' We usually have to lead him with suggestions, like "Would you want a price range adapted to today's selling prices? Large figures and graduations? Correct reading regardless of tall or short clerks…or those with defective eyesight? A scale that would protect your profits and satisfy your customers?'

When the merchant agrees that if he made specifications for a scale he would indeed want these features, he commits himself five times! And you're still left with other strong arguments to close the sale."

Enthusiasm built from there. Others talked about the best way to hold a penny on a piece of adhesive tape inside the lens frame to show how big the penny looks, magnified by the Duplex lens.

Bennett leaned over to sales manager Colenback and said, "This is the real value we get out of these meetings. These guys help each other by passing on new selling approaches that have worked for them. It's not us telling them what will work; it's other salesmen who have been successful using these techniques that are telling them. We never hear these ideas at the home office. I really expect Duplex sales will increase as a result. Let's remember to look at the figures the next few months."

The 1932 100% Club convention at Rattlesnake Island was a huge success.

Marion Klapp of Davenport wrote, "Never has it been my good fortune to enjoy such an ideal vacation as the one held by the 100% Club at Rattlesnake Island. This island is a perfect site for such outings. The fine hospitality, good rest, jolly companionship and valuable selling ideas have given me renewed energy toward qualifying early in the next 100% Club."

J. S. Munson of New York wrote, "Rattlesnake…the most delightful place at which I have ever been entertained…a perfect host…the crowd enjoying their holiday like boys on Treasure Island."

"It was a real pleasure to meet the various company officials and leading salesmen whom I had wished to know personally for years," wrote Tom Keefe of Cincinnati. "Experiences that stand out included my first plane ride along with Bill Crowley, Marion Klapp and Len Hoefgen, and trimming Foster Waltz playing horseshoes. The week was enjoyable and instructive. My hope now is that it may be duplicated by all of us again next year at Rattlesnake Island."

Under his photo in the next System magazine, Bennett answered Keefe's hope:

TO TOLEDO SALES REPRESENTATIVES

It was a distinct pleasure to have the members of the 1932 100% Club as my guests at Rattlesnake Island for a week. I hope the men who were there enjoyed themselves as my guests as much as I did as their host.

The 1932 Club convention asked to have the week at Rattlesnake Island retained as an annual 100% Club reward, which I am pleased to approve. Every effort will be made to make the 100% Club week at Rattlesnake Island in August 1933, even more enjoyable than the one which has just passed.

I want to extend every Toledo Sales Representative a hearty welcome to Rattlesnake Island next August.

H. D. Bennett

CHAPTER 13

Plaskon

Three months after the 1932 100% Club convention, Franklin Delano Roosevelt was elected President of the United States by a huge majority. The nation wanted change. It needed action to recover from the deep economic Depression and felt that Roosevelt would supply that action.

Roosevelt was inaugurated on March 4, 1933…the nation's last March inauguration. He did indeed act fast. Runs were being made on banks and many were failing all over the country. He needed to stop the panic.

Two days after his inauguration, Roosevelt declared a national emergency and closed all American banks. It was called a Bank Holiday. At the same time he placed an embargo on gold to prevent hoarding.

The Toledo Scale management—along with the management of virtually every American company—was deeply concerned about the affect the bank closings would have on the small amount of business still to be had. Bennett gave serious thought to canceling the 1933 100% Club convention to save its costs. It soon became clear, however, that the American people had confidence in Roosevelt.

Little or no effect on Toledo sales was felt from the bank closings…in fact the nation's morale improved well before business improved. So Bennett decided the 1933 100% Club would proceed…with one change to provide an increased incentive to qualify.

The 1933 World's Fair was scheduled to open in Chicago in late summer. Its Century of Progress Exhibition plans had received widespread, favorable publicity. Many were eager to attend. Bennett announced that they would open the 1933 100% Club convention in Chicago, tour the World's Fair for a full day, catch a late train for Toledo, and then travel to Rattlesnake Island for the rest of the week.

There were 49 Toledomen who qualified for the 1933 100% Club…up from 35 the previous year. The World's Fair incentive worked, it seemed. All day Sunday trains from around the nation delivered the 49 outstanding producers of the year to Chicago. They were greeted at the train station by home office executives and delivered to the convention hotel for an evening reception.

The delegation assembled at the Chicago office the next morning to see the Toledo Research Exhibit which had toured the country all year. The exhibit contained vibration filling devices, electric cut-off adaptations, Plaskon molded products and other new developments. Most saw them for the first time.

Then the group moved to the World's Fair. Their first stop…the spectacular Century of Progress Exhibition they had heard so much about. Next, specially conducted tours had been arranged to see the Transportation Building, the Hall of Science, the General Exhibit House and the Florida House.

After this, the men were free to roam the grounds to visit those parts that interested them the most. Then at midnight, the entire group boarded a Pullman sleeper train for Toledo.

When they arrived in Toledo the next morning, they were transported to the University Club for breakfast, then to the factory for a quick trip through the plant. They were shown more new developments. At Toledo Precision Devices they inspected new testing, checking and weighing devices; at Toledo Synthetic Products they saw Plaskon made and small products molded from it; at Toledo Porcelain Enamel they saw the porcelain process used on Toledo Scales and Toledo-Berlow store signs.

At noon they had lunch at the Toledo Club…then were whisked to Catawba Cliffs where they boarded boats for the short trip to Rattlesnake Island. After settling in, they quickly took over the Rattlesnake Broadcasting Company, activated the jail and issued ever-changing passwords to get service at the Tea House since prohibition was still the law of the land.

Activities again began…bass fishing, dice games with millions in script, boat cruises around the islands, tennis, volleyball, horseshoes, and golf at the Catawba Cliffs club on the mainland.

There were business meetings of course…conducted in the mornings. Bennett gave a briefing on the proposed National Recovery Act. Western Zone manager Frank Ditzler discussed the adjustable reading device on the Duplex scale. The Fan Scale line was presented by Northwestern Zone manager Smith, and a discussion of drive-in markets (a West Coast trend) was led by the Los Angeles District sales manager.

A new Selected Figure Printweigh that eliminated weight disputes was introduced by Toledo engineer Williams, who had developed it. Meat packer accounts were talked about by the Chicago District sales manager. Chicago was still "Hog butcher for the world."

Saturday morning, Bennett closed the convention with a talk on the glowing possibilities for the future of the Toledo organization with the many new developments research had recently produced. Bennett was an inspiring, highly skilled speaker and the crowd was with him. As one field man put it, "It made the whole convention worthwhile."

For the second year, the 100% Club convention held on Rattlesnake Island was a marked success.

Meanwhile, other news was being made around the world. In January 1933 Adolph Hitler became Chancellor of Germany. By June, the Nazis were now Germany's only political party. Also in June, President Roosevelt signed into law the National Recovery Act giving the government control over industry in an effort to bring the nation out of the Depression.

And on December 5, 1933, Prohibition was finally repealed, as the 21st Amendment to the Constitution became effective, when

Utah became the last of 36 states to ratify the Amendment. The following May, Bonnie and Clyde were killed in a police ambush. And in July, the nation was captured by the news that "Public Enemy #1" John Dillinger had been shot and killed as he left the Biograph Theater in Chicago after being set up by his paramour, "the lady in red".

Deep in the Depression, the nation was hungry for any kind of news. Good news was hard to come by. Newspapers reported on soup lines and hobos riding the rails in search of any kind of work. The Amos and Andy Show was popular with a wide radio audience.

The top radio newsman was Lowell Thomas who had a 15-minute news show every evening, ending with "So-o long until tomorrow!" Tabloid-style radio news was delivered by Walter Winchell in his staccato manner opening with, "Good-evening-Mr.-and-Mrs.-North-and-South-America-and-all-the-ships-at-sea-let's-go-to-press!"

The 1933 100% Club convention proved to be the last one held on Rattlesnake Island. The Depression was holding fast and virtually every field salesman was cash poor, living hand-to-mouth. When they were given the option of receiving cash awards based on volume versus holding a 1934 convention, they opted for the cash awards.

They needed the money. The 100% Club continued, but for many years only the Club officers and directors—the top selling seven salesmen—were invited to Toledo to receive their awards.

In 1933, Chevrolet sponsored the first Soap Box Derby. Because of Toledo Scale's reputation, Chevy selected it as the official weighmaster at over 100 locations in the U.S. and at the finals in Akron. Soon over 75,000 boys were building race cars in the 100 cities.

The Soap Box Derby expanded into an international event. Chevrolet remained the sponsor for almost half a century and Toledo Scale remained the official weighmaster.

Then in 1934, a company that Toledo had been cooperating with became a tough competitor. In June, IBM sold their Dayton Scale Company division to the Hobart Manufacturing Company of Troy, Ohio. Toledo's relationship with IBM's Dayton division had been trouble-free since Bennett and Thomas Watson, Sr. had made their "gentlemen's agreement" eight years previously. Now IBM had sold Dayton.

Hobart manufactured meat choppers, slicers, coffee mills, vegetable peelers, and commercial dishwashers. Now they were in the scale business too. Hobart was now a competitor.

For many years Hobart and Toledo had cooperated closely in the sale and service of both product lines since they served the same market and did not compete with each other. In many places Toledo offices sub-leased space to Hobart, furnishing stenographic and telephone services. In some Western states Toledo sales and service representatives even sold and serviced Hobart products.

When the sale was announced, Hobart immediately vacated the Toledo offices where they had rental agreements.

A few weeks after Hobart's entry into the scale business, Toledo sales manager Colenback got a call from the general sales manager of the U.S. Slicer Company, expressing an interest in having Toledo act as selling agent for their slicers in the U.S. and Canada.

U.S. Slicer was owned by the Van Berkel Company of Rotterdam, Holland. For years Toledo-Berkel manufactured and sold Toledo scales in Europe under license from Toledo. Toledo was familiar with the U.S. Slicer line. They thought it to be equal in quality to Toledo products, and did the best slicing job on the market.

Colenback took the message to Bennett. They were both put out that after years of friendly cooperation, Hobart would take on a scale line. The idea of selling slicers was discussed in the next staff meeting. With only a few reservations, everyone seemed inclined to the idea. Bennett said, "By God, I like the idea. If Hobart is going to sell scales, we'll sell slicers!"

A few days after the contract was signed with U.S. Slicer, Sylvan Braun, the general manager of Enterprise Manufacturing Company of Philadelphia, came to Toledo to meet Colenback. He explained that he had been talking to U.S. Slicer about a joint effort to compete with Hobart and learned of their new arrangement with Toledo. He came to see them, he explained, to interest Toledo in selling Enterprise Choppers and Coffee Mills on a basis similar to the U.S. Slicer arrangement.

Colenback took Braun in to see Bennett. Braun explained his proposal again. Bennett agreed that Enterprise was an old, well-respected company, but their product designs were badly out-dated. Braun said, "I have to agree. But I'm willing to have them redesigned if you will take on the line. In fact, if you give me the name of your design firm, I'll ask them to do the work."

Toledo employed J. M. Little & Associates for their standard prod-uct designs. Little was a local firm of industrial designers, and Braun hired them to redesign his products. A line of choppers and coffee mills resulted that looked similar to Toledo's family of products.

One chopper was designed by Van Doren & Associates with a Plaskon housing to identify it as much as possible with Toledo's upcoming Plaskon Duplex scale. Van Doren was the design firm for Plaskon products.

An agreement was reached. Braun did everything possible to help. A fine line of choppers and mills resulted. Now Toledo products com-peted with a large part of Hobart's line. The battle was joined.

The battle became bloody...seldom a fair fight on either side. Hobart would send a group of seven of their best salesmen to a city they had targeted to increase sales. Toledo came to call the team "the locust group." Local Toledo offices claimed the group would descend on a city like a swarm of locusts. The group would call on virtually every merchant in the city.

After their visit, Toledo service calls increased dramatically. Toledo servicemen would often find sugar in the dashpot of a To-ledo scale...which slowed down the scale's action and eventually tied it up. Chewing gum would be found packed in a bearing under the open base of a cylinder scale.

Individual Toledo salesmen would retaliate. Sabotage occurred on both sides for years. Former friends became vicious competi-tors. World War II eventually slowed down the sabotage.

In August 1935, President Roosevelt signed into law the Social Security Act. It was intended only for those in commercial or industrial jobs and was to be funded by a payroll tax.

The depression continued. Bennett was constantly seeking ways to build business. So far during the Depression, sales had dropped about 70%, causing a huge operating loss. In just the first three years of the Depression, the company lost all but about 10 cents per share of its earned surplus. Its common stock stood at about $20.10 per share. Par value was $20.00 per share at the time.

Colenback spoke up at a staff meeting. "I'd like to ask you all for thoughts on how we can get more business...any ideas at all." Geoff Bennett was the first to respond. "Well, Lloyd, we know that demonstrating helps sell scales. In fact demonstrations are vital. Let's see if we can figure out some ways to do more demonstrations like we do at trade shows."

Reeves said, "Maybe we could find a way to take a Toledo Scale trade show directly to selected customers. Fit out a truck or a van..."

A novel new way to generate more sales resulted from the meeting. Bennett especially wanted to get the market acquainted with the company's many innovative special purpose scales. Toledo bought two exhibition cars. They were similar to modern mobile homes except the entire interior was devoted to a display of special purpose scales and force measuring devices. An experienced sales engineer was assigned to each one. They called them Aero-Cars.

The Aero-Cars were routed through each zone, scheduled months in advance. Industrial salesmen would line up prospects in their respective territories. They made appointments with engineers, purchasing agents and plant managers. The Aero-Car would park in front of the plant and guests were given an actual demonstration of the special devices. They took the showroom to the prospect.

It was a novel idea and worked to create a great deal of interest in the special devices. Sales improved in each zone after an Aero-Car visit. It also familiarized industrial salesmen with the many precision devices and the job Toledo Scale engineering could do for industry. Toledo had an engineering force larger than the combined engineering forces in the entire scale industry.

The Aero-Cars were regularly refurbished and had new equipment installed. The equipment was tailored to the territory the Aero-Car was bound for next. Among others, Harry Maycock served in the #1 car. Maycock would be on the road for about three months before he returned for new equipment. Maycock later had a long, successful career in Toledo's home office service department.

Bert Dickey was assigned to car #2 and traveled through the South and Mid-Atlantic states. Dickey would later serve as the industrial marketing manager before he became the Toledo Scale distributor in Tampa, Florida. His distributorship grew to become one of the largest, most successful of all Toledo distributors. Aero-Cars operated successfully with various people until the war.

Toledo's home town was proud of the company. A local newspaper assigned their top feature writer, Allen Saunders, to do a complete feature on weighing and Toledo Scale. Saunder's story was given a full page for each of five consecutive days, Monday through Friday. Titled "The Weigh of the World," the series was incredibly thorough, excellent publicity for the struggling company. Saunders began his first piece on Monday with:

Scales Carry Toledo's Name Into Every State
and to Fifty Foreign Countries
Accurate Measurement of Weight is Factor in Civilization
BY ALLEN SAUNDERS

"Much history has been made with a sword and inscribed with a pen, but the story of human progress has been most significantly recorded in the leisurely rise and fall of the scale balance.

From the moment you roll complainingly out of bed to that blissful instant when blessed sleep blots out the blight of the day, you pay unconscious tribute to pivot and bearing.

You don't believe it? Then consider these facts: The cotton batting of the comforter you throw back so reluctantly was weighed before it became bed clothing. The leather of the slippers into which your bare toes snuggle passed over a scale on its way to the cobbler's bench. You turn on a bathroom faucet (parts of which were weighed at the factory) and douse your face with water that contains a proportion of chlorine determined by scales.

Scales weighed the milk you carry in from the front step; scales packaged the cereal, sugar, coffee and salt on your breakfast table. The clothes you don, the parts of the auto you drive to work, the street surfacing over which you pass, the newspaper you read…and on and on ad infinitum…all that you eat and wear and handle and much that you look at, once caused a quiver of an indicator on the chart of a scale…"

Saunders last page on Friday concluded:

"Toledo has become known in recent years as a city of craftsmen, and nowhere is the reason for that more apparent than in the Toledo Scale Company. You find here quality production, but not, in its accepted sense, mass production. The individual unit product gets as jealously keen scrutiny as a Swiss watch. The workman takes a distinct pride in his product and in the skill and knowledge on his part that made the product possible…"

Later in the 30's, Allen Saunders became independently successful as the author of two nationally syndicated comic strips…"Mary
Wirth" and "Steve Roper" which now features Mike Nomad. The two
strips still appear in hundreds of newspapers. They're written today
by Allen's son, John Saunders, a Toledo radio and television personality until taking over the strips from his father.

In spite of much good scale publicity, the major financial bright
spot for the future was Plaskon. Van Doren and Rideout, the industrial designers Bennett had sponsored, had developed many
successful designs that were selling.

The automobile companies were buying many Plaskon auto
parts. Thousands of electric light shades made from Plaskon were
commercially sold. A radio manufacturer used Plaskon for a new
clock-radio. By 1935, Plaskon molded color was putting new life
into old products for hundreds of manufacturers and opening broad
new markets.

And in 1935, through the cooperative efforts of Toledo Scale,
Plaskon, and the plastics division of General Electric, the housing
for the Toledo Plaskon Duplex scale was at last successfully molded.
It was the largest molded part ever made from Plaskon. Years before, a company decision was made that rather than going into the
molding business itself, Plaskon would make the material available to all plastic molders and ship it in dry granular form. This
decision proved to be a good one.

General Electric was one of the first to buy the Plaskon material. Toledo worked with them and finally succeeded in getting
GE to try to mold scale housings. To do the molding job, GE had
a large press built under their supervision in Ft. Wayne, Indiana,
by the French Oil Mill Machinery Company. The press was huge.
It stood nearly two stories high and weighed 89,000 pounds.

The Plaskon scale housing mold was also large…about 4' x 5'.
GE built two special rooms in the Ft. Wayne plant for the molding operation, since it required absolute cleanliness. The press was
installed in the first room and the second was used to store and
very accurately weigh the Plaskon material to match each mold…on

Toledo scales, of course. Air into each room was filtered and a positive pressure maintained in both rooms to keep out any possible contaminants.

Concurrently, Toledo collaborated with ALCOA to provide exactly the right aluminum alloys for sand castings and die castings and—more important—to provide very thin, defect-free sheets of aluminum to make the new aluminum charts called for in the design of the new Plaskon scale.

ALCOA solved the thin sheet aluminum problem. Toledo would have the only aluminum chart in the industry. All other manufacturers used paper charts. The aluminum chart didn't warp. It wasn't susceptible to moisture or temperature changes. It allowed Toledo to place the reading line very close to the chart…almost touching. This eliminated the need for the double reading line then in use.

The popular Duplex lenses would continue to be used in the new Plaskon Duplex scale.

The impossible had been accomplished. When completed, the weight of the new cylinder scale had been reduced by two-thirds…from a high of about 160 lb to only 70 lb, a 90 lb reduction in weight. Bennett was beside himself with delight. The field salesmen were wildly enthusiastic when the model 3055 Sentinel Duplex scale in a Plaskon housing was introduced. No more tough selling jobs getting help from customers to carry the scale into the store. No more hernias!

All the companies involved in the scale's development hired a New York public relations firm and joined together in a giant public relations effort. Toledo Scale, the Mellon Institute, General Electric, ALCOA, and the Bausch and Lomb Optical Company each had a compelling story to tell.

Press conferences with editors of newspapers and trade journals were held in New York, Chicago, and many large cities around the country.

Over 600 articles were published in all types of news media. All carried the story of the birth of the new scale and all the developments engineered into it…the research at the Mellon Institute, GE's molding the largest plastic part ever, the use of ALCOA's thin sheet of aluminum for the chart, and more. All stories centered on Toledo's new Plaskon model 3055 Sentinel Duplex scale.

The publicity did much to create an interest in the new plastics industry. The existence of the GE plant that could turn out a molded part as large as a scale housing prompted many manufacturers to swamp both GE and Plaskon with a flood of inquiries. Everyone, it seemed, wanted to reduce the weight of his or her product and improve its appearance. Industry began to think of plastics as an established, accepted means of solving their problems.

This public relations effort effectively linked Toledo Research with General Electric and all the other involved companies in the minds of American industry. This built Toledo's image to heights never before attained. And, not so incidentally, helped sell not only Plaskon scales, but also all Toledo scales.

Sales volume began to improve a bit. Bennett was confident enough to trade his aging Sikorsky for a new Beechcraft staggerwing…the first airplane that combined speed and comfort. Many recognized it as the first "corporate" aircraft since it had a cruising speed that approached 200 miles per hour. Bennett first used it to reach cities within 500 miles of Toledo to give luncheon speeches about the new Toledo Plaskon Duplex scale, then would return home the same day.

The Plaskon Duplex scale and the Plaskon meat chopper were both entered in the 1936 Modern Plastics competition. Toledo was give the first place award in the Industrial Application category. Industrial designer H. L. Van Doren was awarded the special designers plaque for both designs.

Research efforts into plastics by companies with vast resources, many times larger than Toledo, caused a flurry of patents to be issued. Patent interference claims were made; one troublesome claim came from I. G. Farben in Germany.

Toledo saw the possibility of a long, expensive patent litigation on the horizon similar to past litigation on scale patents. The prospect was to be avoided at all costs.

Unyte Corporation, the American affiliate of I. G. Farben, indicated its patent position...but its American management also expressed an interest in merging with Plaskon. Bennett was interested. Plaskon was much larger than Unyte. He agreed to a merger and offered Unyte a 30% common stock interest in the combined company. Unyte accepted the offer, subject to acceptance by I. G. Farben and Hitler's German government.

Hitler refused to let I. G. Farben dispose of its American interest for anything but U.S. dollars. However, Toledo's international counsel saw a way to circumvent Hitler's restriction. They caused Plaskon to be merged *into* Unyte. For Plaskon, Unyte gave Toledo 70% of its common shares. Unyte then changed its name to Plaskon.

The existing Plaskon officers and directors continued as officers and directors of the new company. Hitler was furious, but he had bigger things on his mind.

One of them was the Volkswagen, Hitler's "people's car". It was designed and built for him by Ferdinand Porsche. The Volkswagen made its debut in February 1936. Hitler sought to emulate Henry Ford by undertaking mass production of a low-priced car for his people.

Through this merger with Unyte, Plaskon acquired a small plastics plant in New Jersey, which eliminated patent problems between the two companies and also eliminated a competitor. And Plaskon became the largest company in the plastics field for a time.

Hitler was shamed by the outstanding performance of American Jews and black athletes in the 1936 Olympics. Ten Negroes showed up on the talent-laden American team. Jesse Owens from Ohio State won four gold medals in track and field events, which presented an implicit challenge to Nazi theories of racial superiority. The applause was thunderous for Owens when he completed his triumphant performance at the Olympics by winning the 200-meter race in a record 20.7 seconds. By then Hitler had deliberately left the stadium so he wouldn't have to greet him.

No manufacturer sold many scales in the last half of the decade. These were still depression years. But of those that were sold, the new Sentinel Duplex scale in its Plaskon housing outsold them all, and the Chicago office led every other office in sales.

Food stores proliferated and the legendary Jack Dee covered them like a blanket…Toledo was the best-known brand name by far in the Windy City. Chicago had been going places and had captured the nation's attention for everything from World's Fairs to public enemies. Corruption was rampant, often involving the police.

A story made its way through the Chicago office that Jack Dee had created a method of dealing with the Chicago police when he was stopped for one of his frequent traffic violations. He would get out of his car, identify himself as a Toledo Scale representative, visit with the cop a bit and apologize for any transgression he might have made. Then he motioned the officer to his trunk. "Here, let me give you something for your family," he would say as he opened his trunk. He would reach in, lift out a nicely packaged bathroom scale and hand it to the cop.

"Look, it's a Toledo!" he said. "The same brand you see in your grocery store…the best there is. Take it home with my compliments." The officer looked it over. It did indeed say Toledo above the indicator. The cop went away happy with his bathroom scale and Dee escaped another ticket.

But Toledo Scale never made a bathroom scale. How did Dee give away a Toledo? The office finally discovered that he had bought a quantity of a little known brand of bathroom scales and covered the manufacturer's decal with a slightly larger TOLEDO decal he got from the Toledo service department. He always kept a supply of these scales in his trunk. No Chicago cop ever complained.

Chicago was a vital market for both retail and industrial scales. Meat packing was centered there as well as many other major industries that required scales. The office was well managed and everyone enthusiastically supported Toledo.

No one was a bigger supporter than the office switchboard operator and stenographer, Miss Glattharr. In 1937 a literary competition was held in Chicago. Miss Glattharr entered the competition. Everyone in the office was delighted with the news that she had won First Prize for her entry. It was reprinted in System magazine. She titled it:

The Egotist

I am as old as the history of civilized Man; early I joined the traffic of the World.

Abraham used me as he bargained for his burial ground. Joseph relied upon me during the years of the Great Famine. Belshazzar trembled as I read his doom. I am pictured on the ancient temple walls of Egypt and Babylonia.

I antedate the use of money of any sort,—yea, the value of money is determined by me. I handle counting problems with startling rapidity and accuracy. I am recognized by the governments of all nations. I can win or lose wars.

I measure one of the greatest forces of nature. I tell how much coal is mined and burned. I determine the value of all metals, common and precious; lapidaries would be lost without me. I guard the very water that man drinks.

If I were unfaithful to my trust I could bankrupt the commerce of the world. I stand guard in the most unpretentious shops and the mightiest industries rely upon me. I have a part in all the food that is eaten, the clothing that is worn, the soaps, powders and perfumes that are bought. I am important at birth, necessary through life, and useful at death.

I spy on most letters that are written, and govern the ingredients of the ink used in writing them. Papers and magazines are subjected to my scrutiny. I work with the ignorant; I assist with accuracy the investigations of the scientist. Pauper or prince, I serve both alike.

I hold a front seat at every baseball game. I stand at the starting and finishing line of every horse race. Prize fighters are classified by me.

I am known the world over. I am one of the most important necessities of a progressive civilization, yet one of the most neglected,—I AM A SCALE.

Its message is timeless. Now more than sixty years later, *The Egotist* can still be found...framed and hung on the walls of company and distributor offices all over the nation.

CHAPTER 14

The Daily Express

No one was more thrilled than Bennett that aviation had suddenly become popular when Lindbergh made his solo flight to Paris in 1927. Bennett continued to fly his own plane whenever he could. More and more Toledo executives tried to tactfully talk him out of it as "dangerous," especially in the two years since Will Rogers and Wiley Post had died in a crash in Alaska.

Since then the popularity of aviation had gone down. Negative publicity resulted with every crash, but nothing stopped Bennett. He loved to fly.

And by 1937 the Douglas DC-3 introduced just two years previously had helped commercial air travel make a more positive reputation. An inspired public relations move helped. An advisor to an airline suggested they stop referring to "safety belts" and start asking passengers to fasten their "seat belts." Why remind passengers about safety? It seemed to help. They're still called seat belts today.

But what took the pressure off of Bennett more than anything else was the publicity surrounding the first successful round-trip commercial flight across the Atlantic in May 1937.

King Edward VIII had abdicated the British throne the previous year for "The woman I love." His brother, the Duke of York, was soon to be crowned King George VI in an ancient coronation ceremony replete with pageantry. Newspaper publisher William Randolph Hearst wanted to scoop his competitors by printing the first photographs of the coronation in the United States.

At the time, Hearst owned 25 major daily newspapers and several popular magazines. Flying the coronation photos back would truly make sensational news. His competitors would have to wait many days before the pictures would arrive by even the fastest ocean liner. Hearst let it be known that he would pay anyone well who would fly the photos across the Atlantic.

Concluding that it could be a profitable venture, two Wall Street brokers put together a plan for the flight. Their first move was to contact Captain Dick Merrill, the most famous American pilot next to Lindbergh.

Merrill had successfully completed a non-commercial round trip flight to England with comedian Harry Richman the previous year that received national publicity...largely because thousands of Ping-Pong balls had been installed in the wings of the aircraft to keep it afloat in case it went down in the Atlantic.

Merrill was a senior pilot for Eastern Airlines. Eastern's president, World War I flying ace Captain Eddie Rickenbacker, was also a close friend. Merrill discussed the flight with Rickenbacker who gave his enthusiastic approval. They arranged for Merrill's regular co-pilot, Jack Lambie, to be the co-pilot on this first commercial round-trip Atlantic flight.

The backers obtained a Lockheed 10-E twin engine monoplane. Merrill supervised modifications that included extra fuel tanks in the cabin. And this time he added a life raft in place of Ping-Pong balls.

As the flight was preparing to take off from Floyd Bennett field, hundreds of well wishers and newsmen were gathered around the aircraft that Merrill had named the "Daily Express." Both pilots were dressed in conservative business suits, lending emphasis to Rickenbackers's statement that this was a business flight...not a stunt. Merrill was preparing to board the aircraft when he heard a shout, "Hold the flight!"

A Hearst newsman explained. "Captain Merrill, we just heard that the Hindenberg dirigible crashed and burned at Lakehurst. Mr. Hearst wants you to take photos of the crash with you." The giant German dirigible had caught fire moments before while attempting to moor at Lakehurst, New Jersey. Merrill and Lambie waited impatiently. Yet within 40 minutes they spotted police cars escorting a van into the airport and up to the plane.

Merrill accepted the package of photos, waved to the crowd and boarded the airplane. Lining up for takeoff, he moved the throttles forward. The aircraft was about 30% overweight and took most of the runway before it successfully lifted off. The Daily Express was on its way to England.

The usual Atlantic weather problems were faced on the flight. Yet 21 hours and two minutes after taking off from Floyd Bennet Field, they landed at Croyden Airport near London. This was longer than Merrill had hoped for, but still a speed record.

A messenger pushed his way through the crowd. "Where are the photographs?" he shouted. Lambie reached into the cabin and handed him the package. Police escorted the messenger back out through the welcoming crowd.

Both pilots were invited to witness the coronation the next day as special guests. Yet they had to miss it…the return flight was also the next day and many preparations had yet to be made. They received a package of coronation photos and took off from the hard-packed sand beach at Southport for the return flight. Twenty-four hours later they landed at Floyd Bennet Field with 51 enlarged photographs of the coronation. A waiting crowd, that included Rickenbacker, cheered as he taxied to the ramp.

Merrill grinned as he shook hands with his boss. Rickenbacker said, "This is the first time I've been able to smile in hours. Congratulations Dick and Jack…you've proven the concept of transatlantic commercial flight." Morning headlines read, "MERRILL RETURNS HERE IN 24 HOURS." The next day Merrill and Lambie flew to Washington where they were congratulated by President Franklin Roosevelt in the White House.

Dick Merrill continued as a Captain for Eastern Airlines until he was forced to retire when the FAA established a rule that airline pilots could not continue flying passengers past the age of 60. He was already 67 at the time. He had been General Eisenhower's pilot for Ike's first presidential campaign in an airliner the campaign had leased from Eastern. He starred in a movie about his exploits titled "Atlantic Flight" where he met and married movie star Toby Wing. During his long flying career he had flown everything from a Curtiss Jenny to the SST Concorde.

He had logged 36,650 hours when he was forced to retire. Then Rickenbacker appointed Merrill a consultant to Eastern, and he continued to fly many jobs that didn't include flying commercial passengers. He was a featured pilot with Arthur Godfrey on Godfrey's 1966 flight around the world to publicize the Jet Commander, a new corporate jet. His total hours exceed 40,000...which will probably never be matched. Part of his new job required giving speeches, in which he excelled.

Almost four decades after his first commercial transatlantic flight, many Toledo Scale people got to meet Captain Dick Merrill when he was the featured guest speaker at Toledo's TelStar '74 sales convention at Innisbrook, Florida. He was 80 years old at the time. Several hundred Toledomen gave him a standing ovation.

TERR

CHAPTER 15

AeroCars and Weldwood

Pressure on Bennett's flying activities were relieved somewhat by Merrill's flight. At the same time, research resulted in new product introductions that continued to keep him busy throughout the decade. In 1938, Toledo introduced a logarithmic chart for industrial scales and a weighing system to balance aircraft propellers, which would prove especially useful in just a few years.

Aero-Cars had been in use for several years when a new service employee was assigned the job of installing new equipment in them when they returned from the road. Edgar J. Quertinmont had completed service training and worked in the mail room when he was assigned the Aero-Car task. He quickly discovered he was also expected to be a "gofer" for the Aero-Car drivers.

Maycock would say, "Ed, please pick up my laundry for me…I need to get back on the road." He was expected to run other errands for the drivers as well. This was one of the perks they assumed since they were not often home.

Before the Aero-Car job, Quertinmont was a mail boy, delivering inter-office mail between the five manufacturing plants. The main plant was his first stop. He would park near a garage in the back to pick up the mail. Almost every day a car would pull into the garage at about the same time.

A relatively young man in a trench coat would get out of the car and they would walk into the plant together. Often when one was slightly ahead of the other, the first would wait for the other to catch up. They began to engage in friendly banter. It was clear they both enjoyed the moment.

Well over a month later, they walked into the plant together when they passed a foreman. The foreman nodded pleasantly. "Morning, Mr. Bennett…hi Ed," he said. They both returned the greeting. Quertinmont stopped. "Did you say 'Bennett?'" he asked the foreman. "Yeah, that's H. D. Bennett…I thought you knew." Quertinmont was taken aback. "Good Lord! I've been kidding around with the president of the company!" The foreman smiled. "Don't worry…he's really a nice guy," he said.

Ed Quertinmont remembered this as marking the beginning of his career with Toledo Scale…which proved to be a long and successful career, with only two short interruptions.

Research projects turned up several new ideas the company pursued since Bennett was desperate for sales. Though not related to scales, the projects did relate to the food industry. Toledo-sponsored research at the Mellon Institute discovered an effective method of tenderizing beef.

The method used specially made light tubes, which gave off a special "ray." When the light tubes were installed in a meat cooler to shine on sides of beef they did a good job of quickly tenderizing whole sides…much quicker and just as tender as hung beef that had aged for a long time. Using the light ray method, beef could be tenderized at a warmer temperature. This caused the enzymes to build up the proper bacteria needed in the tenderizing process much faster.

The light tubes were made by Westinghouse. They had to be properly placed in the meat cooler by an electrician. There was nothing here for Toledo to manufacture and sell. However, the head of research at Kroger was very interested in the project, as well as other food preservation projects.

Kroger was a long-time exclusive user of Toledo scales, so when Toledo determined there was no equipment they could make for the process, Colenback called the head of research at Kroger. "Tell you what," he said. "We don't see there's anything for us to make and you're a good customer. We'll give you the project if you send a letter saying that if anything comes out of it that could be manufactured by us, we would have exclusive manufacturing rights." Kroger agreed…but nothing ever came of it for Toledo.

Kroger finished the project. They introduced the tenderized beef through all their stores and featured it for decades, calling it TENDER-RAY BEEF.

Another Toledo-sponsored Mellon Institute project determined that vegetables could be kept fresh in display cases without refrigeration by controlling temperature and humidity. It was a mister, called a wet produce system. Again Toledo called on the Kroger research department.

Kroger agreed to an experiment under normal store conditions. Twenty Kroger stores in the greater Toledo area were selected for the experiment…ten would have the Toledo-built display cases and ten other similar stores were control stores to compare results. Kroger would keep a detailed record and give the details to Toledo.

Toledo Porcelain Enamel built the ten display cases with a porcelain finish and delivered them to the experimental stores. They were built something like meat display cases but with sliding glass doors to retain the conditioned air. Ed Quertinmont was assigned to work with the cases in Kroger's Fremont store. He reported early troubles. "They ruined more produce than they protected at first," he said.

Kroger store managers didn't like the sliding glass doors, claiming they reduced their merchandising of the vegetables. Toledo engineers removed the doors and installed a new idea called an air blanket. The air blanket held in the specially conditioned air.

When a customer reached into the case for self-serve vegetables, the air blanket was pierced but the air sealed around her arm. The experiment was finally successful. Results showed that vegetables were kept fresh for over two weeks, spoilage decreased and a slight increase in vegetable sales resulted when compared to the control stores.

Colenback asked Kroger for an order. Toledo determined they would have to sell the cases for about $10 per foot. Most stores needed about 40 feet of display space. This would cost Kroger about $400 per store. With their 2,000 stores they would need to spend about $800,000.

Kroger decided the cost was too high considering the slight increase in sales. They wanted quick turnover, and were not primarily interested in keeping the vegetables fresh over several weeks.

Toledo abandoned the project.

The Mellon Institute had also developed a method of keeping citrus fruit fresh. Citrus fruit was successfully stored for up to six months using the method. Toledo's patent attorneys advised that patent protection would be a problem.

Once again, the project was dropped.

Toledo experienced a problem for years with its cylinder scales used in the deep South. When the scale was at rest, the ribbon was held away from the cam. Cockroaches would often sit on the cam. When the scale was used, the roach was mashed between the ribbon and the face of the cam, causing the scale to show an inaccurate weight.

Toledo assigned a research project to Ohio State University to do something about the problem. OSU developed a semi-solid material that could be safely spread around the store that would attract roaches and exterminate them. The first problem was a shortage of roaches. When the roaches were successfully killed in a location there was a need for more to test the material, so a roach breeding farm was created.

After it looked like the material would work, a large store in Ft. Worth, Texas, was chosen to test it. When the store closed for the day, Toledo engineers painted the paste in all the areas they thought roaches liked.

The next morning the floor was covered with dead roaches. They thought they had a winner. But the next morning the roaches were as thick as ever. They discovered that new roaches were brought into the store every morning with the vegetables and other foods delivered.

Toledo abandoned this project too.

Toledo's research costs for these projects totaled about $135,000. Some real benefits for the food industry were developed but no new products were added. Overall, Toledo research paid off…but they had to write off a lot of expensive losers in the process.

In mid year, Bennett made a trip to Europe accompanied by Dr. Howald of the Mellon Institute, the man who had developed Plaskon. They traveled together to study the plastics industry, especially in Germany.

Bennett took a close look at the volatile political structure in Germany and how Hitler might affect the Toledo operation in Cologne. He was concerned. He tried to move some operations to other parts of Europe, but was thwarted by Hitler's government. He next visited other Toledo distributors throughout Europe.

Independently, Howald had been researching an entirely new concept in glue. He chose to stay in Germany for a few weeks to learn what he could about German glues. When he returned to Plaskon in Toledo, he continued his research until he had developed a glue that satisfied him.

It was truly waterproof, vermin proof, easy to handle, and it set up without excessive pressure. The only problem was that the hardening agent had to be kept separate from the powder until it was ready to use…then carefully measured and mixed with water. He solved this by pre-mixing the hardening agent with the powder in such a way that the glue would became active only when mixed with water.

The new Plaskon glue met all severe laboratory tests. It was ready to produce and sell. They named the glue "Weldwood." But Plaskon had no sales organization capable of developing an entirely new market. The Plaskon sales force was trained to sell plastic powder to molders, not how to develop a new market. They knew nothing about glue.

As they were debating what to do, there was a great flood in the Mississippi River valley. Many lives were lost for lack of small row boats along the river. This prompted the idea to make small row boats out of canvas or burlap, impregnate the canvas with the waterproof glue and stack the boats along the banks of the Mississippi as potential lifeboats.

The company had a canoe brought to the plant for a mold. They covered it with a layer of canvas, painted it with Weldwood glue, and added a second layer of canvas, glue, a third layer and more glue. When the glue had hardened they tried to remove the canoe. But canoes curved inward at the top. They didn't anticipate the problem. They couldn't get the canoe out. It was ruined. Then they did the same construction using a large galvanized tub as a mold. The glued canvas tub reluctantly released from the mold. It was put in shallow water and a volunteer "boatman" sat inside…briefly. Someone yelled, "Look out!" The sides had collapsed inward due to water pressure. The tub sank. The volunteer stood up in the shallow water, soaking wet but unharmed. The builders came to recognize a fundamental of boat building…they needed ribs to make it rigid.

Next, a small row boat was brought to the plant. It had draft. Before the first layer of canvas was added, they put a thick layer of wax on the bottom of the boat to help it release from the mold. Now the original row boat used for a mold was removed successfully. This time they remembered to add ribs to make it rigid. They finally had a real boat.

Thought not very attractive, the new plastic boat was functional. It was taken to Rattlesnake Island for testing on Lake Erie. A five horsepower outboard was attached to the stern. The plastic boat was used most of the summer for fun, fishing, and short trips to Put-In-Bay.

During all this testing, the Mississippi had returned to its normal banks. The crisis was over. Nothing came of the boat idea for the Mississippi River.

Marine-grade plywood was also successfully made with Plaskon's Weldwood glue. Chrysler Marine built a cabin cruiser using the special plywood and successfully operated it as an experiment out of New York for at least one season.

At the same time, a shoe manufacturer used a sample supply to glue the soles of ladies shoes together. Tests showed the shoes withstood hard wear in rainy weather. But when Plaskon asked for the order they were told in each case, "Send us more samples."

General Motors "all steel" auto bodies had over 40 pieces of wood in them. These pieces were glued together. This was ideal for Plaskon glue…a Plaskon glued joint would not break. The wood broke first. GM tried it and all tests were successful. But once again, when Plaskon asked for the order, they were told, "Send us more samples."

Plaskon's management knew that all these samples would eventually result in orders. But in the meantime they were suffering a loss in the glue operation. They were getting discouraged. So they decided to manufacture the glue themselves and distribute it through another selling organization that knew how to market glue.

They next made an agreement with the Borden Company who sold the glue under the trade name "Casine". Borden sold a lot of Casine glue. Plaskon's glue finally began to show a profit.

Howald had another idea for his glue. Glass fibers were relatively new, and he was sure that fishing rods could be made of fiberglass impregnated with Weldwood. Plaskon management didn't think the market would be large enough to justify the research. Howald insisted.

To satisfy him, the company gave him the right to do the research on his own and anything that resulted would be his property.

Up until then, fishing rods were made of either split bamboo or steel. In either case the "action" varied. Some were too stiff…some were too nimble and broke easily. Howald was successful in his research. His rods could be made to control the action by using varying amounts of fiberglass and Weldwood in the manufacture. Fishermen could have a strong, waterproof rod as stiff or nimble as they wanted.

He sold the right to use his process to Shakespeare. Soon after, Howald walked into Bennett's office with a fishing rod. Bennett looked up and said, "Whatcha got?" Howald showed him the name scribed on the side of the rod. "Look," he said, "Shakespeare calls it their 'Wonder Rod—Howald Process.'"

The new Shakespeare Wonder Rod swept the market. Fiberglass fishing rods became the standard for the next 50 years.

CHAPTER 16

A New Plant

At mid-year, a surprise visitor appeared at the Toledo headquarters on Monroe Street. He introduced himself as Louis Kahn, a senior partner in the Detroit firm of architects, Albert Kahn, Inc. He asked to see Walter Fink. The Albert Kahn architectural firm was well known and highly respected. Fink was curious. He walked out to the reception area to meet him and led him to his office.

Louis Kahn explained to Fink that his firm wanted to design Toledo's new plant on Telegraph Road. He knew that the plant had been delayed time after time, but brought a special offer with him. Fink was the company treasurer…he knew Toledo didn't have the finances required, nor could it be borrowed from local banks on the long terms that would be required. But he listened.

Kahn said, "Here's what we propose, Mr. Fink. We will design the plant, write the specifications, and get a firm bid from a reputable contractor. If you accept our plans and go ahead with the building, you will pay us our regular fee. But if for any reason Toledo Scale doesn't go ahead with the project, you owe us nothing! For any reason…I want to be specific on that."

Fink took the offer to Bennett. They both were enthralled. Bennett asked, "Walter, can you think of any possible way that we can get a loan to do this? We need a new plant so badly."

"Well, I don't see any way we can get the financing locally," Fink replied. "But it might be possible through some insurance company, or an out-of-town savings bank in a large city. I just don't know. But I think I'd better start looking!"

His inquiries were mildly encouraging. On the strength of this, and with the "no build—no architectural cost" agreement, they arranged for Kahn to do a preliminary plant layout. The design included 20% more floor space than was currently being used in all seven existing plants scattered around the city, to allow for expansion.

Next, Kahn received a firm bid to build the plant for less than $400,000 from Toledo contractor A. Bentley & Sons. This bid contrasted greatly with the 1929 estimate of $1.5 million for the Norman Bel Geddes designs for several smaller structures with less total floor space.

Over the years Toledo had spent more than $350,000 for surveys, plans, and specifications without ever getting a plant. Now things were looking up. Bennett told Fink he wanted him to look into financing, but to hold off on any deal until something else was settled first.

Bennett had another trick up his sleeve. He wanted to complete another acquisition before seeking financing for the new plant. He wanted a done-deal first. And on the last day of the year he wrote to everyone announcing the news:

Toledo Scale Company
Toledo, Ohio
U.S.A.
December 31, 1938

TO THE TOLEDO SCALE ORGANIZATION:

I don't have to tell you that the Toledo Scale Research Program is working. Since this program was set up 10 years ago, you've seen a steadily increasing procession of new developments—Computogram—Sentinel—Printweigh—and many more. Within the past year you've seen the Guardian, the SpeedWeigh, the 0867, to name a few.

But, so much for the past. Even more important is what Toledo Research means to the future—your future. It is assurance to you that the Company is making the investment necessary to keep Toledo Scales fully abreast of the times today, and for the future.

December 22 we made an investment in added plant facilities that places us in a better position than ever to manufacture almost anything that might be required. On that date we acquired the Defiance Machine Works at Defiance, Ohio. This possesses a splendid foundry, and heavy duty production equipment. Foundry facilities are especially important to us in the production of scales of higher capacities.

This new plant also permits further expansion of our line of testing and force-measurement devices. In addition, the machine tools made by Defiance Works will be continued and further developed—with sales through machine tools distributors as at present.

For 1939, our research and engineering program continues at an accelerated pace. We've made an investment in greatly increased plant facilities. This is tangible evidence of our confidence in the business future. I count on your support to help DRIVE AHEAD in 1939.

Sincerely,

H. D. Bennett

President

The plant was officially designated the Defiance Division of Toledo Precision Devices, Inc. It occupied an area of about two city blocks near the center of the town and contained about 173,000 square feet of floor space. Officers of Toledo Precision Devices were Hugh Bennett, president; Geoff Bennett, vice president; and Walter Fink, secretary-treasurer. These were essentially the same titles the three held as officers of Toledo Scale Company.

For years Defiance Machine Works had manufactured some heavy capacity cast levers for Toledo as a vendor. Now Toledo concentrated all foundry work at Defiance, adding many small and medium castings to the large castings that were manufactured there. The acquisition meant that a foundry would not be needed in the planned new Toledo Scale plant...next on the required list.

When the Defiance deal was settled, Bennett called a board meeting to present the Albert Kahn plans and specifications. The board discussed them thoroughly. They were impressed with Kahn's proposal to hold off any fee unless Toledo actually built the plant.

The board then approved the plans and agreed to have the plant built, provided the project could be reasonably financed. They appointed two people to a committee to work on the finances, director John T. Rohr and treasurer Walter Fink.

Fink lost no time. The next day he arranged a meeting with Harlan Newell of the Society of Savings in Cleveland...a large savings bank he had previously queried. He discussed the project with Newell. The meeting was friendly. Newell asked, "Okay then, Mr. Fink, just what do you propose?"

Fink laid it out. He already had Rohr's approval for his plan. "We request a loan of $500,000 . . . enough to build the plant and cover moving expenses. We're willing to pay 5% interest on the loan. We propose to pay off the loan in ten annual installments with the right to prepay on the front end of the loan, plus the right to pay it off at any time without penalty."

"What about collateral?" Newell asked.

"Rather than a mortgage on the building and real estate, we're prepared to offer collateral which we believe will be more acceptable,"

Fink said. "Toledo Scale owns an 87.85% interest in a separate firm, the Toledo Porcelain Enamel Products Company. We offer our complete stock interest in this company as collateral. Should we default, it would be easier for you to sell this stock than sell the plant." Newell was clearly interested. He took Fink to meet Society's board chairman who asked about the history of Toledo Scale. Fink spent several hours with them, talking about the company's long fight for Honest Weight, the development of the Toledo Porcelain Enamel Products Company, Toledo Precision Devices, the Plaskon story and company, the sales organization, and more.

Society's chairman asked Fink to write a brief history of Toledo Scale and send it to Newell. When Fink returned home he told John Rohr about his experience, who agreed that Fink should write the history. Fink wrote a seven page letter containing a brief history and sent it to Newell.

Within a few days, Newell visited all of Toledo's plants. He met with Hugh Bennett and several other company officers in the Monroe Street headquarters, then returned to Cleveland. Several weeks later Fink got the word. The loan was approved...and on the exact terms Fink had requested. Toledo Scale would have a new plant. All manufacturing would be under one roof.

In March 1939, the building contract was signed with general contractor A. Bentley & Sons. The local newspapers covered the news and published the architect's rendering of the plant. This publicity prompted a letter from a prominent Toledo merchant, Julius Lamson, which rather supports the theory that new inventions often come from different people at much the same time. Lamson owned and operated one of Toledo's largest, most successful department stores. He wrote:

Mr. H. D. Bennett, President
The Toledo Scale Company

Dear Sir:

I have noticed with considerable interest the statements in the paper in regard to your expectation of building a new plant and concentrating the various parts of your business in one location instead of being scattered as they are now. I want to congratulate you on the wonderful growth of your company. I have often remarked that the Toledo Scale Company and their products were the best advertisers of Toledo that we have here. Wherever I have traveled, at home or abroad, I have been pleased to see on shop counters in bold letters the word TOLEDO on the front of the scales they use. But I'm interested from another viewpoint.

When I was a boy, fifteen years old, I went to work in a general country store where we sold all kinds of merchandise and used a variety of weights and measures. Our trade was made up largely of rural trade. We bartered with the farmers and took in exchange their eggs and butter and some other commodities. For instance, if a farmer's wife came in with two or three rolls of butter nicely laid out on a platter, we had to weigh the platter with the butter on it and then weigh the platter after removing the butter; then subtract one weight from the other and figure out the price we had to pay in exchange for the trade.

I noticed there were quite a class of people who were continually watching the scales. We had some spring scales, and they didn't want anything sold to them weighed on a spring scale because they did not trust them. They wanted us to use weights on one end of the balance and their product on the other end. As a boy I thought a great deal about it and wondered why there was not some sort of weighing apparatus that would automatically give the weight of the product when it was placed on the scale and one that did not have springs.

I finally evolved in my mind a scale to be made with a slot in the counter top through which would hang a pendulum with a pointer attached above the fulcrum with an arc marked in pounds and ounces in front of a chart. The pointer would indicate the weight on the arched scale above. The principal could be adapted for any kind of business and would be always accurate and in plain view of both the buyer and seller.

I made a drawing of the apparatus. I thought that some day, when I got enough money, I would get it patented. I came to Toledo in 1873 and brought my drawing with me and kept it carefully still wishing for the time when I could get it patented. Some time afterward I went into a stationery store and found on the counter a postal scale for sale, which worked on the same principal that I had planned and realized that someone got ahead of me on the patent.

I don't know who patented your scale or when it occurred but I have always been interested in your scale company because it has grown out of an idea which I had when I was a boy, so I thought I would tell you about it.

Yours very truly,
Julius G. Lamson

Bennett was slow in answering Lamson's intriguing letter because construction began immediately. Within days of signing the contract, the plant location was staked out on the 80-acre Telegraph Road site and construction began. It was completed by August.

About this time, Norman Bel Geddes was in the news again as his widely popular designs for the 1939 New York World's Fair were revealed. Called the World of Tomorrow, the centerpiece of the World's Fair was Geddes' 700-foot Trylon and 200-foot Perisphere in General Motors "Futurama" exhibit. Bennett had loved Geddes' original, creative designs for a new plant from ten years ago but there was no question he would stick with Kahn's design now.

Arrangements were made to move scale manufacturing operations from the seven scattered plants then in use. Box making and lumber storage would remain on Fitch Road. Bennett did not need a landing strip at the new plant because National Airport had opened for general aviation less than a mile away at the corner of Telegraph and Alexis Roads.

Parking had been a problem at the old Monroe Street plant. Many supervisory employees rented space inside the Auburndale garage across the street. They liked the inside parking. Since they were used to renting space, the company built an open garage for 32 cars.

To pay for the garage, they rented each spot to supervisory employees for $3 per month. Because of the high demand, second and third garages were built later on the same rental basis. Even then there was a waiting list.

The company knew that food service would be a problem since there were no restaurants within two miles of the new plant. Toledo had operated its own restaurant at the old plant for years and knew the cost and problems of serving food to the same people every day.

They built a cafeteria on company land just outside the plant's fenced-in area and named it the Weigh-Side Inn. Later it was re-named the Hickory House. Since it was outside the fenced area along Telegraph Road, they hoped it would attract lunch and dinner business from the public to make it more cost efficient. Yet virtually no dinner business resulted and they soon opened only for lunch.

To assure high food quality standards, Toledo leased the building to a woman who had managed the dining room at the Highland Meadows Country Club in Sylvania. Toledo furnished the building, utilities, equipment, maintenance and janitorial staff. The leaseholder furnished cooked food at reasonable prices. A small amount of lunch business came from nearby plants.

Theobald had first dreamed of a new plant in the mid teens. Bennett carried on the dream…in fact he had board approval almost ten years ago, but stopped due to the Depression. Now at long last the dream was a reality. And for the first time the building was owned by Toledo Scale. All of the other plants had been leased. It was built at a cost below the budgeted amount approved by the board. The new factory cost just over 80 cents per square foot, an incredibly low construction cost for Toledo, Ohio.

The dream was now reality. Just before the move, all employees and their families were invited to see the new plant. August 12 was a hot and sticky day. The dog days of summer had arrived. No formal program was planned, yet great groups streamed through the building.

Employees were clearly enthusiastic about their new home. They were greeted by Hugh and Geoff Bennett, Walter Fink, Lloyd Colenback, and other excited management executives.

Manufacturing operations from the scattered plants were moved within the next few weeks. The Plaskon facility was deliberately not included due to its many extra requirements. The move entailed transporting equipment ranging in size from tiny precision tools needed to manufacture delicate, light capacity scales to moving giant four-ton lever boring machines.

Gas furnaces, plating equipment, metal supplies; office equipment, files and records were moved by trucks and flat cars. The move was smoothly completed the last day of August. Newspapers pronounced the plant "The last word in factory construction."

The next day, September 1, 1939, became a historical day. The news marked the beginning of a conflict that would change the world. In a surprise move, Hitler's army invaded Poland. His blitzkrieg rapidly overran the Polish army with its horse cavalry and antiquated aircraft. Within days England and France declared war against Germany. World War II had begun in Europe.

Great Britain's Prime Minister Neville Chamberlain had met with Hitler in Munich the previous year. In an address from 10 Downing Street upon his return he said, "I believe it is peace for our time."

Almost alone, Winston Churchill did not believe him. In a speech in the House of Commons on the Munich agreement he responded, "The German dictator, instead of snatching the victuals from the table, has been content to have them served to him course by course."

Soon after the war started, Chamberlain resigned under mounting pressure from Labor and his own Conservative Party. On May 10, 1940, at the age of 65, Winston Churchill became Prime Minister. Churchill knew the road would be long and hard. In his first speech in the House of Commons as Prime Minister he said, "I have nothing to offer but blood, toil, tears and sweat."

It was the first of Churchill's many great war speeches. Over 20 years later, Churchill was granted honorary U.S. citizenship. In his words accompanying the grant, President John F. Kennedy said of Churchill, "He mobilized the English language and sent it into battle."

Hugh Bennett was one person who did not need convincing that the U.S. would be drawn into the war. In spite of the isolationist mood then alive in America, Bennett was convinced that the United States would enter the war too…and hoped that Britain could hold out alone in the meantime. France had been overrun and defeated by June 1940.

German troops paraded through Paris as French men and women wept openly. Italy had entered the war on Hitler's side. Virtually all of Europe was under the control of the Axis powers. Bennett moved to prepare Toledo Scale…first with a major decision involving Plaskon.

Through the 30's Plaskon had grown by leaps and bounds. It was a true growth company in a growth industry. But Toledo was concerned about the potential competition. Many large, well-financed chemical corporations were now working in the plastics field. DuPont, Monsanto, Union Carbide, and more…all very much larger and better financed. There was a chance that one of them would come up with a better product. A war would only serve to accelerate their interest in plastics.

Plaskon desperately needed a new plant too. They had long outgrown the plant on Fitchland, as well as the plant they had acquired in New Jersey. Three to four million dollars was estimated as the cost to build one. And the research cost to keep ahead in the fast growing plastics industry was very high.

The Toledo Scale board of directors saw this as high risk, especially with their half-million dollar debt for the new Toledo plant. They voted to sell the Plaskon company. Bennett agreed, even though Plaskon was his single most successful achievement.

He no longer held a majority of Toledo Scale stock, but deep down he agreed with the decision. The board told Bennett to find a buyer.

Plaskon was then the largest single factor in the plastics industry. Many companies were interested in buying it. Monsanto was especially interested. Monsanto's president Queeny came to Toledo to discuss buying Plaskon. The talks became serious.

Monsanto made a tentative offer of $7,000,000 for 100% of Toledo's Plaskon stock…but in Monsanto common stock with restrictions on the number of shares that could be put on the market at any one time, and in total for one year.

Toledo needed cash…not stock with selling limitations. Discussions with Monsanto were dropped.

Glass was a major Toledo industry. Owens-Illinois, Libbey-Owens-Ford, and the relatively new Owens Corning Fiberglas were all glass companies with headquarters in Toledo. Their management all knew each other well. In fact, Mike Owens, the mechanical genius who invented the bottle blowing machine, among other inventions for glass production, had been involved with all three at one time or another and was the Owens in all three company names.

Several local bankers who owned Toledo Scale stock and served on its board also served on various glass company boards. Toledo Scale stock owner and board member W. W. Knight, Sr. also served on the boards of Libbey-Owens-Ford and Owens-Illinois.

Many speculated that this is what led to the discussions with Libbey-Owens-Ford. Talks were held with L-O-F based on a cash sale of $3,500,000 for Toledo's Plaskon stock. Auditors claimed that Toledo would realize a profit on the sale of nearly two and a quarter million dollars. That was reason enough. Toledo sold their Plaskon shares to L-O-F. The cash was used to retire a preferred stock issue and for added working capital.

Out of Toledo's search for a lightweight material for scale housings came an entirely new industry…developed so a salesman could carry a scale into a store without getting a hernia. Toledo Scale had been paid over $500,000 in cash dividends over the years and realized a final profit of $2,111,156. Toledo research paid off. And Bennett didn't forget his success with plastics.

After the first scale was housed in Plaskon, Toledo moved to include the rest of the line. Within a few years the entire line of cylinder scales was also housed in Plaskon. This caused the need for a porcelain finish to decrease until only a small number of parts were finished in porcelain.

This meant that the Toledo Porcelain Enamel Products Company was no longer closely related to the scale business. It had evolved into a true job shop operation for a wide variety of products. Toledo Scale had used their 87.85% interest in Toledo Porcelain as collateral for the loan on the new plant building. In order to sell it, they negotiated a different collateral with the Society of Savings.

Fink discovered that the employees of Toledo Porcelain who had operated it since its inception were interested in owning the business. Employees had owned 12.15% of the stock from the beginning and now wanted the rest. In early 1940, Toledo Porcelain Enamel Products employees bought Toledo Scale's interest for cash based on the book value of the company. The cash helped pay down the loan on the new plant.

CHAPTER 17

World War II

Bennett felt the winds of war blowing ever stronger. In spite of the nation's isolationist mood, he was sure the United States would enter the conflict. He began to prepare Toledo Scale for war by concentrating development efforts on those products he knew would be required. Using the Toledo double pendulum mechanism, Toledo greatly refined force measurement devices.

They would be used in dynamometer scales to measure the torque of large aircraft engines and to test diesel engines for landing craft. Toledo dynamometer scales were installed in Pesco Products at their Cleveland plant to test precision pumps that control fluid motion harnessed to activate airplane mechanisms, operate brakes, clutches, jacks, hoists and remote controls.

Custom equipment helped balance propellers, was installed in wind tunnels, checked piston rings, and tested springs for tension and compression. Continuous weighers tested the uniformity of tire tread stock. Toledo hopper scales batched ingredients for newly developed synthetic rubber...now vital since almost all sources of natural rubber were cut off.

Self-gauging pivots for truck scales came along, as well as a rapid moisture tester.

Meanwhile Ed Quertinmont was assigned to various field offices as a serviceman. He was first sent to Columbus, then Pittsburgh and next to Buffalo, returning to Toledo briefly between assignments. Like many good servicemen, he soon accepted a sales territory as a commissioned salesman in Buffalo. His territory was Niagara Falls County, which contained many chemical plants.

Quertinmont was immediately successful. "Man, did I sell scales," he said. "My first year I made over $40,000 in commissions." This was a huge income at the tail end of the Depression. "It scared the hell out of me," Quertinmont said. "I was used to being paid a salary...not commissions. So I just banked the commissions and paid myself a salary."

His district manager in Buffalo was Don Boudinot. District managers were paid a salary with an override bonus and Quertinmont was making a lot more money than his boss was. Boudinot called him in. "Ed, I've decided to change several of your accounts into house accounts."

This practice was not uncommon at the time among many U.S. companies that used commissioned salesmen to reach their markets. It reduced the cost of sales to the company and boosted the manager's bonus. Boudinot listed three or four of Quertinmont's best chemical accounts that he would make house accounts.

Quertinmont was angry. "Don, when you take the first account, you can have them all!"

When Boudinot persisted, Quertinmont resigned. He quickly got a salaried job with the Carborundum Company in Niagara Falls, which had been one of his accounts. Carborundum had over 400 Toledo scales and Quertinmont became manager of their weights and measures department. While his salary was much less than he had been earning in commissions, he was comfortable being back on salary.

Several months later his phone rang at about two in the morning. Quertinmont picked it up, worried that a middle-of-the-night phone call could be serious. A voice slurred, "Ed, what the hell is this I hear about you not being with the company anymore?"

Quertinmont recognized the voice immediately. It was Stanley Q. Bennett, Toledo Scale's national service manager (no relation to Hugh and Geoff Bennett). He could tell that Bennett had been drinking. "Stanley, why are you calling me in the middle of the night?"

"I just found out you were gone. That's a bunch of crap! You don't belong anywhere except Toledo Scale, and I want you back here, dammit," Bennett said. "And I want to make an appointment for you to come and talk to us right now!" Quertinmont started to reply—"I got a job at Carborundum…"

Bennett interrupted, "I didn't ask you where you are working. Dammit, I wanna know when you can come for a talk. You belong at Toledo Scale, dammit!"

Quertinmont knew Stanley Bennett was deadly serious even though he was clearly in his cups. He finally agreed to an appointment. He was greeted enthusiastically in Toledo, and got a job offer. It included an increase over what he was making at Carborundum, plus an agreement that the time he was gone would be treated as a leave-of-absence with no break in his employment. The offer was for a job as assistant to Red Miller, the manager of Toledo's training department. Quertinmont accepted.

So just before the war and after a three month hiatus, Quertinmont was back with Toledo Scale…and back in Toledo, Ohio working in the training department at the new plant.

Two years after the main plant was built, Toledo already needed more space…in spite of the fact that the main plant was built with 20% more space than was forecast to be needed. A 65,000 square foot addition was added to the back of the plant. The addition included another boiler house, needed for the added capacity. It was completed in mid 1941.

On a quiet Sunday morning, December 7, 1941, Bennett's prediction came true as Japan bombed Pearl Harbor in a surprise attack. President Roosevelt called it, "a day that will live in infamy" as he placed the nation on a full war basis. The next day the United States Congress declared war against the Axis powers, Japan, Germany and Italy.

The surprise attack on Pearl Harbor caused the entire nation to immediately support the war effort. On that fateful Sunday morning, the Chaplain of a battleship in Pearl Harbor was preparing for divine services on the afterdeck. Suddenly Japanese planes began to attack the ship without warning.

The Chaplain dropped his preparations, ran to a machine gun and began firing on the attacking planes. Moments later he was heard to say to one of his assistants, "Praise the Lord and pass the ammunition; I just got one of the sons of bitches."

Praise the Lord and Pass the Ammunition became the title of one of the first popular songs of the war. The battle cry was "Remember Pearl Harbor". The United States was indeed united…including the former isolationists. American media identified the world's greatest villains as Hitler, Mussolini and Hirohito.

Ration stamps were quickly issued for all vital commodities. Gasoline rationing was soon initiated. The company was concerned that there might come a time when it would be impossible for salesmen to get gasoline for their cars. So Toledo Scale asked area manager W. M. Randolph to conduct an experiment down in Dixie to see if sales could still be made using only public transportation.

Retail representative Bob Schick was sent from Atlanta to Augusta, Georgia, by train to spend a week there on retail sales. Six pieces of equipment were shipped to him in care of his hotel.

On Monday morning, Schick took a bus out to the end of the line. He worked his way back on foot and called on stores along the way. When he located a prospect, he would return to the hotel, call a taxi and take a scale or food machine out to the merchant's store. He repeated this process all week.

At the end of the week total sales were slightly above average. Taxi and miscellaneous expenses for the week were less than ten dollars. Area Manager Randolph wrote, "We now know definitely that should a situation develop where gasoline is impossible to get, we will still be selling retail scales."

Very soon Toledo Scale began to execute government ordnance contracts for precision fire-control equipment. Special Toledo equipment checked the balance and loading of huge bombers. Even the much maligned ration stamps created to ration food, gasoline and other consumer goods were counted on special Toledo Scales.

The government moved to locate war plants in remote locations to minimize the damage in case they were bombed. Toledo's nationwide service coverage was successfully put to use to serve these remote locations under sometimes severe handicaps.

The plant adapted to war production. The War Production board next ordered Toledo to discontinue manufacturing retail scales and food machines. This made the public transportation test conducted by Bob Schick in Augusta, Georgia, completely moot. Only industrial scales that were declared essential to the war effort were permitted to be manufactured.

The Defiance plant was converted to making castings for war production as well.

Material handling equipment was installed at the Reynolds Metal Company to speed vital war materials. The Geo. K. Garrett Company used newly installed Toledo conveyor weighing equipment to accurately load boxes of lock washers that would be used in weapons moved by a vibrator mechanism, then moved the boxes to a box weighing position to precisely check the weight.

Many metal working shops were soon adapted to make high-explosive shells. Toledo SpeedWeigh scales were ordered for them by the war department to hold shell weights within close tolerance as part of the inspection process. The process included checking the weight, length and outside diameter of each shell and the identifying data stenciled on each one.

At the Square D plant in Milwaukee, various models of Toledo counting scales were matched to jobs to count the company's electrical control equipment that would be used in a variety of war machines. Toledo counting scales were sent to many companies that produced munitions for the war effort.

At the Harley Davidson plant in Milwaukee, Toledos were added to those already there to quickly and accurately furnish necessary weights for production and weight control. The name Harley Davidson meant motorcycles the world over, and the plant worked at top speed to put wheels under the Army's motorized units. This plant was where motorcycles were produced for the Armored

Division's motorized scouts as well as for reconnaissance and message carrying for all services.

And at one of Republic Aviation's huge fighter plane plants, Toledo installed a new aircraft scale to weigh the Republic P-47 Thunderbolt, the fastest, most powerful high-altitude fighter of the day, capable of reaching 400 miles per hour in level flight.

Proper weight and balance is vital to aircraft. The Aircraft scale was actually three pit scales, one each in fixed positions to measure the weight on the main wheels, and one installed in a long pit at a right angle to these, in which the scale could be moved forward to weigh nose-wheel aircraft, or to the back end of the pit to weigh tail-wheel aircraft like the Thunderbolt.

Aircraft scales were next installed in Ford's great Willow Run plant to weigh Consolidated Aircraft's huge, 4-engine B-24 Liberator bombers, being built there. Planes of such massive size had never been produced in a production line before. The scales had to determine the gross weight and weight distribution of these heavily armed bombers.

Variations from set standards seriously affected the Liberator's maneuverability and made them useless for combat. Toledo engineers quickly solved the weight distribution problem. Thousands of B-24's were manufactured at Willow Run during the war.

A top-secret project was Toledo's work on the super-secret Norden bombsight as a subcontractor to the Sperry Corporation who made it. Toledo was assigned the project because of their expertise in precision ball bearings and races and their skill in machining pinions; both used in small scales.

These ball bearing races were used in the Norden bombsight guidance system…held steady by a gyroscope full of precision ball bearings.

The Norden bombsight was a closely guarded secret since it was considered to be vastly superior to the bombsights used by the Axis powers. The Norden bombsight contained a self-destruct mechanism that was to be activated should the aircraft be shot down over enemy territory.

Toledo's work was done in a separate, secure building leased from the Buckeye Winery next to the main plant. Security was tight…only those assigned to the project were permitted inside the building. Weighing demands of war industries and ordnance plants increased. Civilian agencies were called upon to perform this service. The War Department arranged for new identification cards to help Toledo servicemen gain admission to vital industries and war plants. The cards were issued by Toledo Scale, signed by the national service manager and countersigned by a military security officer.

They contained a complete description and thumbprints of the serviceman. The government was serious about security in plants for war production.

Hitler violated his non aggression pact with Russia with his June 1941 invasion. When the U.S. and Britain entered the war six months later, Russia joined the Allies. Food was in short supply in Russia and the U.S. made a Lend-Lease agreement with them. "Cbnhar Tywohka" was their name for a basic ration of pork supplied to them under the agreement. The Cudahy Packing Company plant in Omaha was one of the meat packers who supplied the Cbnhar Tywohka.

At Cudahy, pork was cut in two inch cubes and hand packed in cans. Government inspectors insured each can was accurately weighed on Toledo SpeedWeigh scales. At the bottom of each can the operator placed two bay leaves, three peppers and 0.28 ounces of salt. Then from five to nine chunks of lean pork were added to the can which was then topped with an ounce of melted lard and sealed. Cudahy concluded immediately that Cbnhar Tywohka did not represent a potential new product for the post-war U.S. market.

Within a few months of the Pearl Harbor attack, Bennett set up a separate research division remote from the plant in a two-story building at 300 Ontario Street in downtown Toledo. Security was tight in the main plant and he wanted to keep research going both for war-related projects and civilian products to prepare the company for when the war was over.

Called Tolco, the division conducted a number of research projects. Research work already under way at the Armour Institute and at Batelle Memorial Institute was directed by Tolco. They conducted research on many varied assignments.

At Tolco, engineer L. S. Williams developed the first mathematically calculated double pendulum counterbalance system. Williams worked for many months on the mathematical calculations, which today could be done by a computer in minutes. Tolco developed the first Toledo SpeedWeigh scale with an all aluminum housing. It was immediately placed in production.

Even though the Plaskon company had been sold, Bennett and Toledo Scale kept getting good publicity for it. During the war United Air Lines sponsored a weekly feature entitled "In Time To Come" on CBS radio in which they saluted America's industry and its leaders.

One complete program told of the development of plastics and the role played by Toledo's president, Hugh Bennett, in this new, but fast-growing industry. The script read:

"Tonight, 'In Time To Come' will tell you some of the high spots in an industry less than seventy-five years old...plastics. It all began with an accident. Often we have wondered how many great discoveries were just that...accidents. But in 1869 a young chemist named Hyatt was working in a grimy laboratory...explaining a theory to a young protégé. 'The beaker contains cellulose,' he explained, 'and nitric acid. Reacted with heat it gives us nitrocellulose...pretty dangerous stuff...it's an explosive...powerful enough to blow us both to Kingdom Come...here...I'll add some more acid...stop fidgeting will you...

The bottle fell out of his hands but didn't explode. The experiment was ruined...but the product on the floor was a new substance...the first true synthetic plastic...celluloid.

The next great step in plastic research came in 1905...this time it was no accident...merely a case of mistaken values...and a worried young man called Bakeland. He invented Velox...a photographic paper, sold it to Kodak at their price...a million dollars. He would have taken ten thousand. Using this money for research he retired to a laboratory for three years and developed Bakelite…the second great plastic discovery…a new substance from coal, tar and wood.

Then in 1929…1930…in the offices of the Toledo Scale Company…suggestions were coming in…not from customers…from the salesmen who sold the famous Toledo Scale…For instance…'That porcelain scale weighs over 150 pounds…I walk into a prospect's store…stagger in I should say…lugging the scale…and he says to me…'Here…nice scale…set it up here…mind those displays…Hey! Look out! Then the counter broke and everything fell. So that's what happens. Lost me a sale. We gotta do something about it.'

President Bennett of the Toledo Scale Company did something about it. He went to the Mellon Institute and financed research in a durable, lightweight housing to replace the cast iron construction of the world-famous scale. Research came up with an answer…Plaskon.

Plaskon…another stride forward in the plastics industry. Today, plastic products reach into all our lives…all children of Hyatt's laboratory mistake…of Bakeland's experiments…of Bennett's lightweight scales."

Not long after the broadcast, Hugh Bennett was called to Washington by the head of the War Production Board. He served two years as a "dollar-a-year" man in the machine tool division of the board. His brother Geoff assumed control of the company in his absence as Executive Vice President and General Manager. Geoff Bennett managed another addition to the plant, made necessary by the large volume of high priority war work assigned to Toledo Scale during the early years of the war.

Toledo Scale kept advertising during the war, though on a reduced level. The messages were institutional, intended to keep the name alive and ready for post-war business. In one popular ad the illustration showed a globe of the earth held in a hand…and asked the intriguing question:

How Much Does The Earth WEIGH?

Scientists have calculated the weight of the earth at 6,000,000,000,000,000,000,000 tons. However, we feel a bit like Archimedes of old, who, in illustrating the principle of levers said, "Give me a place to stand and I will move the world." If we could but find a place to install such a gigantic scale, we're confident that our engineers could build one to weigh the earth down to the last ton!

A bit fantastic you say? Right. But then a lot of present-day industrial Toledo Scale applications would have seemed fantastic a decade or two ago.

It's surprising to look over the vast number of ingenious weighing, classifying, and testing jobs Toledo Scales are performing today in our country's war production for victory. There are scales for balancing propeller blades, measuring wind tunnel stresses on aircraft, dynamometer scales checking engine horsepower, ammunition classifying scales, batching scales for synthetic rubbers, and scores of other weight-control applications that read like a page out of America's Industrial Progress Book.

A peek into the laboratories of our Research Department would reveal developments under way that will in the future bring about a new age of industrial weight control. Fantastic as it may seem to think about a scale that could weigh the earth, it illustrates merely the wide scope of things to come through better industrial weighing with Toledo Scales.

TOLEDO SCALE COMPANY

TOLEDO • OHIO
"NO SPRINGS—HONEST WEIGHT"

After Mussolini was overthrown in 1943, American policy changed. Japan's war leader, Tojo, replaced Emperor Hirohito as the real Japanese villain in all national publicity. American leadership apparently concluded that Hirohito should not be named a villain in the hope that he would help smooth the peace process when the conflict was over. He did, in fact, intervene to stop the war when the second atom bomb was dropped and his war leaders still wanted to continue to fight to the death.

In spite of the Toledo operation being named a vital industry, many factory employees were serving in the Armed Forces…most by their own choice. Many more from field offices were also serving.

In World War II, GIs found recognition all over the globe when mentioning Toledo as their home town. "Oh yeah! No Springs—Honest Weight" they heard.

By 1943 System magazine published the names and home towns of 133 Toledomen from the field sales and service organization in the Armed Forces. Already, six of these were listed as killed in action.

Some research continued during the war for post-war products. Engineer George Wood developed a coffee mill to grind coffee at the point of purchase. When coffee was freshly ground it was perceived by housewives to be superior. To test the prototype it was installed in Felker's Market on Ashland Avenue. Herbert Felker's father had used the first DeVilbiss scale in his market on Adams Street and he was proud to be chosen for the test.

The coffee mill had a distinctive appearance. As much as three pounds of coffee beans could be poured in the opening at the top. The ground coffee came out a side spout. Coffee dust was blown away as the ground coffee moved on a short conveyor to the bag. The mill operated trouble free for several years.

Yet vacuum-packed coffee was becoming more popular. Toledo believed the days of fresh ground coffee in the grocery store would soon be over and didn't manufacture the mill.

Tolco was ahead of its time on many projects. They developed an instant coffee by grinding coffee into a very fine powder. The powder was made into a pellet by compressing the amount that would make one cup when hot water was added. It worked. But the first cup of perked coffee tasted better and had a more pleasing aroma than the instant coffee…just as it does today.

The project was dropped and the high compression machine used to make the pellets was given to the Battelle Institute. Other Tolco projects Toledo dropped included cintered (powdered) metal, and a method of adding value to peanut shell waste by grinding them into a soil mulch. Both too soon.

Tolco also developed the first model of the Toledo Gravity-Feed Slicing Machine as part of their food machine development efforts. The prototype had an estimating scale as part of the slicer. Toledo thought that an estimating scale in the slicer would be of real convenience to the butcher, saving him steps from the slicer to the scale when a customer would order, say, a quarter pound of boiled ham. Field tests showed positive results and it was put into production.

It turned out the butcher preferred to walk to the scale with the product he had sliced. He usually cut a slice or two more than was requested, put the slices on the scale, read the amount and asked the customer, "Is that all right?" The customer almost always agreed…and the butcher increased his meat sales. The estimating scale was dropped as part of the unit. It became simply a gravity-feed slicer.

Engineer Bruce Robinson developed a gravity-feed chopper. Jim Brown added a steak tenderizing machine. Both were developed and put into production after the war. Yet more work had to be done and Toledo had no spare engineers.

Toledo urgently needed more food machine products to compete successfully with Hobart when the war was over…especially a meat saw.

Toledo employed a professor of mechanical engineering from the University of Michigan during his summer vacation to work on designing a meat saw, following ideas given him by Toledo. Before the summer was over he had designed Toledo's first experimental model of a meat saw with some unique features.

The saw blade tension was provided by the weight of the electric motor. This eliminated the need for the knurled tension knob used on competitive saws...always slippery from the meat juices on butcher's hands. It also contained an electric light recessed into the underside of the head, which lit up the entire table surface for the butcher. Various sizes were eventually put into production.

Probably the most fascinating Toledo Scale project during World War II involved three Toledo employees who had been assigned special sensitive, essential duties. Red Miller, Ralph Brimacombe and Ed Quertinmont were named project service engineers. They were first sent to high-risk munitions plants all around the country to keep their scales working properly.

Each had been investigated by the FBI and they were given top-secret clearance. Their jobs were declared essential to the war effort. They always knew what kind of plant they were going to work in...until they were ordered to Richland, Washington at different times to work in a plant being built in nearby Hanford along the Columbia River in a remote, desert-like area.

The whole operation was managed by DuPont. The city of Richland was built virtually from scratch to house the thousands of workers on the project. Housing facilities, supermarkets, theaters and everything else that made up a city were built for the operation. At one time as many as 60,000 people worked on the project...and not one of the workers knew what the plant was for.

The plant at Hanford was being built in two parts. The first part, called a canyon, housed tanks, hoppers, cranes and tank scale levers. The canyon was designed to be flooded by water from the Columbia River after it was completed. Everyone assumed the water was to cool whatever process was to take place in the canyon. Every metal part was stainless steel.

A building called the gallery was built adjacent to the canyon. It was separated by a concrete wall nine feet thick with a built-in lead shield. The gallery side contained all the controls for the equipment in the canyon including the scale heads. Over 400 Toledo tank scales were installed in various parts of the plant and the three Toledo project service engineers took turns installing and servicing them.

Each of the three spent many months working at Hanford. As the plant drew nearer to completion all the workers were told to simply stand by. Work was suspended and everyone just stood around for days, shooting craps and playing poker. Then layoffs would be announced and the work force reduced.

This process occurred several times. The closer the plant came to completion, the more the work force was reduced.

Since scales were essential to the project, Toledo project service engineers worked right up until the end. Quertinmont alone worked there a total of 26 weeks on three separate occasions. Yet none of them ever found out what the plant was for. When anyone asked they were given a silly answer.

Quertinmont recalled one answer. He heard a DuPont executive say, "The plant will make Vaseline." When the questioner said, "Come on, no one needs a plant like this to make Vaseline." "Well, Mr. DuPont thinks so," the executive replied. "One of FDR's sons is going to marry his daughter. And Mr. DuPont says he's going to need a whole factory of Vaseline if he's as big a prick as his father!"

It wasn't until the two atom bombs were dropped on Japan and the war was over that they realized they had been part of the Manhattan Project. The first bomb used uranium…the second plutonium. As more information was released they finally understood the Hanford plant was built to make the plutonium in the atom bomb dropped on Nagasaki.

Quertinmont said, "This was probably Toledo Scale's biggest single contribution to the war effort."

CHAPTER 18

Transition

In 1944 Paul Block, Jr., the 34-year-old co-publisher of *The Blade*, was deeply concerned about Toledo's future after the war. Block remembered the original Toledo Scale plant designs by Norman Bell Geddes and his Futurama designs at the 1939 World's Fair. He was impressed with Geddes' futuristic ideas. Block asked him to return to Toledo and look at it to see what it needed for its future.

He asked Geddes, "How can we show the people—especially those coming back from the war—that there is a future here?"

The result was "Toledo Tomorrow", a dramatic 61-foot-long model of Toledo complete with lights and sound effects that showed what the city could look like in 50 years. Toledo's existing buildings were on the model in perfect scale, along with the future improvements.

It was a $500,000 project, funded by *The Blade*. The exhibit was the largest scale model of a city ever built. Toledo Tomorrow was unveiled on the Fourth of July, 1945, about a month before the end of the war.

Life magazine did a six-page story entitled "Toledo: City of the Future". Eleanor Roosevelt wrote in her syndicated column, "Toledo sets an example for the rest of the country." Some people called the plan too futuristic. But it was a plan that helped transform the city at the end of the war by setting the stage for a series of major projects—a train station, airport, seaport, express roads, downtown pedestrian walkways above the streets, and a series of parks along the river.

City planners came from all over, sparked by the *Life* magazine story. Indianapolis, St. Louis and Portland, Oregon, took back many of the ideas and implemented them in their own cities. For Paul Block, Jr., sponsoring Toledo Tomorrow launched his civic leadership that led to the construction of Central Union Terminal, Toledo Express Airport, the SeaGate downtown developments, Medical College of Ohio, the Government Center, and more. He helped propel Toledo into the modern age.

Civic planners are now rediscovering some of the planning principles first proposed by Norman Bel Geddes. He was a creative power...with an artistry that evidently runs in the family. One of his daughters, Barbara Bell Geddes, became a well-known actress with a long successful career. She eventually starred in the TV show "Dallas" as Miss Ellie, J. R. Ewing's mother.

As 1945 approached, it looked as if the war would be over before long. There would be a huge backlog to fill...especially retail scales and food machines. Toledo had under development an entirely new line of both industrial and retail scales and food machines just waiting for the war to end. And manufacturing operations had become quite disorganized from all the war projects. There would be a large retraining effort required as men returned from war service.

Bennett had not held a majority of Toledo Scale stock for some time. Now a majority was controlled by bankers led by W. W. Knight, Sr. and others who had been Bennett's original investors and had also bought out the stock of the original eastern owners. It was rumored they were pressuring Bennett to pay off the loans he had obtained to expand the plant and convert it to war production.

There was no way Bennett could do it while the war continued. The majority stockholders wanted to change the direction of the company to prepare for post-war activities. They came to believe that Hugh Bennett did not share their vision. He talked about opportunities in machinery for plastics.

Many manufacturing methods were obsolete, based on war production needs. The company needed someone who knew how to modernize manufacturing in order to compete successfully after the war. To assure themselves that this would be done, they arranged to bring in a highly qualified manufacturing executive who, not so incidentally, was W. W. Knight's son-in-law.

Harris McIntosh was hired on February 1, 1945 as vice president of manufacturing and product engineering. McIntosh quickly rearranged factory departments. He changed an obsolete method of assembly in which one man built one machine to an assembly line production method, preparing to convert from war work to regular line production.

Executive vice president Geoff Bennett resigned. Hugh Bennett was already showing signs of heart disease. Many Toledo executives thought he looked depressed…assuming it was caused by his brother being forced out of the company. Many thought that it fell on Hugh Bennett to be the one who had to fire his brother. It appeared that the Bennett era was nearing an end.

On April 12, the nation abruptly lost its leader. President Franklin Roosevelt died in Warm Springs, Georgia, of a cerebral stroke at the age of 63. The nation mourned the loss of its popular president, the only man ever elected to four terms in the White House. The war with Germany was almost over and Roosevelt's failing health could not quite carry him to the end.

Relatively unknown Harry Truman, who had served only a few brief months as Vice President, was sworn in as President vowing to carry on Roosevelt's policies.

About two weeks after Roosevelt's death, Italian partisans in Milan executed "The Father of Italian Fascism," Benito Mussolini. His bullet-riddled body was hung by the heels beside the body of his mistress and two compatriots executed with him.

A few days later the news of Hitler's suicide on the first of May in a Berlin bunker reached the American people. Less than a week later the war in Europe ended with Germany's surrender on May 7, 1945, called VE Day.

Then, three months later on August 6, the atomic age was ushered in when the B-29 Enola Gay dropped an atom bomb with a

power equal to 20,000 tons of TNT on Hiroshima, Japan. When the
second atom bomb was dropped on Nagasaki a few days later, the war
with Japan abruptly ended. VJ Day was celebrated on August 15.
Our servicemen came home and peace returned to the world.

For the United States, 1945 was the most momentous year of
the century. Within three months, Roosevelt died in Warm
Springs—Mussolini was shot—Hitler died in a Berlin bunker—
the war was won in Europe—the atomic age was ushered in at
Hiroshima and Nagasaki—and World War II was over.

Many Americans who lived through the times still refer to
World War II as "the last good war." It was a clear struggle between
good and evil. Hitler and Tojo had to be defeated…there was no
doubt. It transformed the nation into a superpower. Beginning
with an army of 1.7 million men and a navy of only 160,000 on
Pearl Harbor Day, America's armed forces grew to 12.3 million
men and women by VE Day. Plus another huge army of universally supporting citizens back home.

When the war ended, all was not peaceful at the top rungs of
Toledo Scale. Hugh Bennett continued to negotiate with the majority stockholders. They agreed the broad post-war fields would be different for Toledo Scale and Defiance Machine Works. There were different opportunities for both and would require separate structures.

Bennett had an outstanding record in plastic research. He saw
a bright future for plastics but believed the machinery handling
end of the industry had not kept pace with the material end. He
had many ideas for plastic handling equipment. He saw the need
for plastic preforming machines and extrusion molding machines.
He believed that powdered metal had a bright future…parts could
be molded to close tolerances without the need for a machining
operation.

Bennett thought that plastics handling machinery could be
developed and manufactured by Defiance Machine Works. In
December he reached an agreement with Toledo Scale's majority
stockholders and traded his financial interest in Toledo Scale for
100% interest in Defiance Machine Works.

On December 31, 1945, Harris McIntosh was elected president of Toledo Scale Company.

Bennett's achievements were many. At the start, he took over an accumulation of problems, which included the huge debt caused when Toledo Scale lost the lawsuit to Dayton because a Phinney scale couldn't be found.

He led the company through a ten-year depression when there was often grave doubt that it would survive. Even as late as 1939, there were still 9,000,000 workers unemployed.

He built the new, modern manufacturing plant first dreamed of by Theobald many years before. Within two years of the plant being completed, he had to lead the company through a great world war in which most of his activities were dictated by the War Production Board.

His enthusiastic support of research led to many new inventions…industrial printers, Duplex reading scales, aluminum charts, more prices per pound, plastic housings, a vastly expanded line of industrial and special purpose scales, and several new companies including Plaskon.

Bennett was a true entrepreneur. Hugh and Geoffrey Bennett enthusiastically took over the Defiance operation and began to implement their plans. They developed a unique press to preform plastic materials. Geoff Bennett took over more of its development as Hugh's heart disease worsened.

Four years later, just as the company was ready to prosper, he suffered a fatal heart attack.

Like Henry Theobald before him, Hubert D. Bennett was just 56-years-old at his death. And like Henry Theobald, he was buried in Woodlawn Cemetery, not far from the founder's grave.

PART III

McIntosh

"Diverse weights are an abomination unto the Lord and a false balance is not good."
Proverbs, chapter XX, verse 23

CHAPTER 19

A New Leader

Harris McIntosh was born in Cayuga, New York in the Finger Lakes Region of the state. Cayuga is near the northern end of Cayuga Lake, miles north of Ithaca at the southern end. He owned a farm in the area with an apple orchard. The orchard raised—what else?—Macintosh apples.

Throughout his career at Toledo Scale, he would bring apples into his office at harvest time and pass one out to any of his factory worker friends who came in for one. They enjoyed getting a Macintosh from a McIntosh.

He graduated from Yale in 1927 and became a security analyst with a bank in New York City. McIntosh first came to Toledo in 1935 as assistant to the president of the Dura Corporation. Later he became president of Fostoria Screw Company.

In 1942, shortly after the war began, he went to Burbank, California as an executive for Lockheed Aircraft where he learned many of the production methods he brought to Toledo.

Harris McIntosh was 41-years-old when he was named president of Toledo Scale. He was proud of his Scottish ancestry. Even though the trend in business was for executives to use initials, he wouldn't permit it in his case…not even a middle initial. He was simply Harris McIntosh…no exceptions.

A month or so after the war in Europe had been won, an Army Lieutenant showed up at Toledo Scale asking to see the president. He explained that his visit was not official…that he had a message from Germany that he was asked to deliver. His home was in Northwest Ohio, he explained, and he just got home for a furlough before being sent to fight the Japanese.

McIntosh greeted him. The Lieutenant said, "I had an unusual experience a little while ago. My unit was fighting its way to Cologne when we came across a large cave. It appeared there were people in the cave. We didn't know if they were soldiers or civilians. As we prepared to dig them out, a very thin, older civilian ran out with his hands up yelling 'Me Toledo! Me Toledo!' He was grungy, with long hair, obviously having spent some time in the cave. At first, I couldn't understand what he was trying to tell me."

McIntosh asked, "What did you do? Did you find out what he meant?"

"Yes, he could speak English, though not too well. He said his name was Theodore Pruemm, and before the war he operated Toledo-Werk, Toledo Scale's German operation in Cologne. Well, I knew of Toledo Scale, of course…"

McIntosh interrupted. "Pruemm! I know the name from our files, but I never met him. I'm new here. But I understand that a man named Pruemm was our German Licensee before the war. What else did he tell you?"

"Well, he said that he and his family, along with several dozen other German civilians, had moved into the cave to escape the bombing. He told me that when the German army left the city, he was able to rescue some machine tools from Toledo-Werk and transfer them to the cave for safekeeping. This turned out to be true…there was a lot of equipment in the cave."

"Did he tell you why?" McIntosh asked.

"Yes, he said he hoped to rebuild Toledo-Werk and make Toledo Scales again once the fighting was over. He pleaded with me to somehow get word to you that he was alive and well, and wanted to resume his relationship with you. He was really glad to hear that my home was nearby."

"Well, I'm glad he survived the war," McIntosh said. "We'll try to get in touch with him through the War Department. But I really want to thank you, Lieutenant, for taking the trouble and the time from your furlough to come in and tell us about your experience. What can we do to thank you?"

"Nothing, really. I've heard about Toledo Scale my whole life. Being from the area, I always wanted to see the inside of this nice plant, and this gave me a perfect excuse to stop by."

McIntosh took him to meet Parmelee in the International Department where he repeated his story. He gave him a plant tour. They arranged to meet later for dinner with the Lieutenant's family in appreciation of his time and trouble.

McIntosh was new to his job. He hadn't paid much attention to International since the war with Japan was not yet over. Later he was able to get in touch with Preumm and arranged to resume Toledo's relationship with him.

After Japan was defeated in August, Toledo-Werk was rebuilt. By 1947 they were able to have a large display in Cologne's first Industrial Fair after the war. Over time, McIntosh and Pruemm— and their families—became good friends. Their friendship lasted several decades. It included visits to each other's homes in Perrysburg and Cologne.

Later, Toledo Scale acquired a majority interest in Toledo-Werk. By the early 1960s it became the largest Toledo Scale facility in the European Common Market.

Unlike his two predecessors, McIntosh appeared to be rather shy and introverted. Still, he made many friends over time among the factory workers and staff by walking through the plant and visiting with them one at a time. He soon let it be known to his executives that no employee with over 25 years of service could be fired without his approval…and he rarely gave it.

Red Miller had a long-time staff employee in his service operation that had a serious drinking problem. It regularly affected his work. Miller tried to fire him time and again. McIntosh always said, "Aw, Red, let's give him another chance." Yet he did not hesitate to replace executive level management people when he thought it was called for.

He invested heavily in new machine tools and introduced new production methods. Even the Toledo industrial line, with its more than 45,000 variations of basic types, lent itself to the new production methods McIntosh brought to the company.

The new line of food machines, which included gravity feed choppers, steak machines and meat saws, was scheduled for production in early 1946. Each product needed extensive tooling. The work force had to be expanded and trained. A problem with the weather surfaced immediately. The winter of 1946 was especially cold. The Ohio Fuel Gas Company couldn't keep up with the demand.

Toledo's plant, along with many others, had to shut down production until the weather moderated. McIntosh had an 18,000 gallon propane storage tank installed so the plant wouldn't be shut down again. This standby supply was used several times in the next few years.

In one of his first moves, McIntosh reorganized the engineering department under an Engineering Steering Committee, which he headed. He divided engineering activities into three parts; research engineering, development engineering and production engineering.

He spoke to the engineers in a group. "Let me define what we're going to expect from each of these three groups," he said. "You research engineers will create the kind of new ideas that will lead to new products. And ideas to improve existing products. That's your primary job."

He turned to the head of development. "Development engineering will make the new ideas practical. You will adapt them to fit our production facilities. Your engineers have to be familiar with our manufacturing techniques…able to design parts and finished products for efficient production."

"You production engineers pick up where development leaves off," he said to them. "You are the people who establish the procedures we need in the plant to build the new products."

Several long-time engineers frowned. They were used to doing all of these jobs from beginning to end. The younger men seemed to welcome the idea that they would have defined tasks. After some questions, the entire engineering staff agreed the structure should help get out new products faster.

Then McIntosh had a 10,000 square foot structure added to the northeast front of the plant to house the research and development engineering departments. Shortly after, a 45,000 square foot bay was added at the north side of the plant. A year later another bay was added to the north side, plus a one story addition to the east end of the bay for the service, technical school and sales training operations. The Toledo plant now had 443,500 square feet of space altogether, with seven bays.

Post-war plans anticipated a large increase in sales…especially for retail scales and food machines, which couldn't be produced during the war. The company set a goal of a million dollars in monthly sales…a volume that had never before been approached. Yet, in the first month in which it was in a position to put forth a real sales effort, Toledo Scale had orders for over two million dollars worth of weighing equipment and food machines…double the anticipated sales pace.

The sales force had been greatly depleted during the war. It was in the process of being rebuilt and retrained. Yet as this was going on, sales continued at over twice the anticipated rate. There was a huge pent-up demand. It was a real challenge for McIntosh and his new management team.

The world was returning to normal. Toledo Scale was the weighmaster again on the 10th Anniversary of the All-American Soap Box Derby as it got under way in 133 locations in the U.S. and Canada. Interest was especially high this year. The 1966 Derby winner accepted an offer from Hollywood director William Wellman and appeared in the movie *Magic Town* with popular star James Stewart.

The U.S. War Department announced they would use an extremely sophisticated calculator called ENIAC created by IBM. ENIAC (Electronic Numerical Integrator and Computer) used over 18,000 vacuum tubes and worked a 1,000 times faster than any calculator devised. IBM also planned to release its less ambitious calculator called the 603 Multiplier for commercial use.

And later in 1946, the Haloid Company in Rochester, NY announced that they had invested in a copying technology invented by Chester Carlson utilizing "xerography" (from the Greek for "dry writing.") He had invented the process years before, but had trouble finding a backer until Haloid picked it up. Neither the Army Signal Corps nor IMB were interested.

New cars were finally becoming available again. Many Toledo salesmen chose to buy increasingly popular station wagon versions since they could carry some smaller scales and spare parts.

Special Toledo industrial scales developed for the war effort became standard. A Toledo dynamometer scale with a capacity of 15,000 pounds was sold to the Bendix Corporation for their brake laboratory in South Bend, Indiana. One of the world's largest dynamometers for testing brakes was installed there. The Toledo dynamometer scale measured a developed brake torque of 302,500 inch-pounds.

The industrial market increased. In one month alone the field reported they sold scales to weigh casting cores, dry cleaning, drums of lacquer, potato chip packages, doughnut dough, rubber parts, lace curtains, dye, rubber bands, processed cheese, sandpaper, electrical parts, nuts and bolts, cotton laps, ice cream containers, beef carcasses, for peanut grading, for counting costume jewelry parts, and many more unique applications. New scales sold everywhere right after the war.

Toledo introduced "The World's Most Modern Power Meat Saw" in 1947. This was essentially the saw developed by the University of Michigan professor hired during his summer break just before the end of the war. It joined the post-war line of gravity feed choppers and steak machines developed in 1945 to expand the line of Toledo food machines and compete more directly with Hobart.

Frozen foods began to become popular after the war. Frozen food processors needed fast, accurate checkweighers in their packaging operations. Frozen food products normally had a high value and small errors multiplied quickly into large losses, which could be controlled by checkweighers.

In-motion checkweighers had not yet been perfected and many Toledo SpeedWeigh manual checkweighers were sold to the industry.

Seabrook Farms was one of the largest frozen food processors in the country. They bought many SpeedWeighs and installed them in packaging lines to checkweigh packages of their peaches, beans, and other frozen vegetables. Seabrook had to be sure their packages contained at least the weight printed on the package, but not contain too much beyond that weight which was pure giveaway.

Automobile and aircraft tires became stronger and longer lasting as nylon was used for the first time.

At the National Aircraft Show in Cleveland, The U.S. Rubber Company used Toledo bench scales to compare the weights of two sets of aircraft tires—one rayon and the other nylon. The lighter nylon tires cost a bit more but meant more payload dollars. A Toledo fan scale was used to illustrate the extremely light weight of U.S. cellular rubber, which had several uses in aircraft construction.

And Chuck Yeager became the first human being to travel faster than the speed of sound. At an undisclosed Army base in California, a rocket plane named Glamorous Glennis (named for his wife) quickly reached a speed of over 600 mph, breaking the sound barrier. A sonic boom was heard for the first time.

In December, Bell Laboratories announced that they had recently developed something that might make the vacuum tube obsolete: the transistor. Bell explained that a transistor is a solid state electronic component. It was faster, lighter and much smaller than a vacuum tube. It generated less heat and required less than one hundredth the power of an early style vacuum tube.

By the end of 1947, scale and food machine production had almost caught up with demand. The huge backlog caused by the war was almost over. McIntosh wanted to remind the sales force.

He spoke to executive vice president Walter Fink. "Walter, I know you're going to write a column in December's *Toledo System* magazine. Let's remind everybody that we're practically back to normal...no more easy orders. It's back-to-selling time."

Fink wrote, "During 1947, we were all conscious of the transition from a seller's market to a buyer's market. But Toledomen have always had the advantage when they could sell our products on merit and performance. Those days are back again. In the past year our competitors have stressed their biggest feature 'spot delivery'. No longer do they have this advantage since we are current on retail scales and choppers, and soon will be on steak machines and the power saw."

He continued, "Let's look beyond our business for a moment. The intense activity of the war years has obscured the very great growth that had taken place in the country. There are 9,000,000 more people here than in 1939. The urban population has increased. More industries are located in more cities. Today the regional differences in the type of equipment purchased are disappearing. We're closer to a national market today than at any time in the past. We're not going back to pre-war, but ahead to new selling opportunities."

He concluded with, "We recognize that industrial scale production is the area where the greatest improvement is yet to be accomplished. You will see steady improvement here, too."

Retail continued to lead in sales, however.

The company introduced an improved retail Duplex cylinder scale in 1948. Named the Guardian "70" Duplex because of its 70 prices per pound, the scale was housed in a Plaskon case and had a duo-pendulum mechanism. The scale was introduced to all sales managers at a meeting in Toledo. This meeting set the stage for a series of more than 30 meetings held within weeks throughout the country.

Service instruction meetings were held at the same time. All details of the announcement were carefully planned...sales literature, field consignment, advertising, and parts stocks and tools were all complete in time for the introduction.

The headline in the first ad called the scale the "World's Finest Food Store Profit Guardian." The scale was ready to go in every sense when placed in the hands of the field organization.

Retail customers were quick to welcome the Guardian "70" Duplex. It was the first new post-war retail scale available. With its improvements, it offered many new user benefits. Because of its Plaskon case the scale soon received the Modern Plastics award for "the meritorious application of plastics."

Export sales were recovering from the war. In 1948, export sales manager Frank Parmelee made his first post-war trip to Central America. In Central and South America, governments were a large user of Toledo scales.

Parmelee first traveled to Costa Rica where he visited the office of the Toledo distributor and sat in on their daily sales meeting. These meetings were attended by all employees. Next he visited the Fabrica Nacional de Licores, a government liquor plant in San Jose. His plant host explained, "In Costa Rica the government makes all the liquor. We use your monorail scale to control the batches."

He visited the custom-house in San Jose that had a Toledo floor scale. "We use it to determine duties," he was told. At the Banco National de Costa Rica he watched as packages of money were checked on a Toledo SpeedWeigh scale in a bank vault. He visited the most modern supermarket in Tegucigalpa, Nicaragua and saw it was full of Toledos. And he visited the custom-house in Manaugua, Nicaragua where a Toledo portable determined duty charges.

From the Caribbean to the Pacific he saw the familiar Sin Resortes—Peso Exacto—No Springs—Honest Weight. He was welcomed everywhere. Latin American customers were glad to see that new Toledo scales were being produced again.

And in November, a feisty Harry Truman surprised everyone but himself when he defeated Thomas E. Dewey and was elected to a full term as President of the United States. All of the pollsters predicted that Dewey would win easily…but they all were wrong.

The *Chicago Tribune* was so confident of the polls that they printed an early edition with the headline, "DEWEY DEFEATS TRUMAN." A famous photograph showed President Truman wearing a big smile as he holds up this issue of the paper.

CHAPTER 20

Golden Anniversary

The following year, Toledo Systems built a glass batching demonstrator for a visit from A.I.E.E. and kept it operating for many days after the visit to show it to other process industry people. A large control panel showed the sequence of operation with flashing lights.

It contained dial scale heads with electric eyes to shut off feeders at various weight hopper cutoff points. The system was fully automatic. It used interlocked relays, counters and timers to control the batch.

Many orders for glass batching systems resulted—and other processing systems as well—because Toledo was able to effectively demonstrate their expertise.

Television sets slowly began to sell in volume as the nation embraced this new mass medium, first displayed at the 1939 World's Fair. The Kimble Glass division of Owens-Illinois used Toledo fan scales to weigh face plate portions of TV screens to make sure they contained exactly the right quantity of glass.

WSPD-TV, Toledo's first television station, presented a feature on Jim Ueblehart's program on the new Guardian "70" Duplex shortly after they went on the air.

Toledo's long effort to encourage state legislators to enact weights and measures laws was winding down. The effort was started by Henry Theobald in 1903. Massachusetts was first in 1907. The campaign lasted almost 50 years.

After World War II, in the late 1940s, Oklahoma, Kentucky and Louisiana were among the last states in the union to pass weights and measures legislation.

In November 1948, Allen Chappius, the new Director of the Louisiana State Division of Weights and Measures, along with a dozen of his inspectors were guests at the Toledo plant. The trip to Toledo was part of their training program. They were given a formal welcome to Toledo by Mayor Mike DiSalle, who later became Governor of Ohio.

Louisiana's new director had completed a training course outlined by the National Bureau of Standards in Washington. He had also visited weights and measures officials in several states to prepare for his duties. At the Toledo plant the group was instructed on the principles of scale design, and the features and construction of various types of scales.

Chappius remarked, "This is excellent…it will supplement the classroom training that we've already conducted for our inspectors in Louisiana."

Now all states had passed weights and measures laws. Toledo people whispered to each other, "There's a ghost of a smile now on Theobald's portrait in the lobby."

McIntosh then made his first acquisition. He bought the Sterling Division of the Anstice Company in Rochester, New York. It became the Kitchen Machine Division of Toledo Scale. Instantly Toledo was into the commercial dishwasher business. The product line also included vegetable peelers, vegetable dicers, and a large line of other products sold to the hotel, restaurant and institution field.

Toledo acquired a modern plant in Rochester, New York, along with some adjacent vacant land. Toledo Kitchen Machine products were distributed through selected restaurant equipment dealers. Service was furnished by factory-trained servicemen through all regular Toledo Scale offices.

In 1950, the Buckeye Winery, just north of the main plant on Telegraph Road went out of business. During the war, Toledo Scale had leased this building for high security work on the Norden bombsight and other classified ordnance work.

Toledo Scale bought the building with six acres of land the next year. The plant was immediately renovated with the addition of 40,000 sq. ft. of space. It became Toledo's ordnance building, used for work on military contracts, which expanded when President Truman initiated the Korean "police action" in June 1950. These military contracts lasted throughout the Korean conflict.

After the Korean War, the main part of the ordnance building became the Toledo Scale Training Center. It was used for both sales and service training. A smaller part at the south end became the company print shop, mailing operation, and warehouse for all catalogs, literature, paper and office supplies.

Sales manager Lloyd Colenback had experienced a checkered career with the company. He had been Bennett's sales manager since early Depression days but left the company during the war. Then he returned to the company in the Canadian operation. He did well and was soon returned to Toledo as general sales manager.

It was rumored Colenback had a drinking problem. Norman Vincent Peale spent some time in the Toledo area very early in his career before he moved to New York and became a famous clergyman. Somehow, Peale had met and befriended Colenback. He counseled him about his drinking. The counseling seemed to work.

Even after Peale moved on to New York, Colenback would catch a train and visit him in New York whenever he felt his urge to drink was getting too strong to resist. With Peale's help he was able to stay on the wagon for longer and longer periods. But he would always start again. The demons that caused him to drink finally got the best of him. One morning Lloyd Colenback was found dead in his home. He had hanged himself with his belt.

Colenback had been an effective sales manager. He was widely respected for his knowledge of scales and was mourned by those who knew him best.

Colenback's suicide created a hole that had to be quickly filled. In June, McIntosh brought Ed Jackson in from the field as general sales manager. Jackson had been the Toledo Scale sales manager in New York City before coming to the home office. In March 1951, he was promoted to sales vice president.

By 1951, it had become common for Chicago retail sales manager Jack Dee to personally bring his orders into the home office at the end of every month. Chicago's "Mr. Toledo" usually brought orders every month that totaled well over $100,000. He expected to be always greeted by Ed Jackson—and was. In Jackson's absence, executive vice president Walter Fink or Harris McIntosh greeted him.

Dee expected it. He saw it as his due. He played the role of a VIP visitor with style and panache.

Many believed that Dee used his briefcase full of orders to negotiate special sales promotions or better deals for favorite customers. When he didn't get the deals he wanted he kept some orders back…holding some in his briefcase.

He knew which of his customers would wait and which ones wouldn't. So he would simply hold selected orders for the next month and try again. This worked for him especially well when the company was hungry for orders to close out the month.

Dee was already a legend. He sold hard and negotiated hard all of his career.

In June, Toledo's Brazilian distributors, Eric Haegler and his son Ricardo Haegler visited the plant. Their firm, S.A. Haegler de Maquinas e Representacoes, had represented Toledo since 1940. The family would prove to play a significant role in the future of the Toledo Scale name.

Also in 1951, Toledo Scale plant foreman Jack Rittenhouse celebrated his Golden Anniversary with the company. He had been with Toledo Scale since its inception in 1901.

Actually he started his scale career with the DeVilbiss Scale Company in 1899 as a factory apprentice when he was only 14-years-old. When Theobald bought the DeVilbiss scale company and founded Toledo Scale, he came with it…so he already had worked 52 years for essentially the same company.

On July 10, 1951 Toledo reached its actual Golden Anniversary date. Both Toledo newspapers printed half page stories about the company's 50th birthday. The papers pointed out that there were only five companies in Toledo with more than 100 employees that could claim a 50-year history.

The company printed and widely distributed an oversize 36-page brochure that covered 50 years of progress. Toledo Scale observed their 50th anniversary with special events throughout the year.

An elaborate public Open House was held at the plant to celebrate. The Open House Committee consisted of 473 people that included employees and family members, and community leaders. Over 5,000 guests visited and took a guided plant tour. As many as 42 displays were scattered throughout the plant to show Toledo products and the way they were made.

Jack Rittenhouse received special recognition as the only employee who had been with the company since its beginning.

Over a ton of beef was served to the crowd, along with a ton-and-a-half of potato salad and baked beans, 250 gallons each of coffee and cider, and 3000 doughnuts. A Toledo Printweigh scale weighed and recorded over 50 tons of Toledo people and their guests. Door prizes were awarded to 50 lucky winners. The 50th Anniversary Open House was an overwhelming success in every way.

The next year, Olympic athlete Bob Mathias competed a second time in the 1952 Olympics. He had won the Decathlon at the 1948 Olympic Games. As the winner of the Olympic Decathlon he was called the "world's greatest athlete".

Early in the year, he had his shot-put and other equipment used in the ten Decathlon events officially weighed and certified on a Toledo SpeedWeigh by the Sealer of Weights and Measures in his home town of Tulare, California. He practiced with precise equipment.

At the U.S. Olympic trials, Mathias piled up 7825 points to break all previous records. This gave him the honor of leading the U.S. Decathlon team in the Olympic Games for the second time. He went on to win his second gold medal in the event at the 1952

Olympics in Helsinki, Finland. His total of 7887 points in the Decathlon set a new world record.

Toledo Scale lost another company pioneer with the death of Frank Ditzler. Theobald had recruited him from NCR in 1908 where he had been their national sales manager. He became Toledo's first national sales manager. Seeing opportunity in the far West, he chose to move to San Francisco in 1910 to organize West coast sales operations. He was a company director when he retired in 1944.

By the time of his retirement, Frank Ditzler's Western Zone had been the top selling zone nine times, setting a record still unmatched in 1952.

His son Hugh replaced him as Western Zone Manager and had a long successful career with Toledo Scale. Hugh Ditzler was one of many successful second-generation company employees. It seemed to pay to grow up in the business.

In 1952, President Truman chose not to run for re-election. During the 1952 Presidential campaign, Eisenhower declared he would "go to Korea" which helped him get elected president. He handily beat Democrat Adlai Stevenson.

Eisenhower negotiated a truce in Korea that ended the conflict in 1953 after the United States had suffered almost 140,000 casualties. Toledo's ordnance contracts ran out soon after the truce was signed. Eisenhower's two terms ushered in an era of quiet peace and prosperity in the nation.

A popular new exhibit entitled "Your Weight on Other Worlds" opened at the Hayden Planetarium in New York City. It was composed of five Toledo model 31-1800 portable scales with special dials calibrated to show a person's weight on the Moon, Mars, Venus, Jupiter and the Sun.

When a 200 pounder stood on the moon scale it showed his weight as a mere 32 pounds. On Mars a puny 76 pounds. Closer to normal on Venus at 170 pounds. On the Jupiter scale it showed his weight as a ponderous 528 pounds, and on the sun an unbearable 5,578 pounds.

Popular Science magazine printed a story about the display in an article called "The Line Forms Here For A Trip To The Moon". The article reported that the Hayden Planetarium already had over 24,000 people signed up for the first trip. Of course, they didn't offer any definite time schedule for the flight.

It's doubtful that any of these 24,000 people could have predicted how quickly it would come true. It took only another 17 years for American astronauts Neil Armstrong and Buzz Aldrin to walk on the surface of the moon.

The "31" in the model 31-1800 scales displayed in the Hayden Planetarium meant that the series was introduced in 1931. It took another 21 years before the industrial scale line was finally improved.

Toledo engineer Warren Hem had left the company to develop a new line of automatic indication dial scales for the Howe Scale Company in Rutland, Vermont. McIntosh enticed him back. Hem then developed an entirely new line of industrial dial scales including portable, bench, truck and person weigher models. It contained many technical improvements, including a vastly improved linear cam that enhanced accuracy over the full scale.

Informally called the "gray line," the 2000 series was introduced in 1953. It remained essentially unchanged until mechanical scales began to be replaced by electronic scales in the mid 1970's.

About the time the new industrial scale line was launched, Toledo's engineering department claimed that the science of metallurgy had made great strides. They reported that spring scales could now be manufactured that solved the age-old inaccuracy problem. The use of springs would reduce manufacturing costs and make the scales more profitable. It was clear that a spring counterforce was coming.

While no spring scales were under development at the time, their potential prompted Toledo to drop "No Springs" from the slogan on all scale products, literature and ads. The slogan became simply "Honest Weight" from that time on.

About the same time, the company hired Geoffrey T. Gray as a senior design engineer. Gray was born and raised in England, where he was educated as a mechanical engineer.

He began his career during World War II with one of Britain's largest aircraft manufacturers. After the war he became chief designer for a firm in Cardiff, Wales, that manufactured chemical process machinery. This company had a contract with B. F. Goodrich in Akron who was manufacturing and selling equipment made to the designs of the British company.

The British company sent Gray to Akron under a six-month contract to work with B. F. Goodrich on the process machinery. While in the rubber center of America, he became acquainted with an industrial design firm that had a contract with Toledo Scale. This design firm recommended him to Toledo.

When it was time to go home to England, he observed, "Here is a country where work might be easier. And besides, these Yankees seemed to be human after all." He was hired to work on a new generation of industrial printers.

The original Printweigh was designed in 1931 and hadn't been redesigned since. Gray helped design the Printweigh 400, introduced a few years later. It was a vast improvement and an immediate success.

It marked the beginning of a long, successful career with the company. Later he designed several custom-built systems, worked as Regional Sales Engineer, as a staff instructor for custom products in the sales training department, as the company's advertising manager, training manager, and general sales manager for Toledo Scale Company of Canada, Ltd.

In 1954 Donivan Hall was hired by engineering vice president Bob Bradley to develop load cells. Hall had earned a BS degree in Engineering-Physics and a Masters in Electrical Engineering from Ohio State University. Load cell development started slowly.

Hall said, "We had trouble coming up with anything for a while until a patent on strain gauges owned by a competitor ran out. Then we made some progress improving on this strain gauge technology."

Working with transducer expert Aniese Seed and others, Hall's engineering team developed a line of 50 lb to 50,000 lb load cells.

The larger cells were used in Toledo's vehicle scales. It wasn't long before Hall had invented several scale improvements, which were patented listing his name as the inventor, with the patents assigned to Toledo Scale.

CHAPTER 21

Electronic Wings

Toledo Scale executive vice president and company director Walter Fink retired in April 1954. He had been hired as an accountant by Henry Theobald in 1918 after Toledo lost a patent suit and faced the payment of a large judgment. He worked closely with him until Theobald's death.

Because he needed detailed financial information when he became president, Hugh Bennett quickly came to depend on Fink as well. He worked with him for about 20 years…Bennett's entire career with Toledo Scale.

Fink handled many special projects for him including all those for the new Telegraph Road plant. And when McIntosh took over leadership of the company, Fink became his good right hand.

Fink had worked intimately with all three company presidents. McIntosh urged him to continue to serve in a consulting capacity and Fink agreed.

Meanwhile McIntosh retained the management consulting firm McKensie & Company to do a study on Toledo's procedures and people. Ed Jackson was the prime force urging McIntosh to retain the firm. A contract was signed. McKensie staff people spent several months interviewing people and examining everything. Then they presented a list of recommendations.

Recommendation number one…replace Ed Jackson. McKensie was also an executive recruiting firm and they had a client they recommended as an ideal replacement for Jackson. The company agreed and McKensie client George McKenna was appointed vice president, sales.

In his turn, Jackson became a McKensie client. Jackson moved to Los Angeles after being placed by McKensie as general sales manager of Axelson Manufacturing, a division of U.S. Industries.

Not long after Fink retired, labor relations took a turn for the worse. Workers were represented by Local 773 of UAW-CIO. About 700 union members went on strike and walked off the job…the third strike in the company's history. The union demanded a large hourly wage increase and other changes in the contract. The 90 members of MESA employed at the plant honored UAW picket lines.

Toledo was a strong labor town, largely dependent on supplying parts to the automobile industry. Economically the city was little more than a suburb of Detroit. It was often observed that when Detroit caught a cold, Toledo got pneumonia.

The United Auto Workers had organized the labor force in many local plants, which produced products that had nothing to do with autos…like scales. The union wanted scale worker hourly rates to more closely approach parity with auto worker rates.

Toledo Scale competitors were largely located in small-town America where the prevailing wage rates were much lower, far removed from high labor rate areas. The company took the position that hourly rates should be based on the ability to compete in their own industry…not the auto industry.

Toledo Scale wage rates were already 10 to 40 cents higher than rates paid by competing firms. The company was willing to continue paying the highest rates in the scale industry…but claimed they couldn't remain competitive at significantly higher auto worker rates. So the strike continued.

Two weeks into the strike the UAW established a strike kitchen for the workers. Strikers were given $15 worth of groceries per week, plus $3 for each child. The union arranged for loans to cover the cost of other necessities.

The Labor-Management-Citizens Committee and a federal mediator became involved. The LMC was pioneered by Toledo mayor

Mike DiSalle to help settle labor disputes in the city. It had a record of success, but their efforts to mediate this strike proved futile.

Two months later a "back to work" faction called a meeting of workers. Strike leaders heard about it and invaded the meeting and took over the session completely, converting it into a strike rally. The anti-strike faction failed and the strike continued.

After nine weeks, an agreement was finally hammered out at a top level meeting attended by Dick Gosser, international vice president of the UAW-CIO, company president Harris McIntosh, and other labor and industrial leaders. The agreement provided wage increases of five to ten cents an hour.

Some believed the experience marked the beginning of a unique relationship between Dick Gosser and Harris McIntosh. Gosser was a labor leader of the old school, uneducated, profane and tough. McIntosh was an Ivy Leaguer, soft-spoken, urbane and introspective. Yet each came to display much respect for the other. They treated each other as equals.

As time passed and more labor disputes took place, many within the company believed the disputes were finally settled in a private meeting between the two.

Each would let their negotiating team work with the opposite team. If the teams reached an agreement Gosser and McIntosh didn't get involved. But if the negotiators reached an impasse, one would call the other, set up a lunch and settle it together. It worked for years. Both sides benefited.

After the strike everybody went back to work. Now they had a backlog to fill.

Orders included scales to checkweigh waste fibers used in oil filters, to regulate the size of crushed rock nuggets for the Indiana Turnpike, to accurately weigh the clothes used in testing clothes dryers and washing machines, to check the growth of a litter of pigs on an experimental farm, to provide the exact printed weight of chlorine sold directly to customers via a pipeline, to determine the uniformity of loaves of bread, to check lots of golf tees, to check the resiliency standards of sponge rubber products...and many more unusual uses for scales that no one had ever anticipated.

After the strike was settled, the company reacted to the competition from a new manual prepackaging scale system Hobart introduced. Prepackaging meat products at the store level—and produce in some chains—was beginning to catch on across the nation. Toledo had not anticipated the trend.

The Hobart 2000 prepackaging system could weigh a package and automatically print a label for it that showed the weight, price per pound and total value of the wrapped package. An operator had only to enter the price per pound on a keyboard, put the package on the scale, and a label would be printed seconds later. The technology used relays to do the calculation, which was then sent to an attached printer Hobart purchased from NCR.

Toledo had nothing to compete with the new Hobart. Engineers were given a rush project. They started with a standard cylinder scale. A printer was designed in-house to print a label. The result was named the Valueprint System.

The Valueprint was launched in January 1955 at a general meeting in Toledo of key field and home office people, followed by field meetings around the country later in the month. Jack Dee in Chicago jumped on the Valueprint, selling many in the first few months. Hobart had been hurting his sales in Chicago even though he had a virtual stranglehold on the market.

Dee quickly fought back with the Valueprint. He sold many to Jewel Tea Company, National Tea Company, and other large Chicago-area chains. However, service problems soon resulted, especially with the label printer. Toledo's expertise was in scales...not label printers.

Ed Quertinmont, then assistant national service manager, said, "If I got gray hair it was because of the Valueprint. I musta spent half my life in Chicago along with a crew of seven or eight servicemen on Valueprints trying to keep 'em working."

The Valueprint problems made it clear that it was going to be a stop-gap product. Toledo assigned a project to Battelle in Columbus to design a better automatic prepackaging scale. The project would take four years to complete. Service problems with the Valueprint continued. Hobart took a commanding sales lead with their prepackaging scale.

Walt Disney opened his dream "Never-Never Land" he called Disneyland in Anaheim, California in 1955. The super amusement park cost some $17 million to complete. Disney's real-life dream world was expected to attract five million visitors a year.

The following year, the developer of IBM, Thomas J. Watson, Sr. died at the age of 82. An IBM Division, the Dayton Scale Company, competed with Toledo Scale in the early years. Watson sold Dayton Scale to Hobart in 1934. Although IBM was not the first to move into computers after World War II, its success in marketing them quickly outdistanced all competitors.

Toledo Scale's research engineering department was expanded to include electronics research activities. Director of engineering Bob Bradley named Bob Bell manager of the expanded department. Engineers Larry Williams, Fred Carroll and Roger Williams were added to the staff. Toledo didn't want to fall behind a competitor again.

In spite of more than a half-century culture built on abhorring the very idea of using springs in scales, improved metallurgy and competitive pressures finally caused Toledo to accept the idea. In the 1950s the company introduced their first low-cost retail box-spring scale, the Model 1361. Even though the counterforce in the 1361 was indeed a spring, the ghost of Henry Theobald prohibited anyone in the company from calling it that.

Ed Quertinmont said, "We couldn't refer to it as a spring. We were supposed to call it a coil. Specifically, an 'isoelastic coil'. Somehow, that took the sting out of it."

Since "No Springs" had not been part of the slogan for several years, there was little negative customer reaction. The 1361 did indeed deliver Honest Weight. It easily passed all weights and measures standards in every jurisdiction.

Weights and measures officials around the country were the only group that gave it special attention. They knew a spring when they saw one no matter what it was called. They used extra care in checking it out for approval. After it was approved, they enjoyed kidding Toledo people about it.

About the same time several new distributors were appointed. Bob Barker was named district distributor in Flint, Michigan. His distributorship covered Flint, Lansing, Saginaw and Alpena.

Bert Dickey was named divisional distributor in Tampa, Florida. First employed in the mid 1930s, Dickey was one of the original Aero-Car drivers. He had worked in several company offices and as industrial sales manager before becoming a distributor.

Bert Dickey retired about 20 years later and sold his interests. The successors kept the name. Dickey Scales, Inc. still operates throughout Florida and parts of Georgia. It's one of the company's largest, most successful distributorships.

David Martin was appointed district distributor for the Grand Rapids, Michigan area. Martin had been with the company since 1941. D. C. Martin & Son Co. remains the Grand Rapids distributor today under the leadership of David Martin's son, Coby. Coby Martin's son works with him, so the distributorship is now in its third generation.

A breakthrough new product came out of research. A new digital-scanning electronic unit transmitted weights to remotely located data handling devices for the first time. Weights could now go anywhere and be reproduced accurately in almost any form.

General sales manager Don Boudinot said, "The achievement has the same significance in the field of weighing as breaking the sound barrier had in aviation." The digital-scanning electronic unit was developed in time for display at the Chemical show in December. It was the hit of the show.

The basic element was a light source that scanned lines exposed on a special chart. The output was a series of electrical pulses that pass through an electronic counter and translator to a remote recording or indicating device.

Called "Electronic Wings", the unit could be used with any Toledo industrial dial scale. It soon became popular to totalize meat and other items over a monorail scale, to remotely record batch ingredients and supervise remote scales from a central location.

It was Toledo Scale's first digital electronic product.

Retail announced several new food machines that were developed through the increased research efforts. A high-speed saw and two new high-speed steak machines were introduced that met the demand for faster, cleaner and more profitable meat processing. Again, they were launched at a general meeting in Toledo of key field and home office people, followed by field meetings around the country.

Early the next year some fresh Toledo Scale publicity came from the Hayden Planetarium in New York City. The great Ahnighito Meteorite, discovered in Greenland by Admiral Robert Peary, had been displayed there since the Planetarium opened in 1935. It was huge. It had never been weighed.

A specially designed Toledo Scale was installed to finally weigh it. The meteorite was lifted in heavy rigging equipment while the scale was installed beneath it. When the installation was complete a ceremony was held for the weigh-in.

Admiral Peary's daughter, Mrs. Marie Ahnighito Peary Stafford, recounted the history of the meteorite from first-hand knowledge. She had been born in northern Greenland and as a small child had christened the meteorite as it was hauled aboard ship to be brought to the United States.

When the meteorite was lowered to the scale platform it was found to weigh 68,085 pounds.

Toledo designed a special dial for the scale. Since a constant weight of over 34 tons was on the platform it was possible to provide ten pound graduations in spite of the very great load. Visitors could then see their own weight added to that of the meteorite with a large sweep of indicator travel. It was a popular display for years.

Back in Toledo, Harris McIntosh was toastmaster at a community welcoming dinner for a group of executives from the Chevrolet Division of General Motors. For years, Chevrolet had operated a small plant on Central Avenue near Willys Overland. The Central

Avenue plant was old and obsolete. Chevrolet purchased property on Alexis Road with a large, modern manufacturing building in place. Known as the "Propeller Plant," it had been built during World War II and was now surplus.

Chevy planned to manufacture automatic transmissions for their cars in their new Toledo plant. Chevrolet's general manager Thomas Keating was presented a key to the city by Mayor Ollie Czelusta. McIntosh introduced him to the audience of 650 business and industry leaders who welcomed him. It was a prime addition to the community. More than 2,000 jobs were planned.

The plant still operates as the Powertrain Division of General Motors.

McIntosh was a community leader. He was proud of the appearance of the Toledo Scale plant. He insisted the large grounds be kept in good condition, and was greatly pleased when the American Association of Nurserymen presented the company a plaque in recognition of its "noteworthy contribution to the beautification of American industry".

The letter, which accompanied the plaque, read in part, "You are one of the very few companies considered by the judges to be worthy of this top national award. It should be gratifying to your whole organization to learn that you have emerged first in this competition."

After this, the maintenance department saw to it that the grounds were kept in pristine condition.

The popularity of frozen foods led to many large freezers being sold to homes all over America. Many Americans were buying sides of beef and other meat products for their freezer. Meat merchandisers began to specialize in processing meats for home freezers. Their beef and pork products were perceived to be of superior quality.

Toledo's line of high-speed power saws, steak machines, choppers for ground meat specialties, and other food processing equipment was ideal for this market. Often a separate retail meat department for over-the-counter sales of fresh meats was part of the operation. Duplex scales were sold for these.

Home freezers appeared to have had an impact on the amount of meat Americans consumed. Meat consumption was 160.5 pounds per person in the U.S. this year, up by 25 pounds in just three years. Federally inspected meat production totaled 20.1 billion pounds...all of it weighed at some point.

Foodstuffs were becoming a better buy every year, taking a smaller percentage of income. A major reason was that production efficiency in the food industry had increased regularly since the war, often helped by special scales.

An example was the six Toledo electronic artery pumping scales sold to Wilson Meat Packing Company in Cedar Rapids, Iowa. These special scales automatically pumped the right amount of pickle brine solution into fresh hams based upon their individual weights.

Previously each ham was handled manually. The operator had to consult a chart and watch the scale until the right amount of brine was added. Now, one operator handled the work four used to do. The electronic artery pumping scales also eliminated the human error inherent in the manual process.

And, at a large bakery in Michigan City, Indiana, a new Toledo batching system permitted the bakery to buy sugar in bulk. The sugar was received in hopper type railroad cars and unloaded into an underground hopper. From there it was routed to an upper floor and into Toledo weigh hoppers equipped with cut-offs set at formula weights. This eliminated the former method of buying in 100 pound bags. Sugar was much less costly in bulk. Labor costs to empty the bags were eliminated.

Supermarkets began to weigh in meat and produce at the back door to eliminate an increasing problem of short weights. Supermarkets would have hanging beef quarters, boxed primal cuts, produce and other products delivered. They would then cut and package these products for their retail cases. Weight tickets from vendors often showed weights higher than were actually delivered.

A Big Chief Supermarket in Omaha, Nebraska, solved the short weight problem with a typical Toledo installation. In their back room, they had a 2181 Toledo bench scale permanently mounted on a stand. In combination with an overhead track scale reading to the same dial, it became a dual weighing system.

Beef quarters and other heavy meat items were weighed in on the track system while smaller cuts, boned meats, and produce were checkweighed on the bench scale platform. Vendors seemed to turn honest overnight.

Honest Weight was still a factor in commerce. Toledo had appointed an executive to work with all the various weights and measures jurisdictions to smooth the path towards approvals for their scales. In recent years Stanley Q. Bennett had held this job. In July 1956 he retired.

Red Miller was then appointed Manager of Weights and Measures. He became widely known in every state and at the National Bureau of Standards, and was a popular visitor everywhere he traveled.

Red Miller also continued his duties in charge of the service training school and service engineers. Over the years, hundreds of servicemen were trained under his leadership.

Automatic prepackaging scales were becoming more popular. Higher volume supermarkets demanded even more automation. A wrapping machine was needed, and an automatic labeler. Toledo had no project under development for a wrapping machine. And they needed one fast.

The Triangle Package Machinery Company in Chicago was a successful manufacturer of filling equipment based on predetermined weights. As such, they were known to Toledo's retail marketing people, who talked to them about wrapping machines. Triangle designed and built a prototype. It looked good. Toledo made a deal with Triangle to become their exclusive distributor for the new wrapping machine.

Called the Toledo-Triangle Cross-Wrap, the machine was manufactured by Triangle and sold exclusively by Toledo Scale. It offered time-saving advantages in wrapping meat and produce for prepackaging displays. It worked with a wide range of package sizes through a single control lever.

The machine adapted to corner or in-line installations to meet layout needs of food store backrooms. The Cross-Wrap worked equally well for flat-board or tray packaging and used the same sizes of film as for hand wrapping. These wrapping machines produced by Triangle solved Toledo's immediate problem, and the arrangement lasted for years.

A new prepackaging scale was introduced for manual prepackaging of meats and produce. The Model 1070 Speed-Pak was, in fact, a spring scale (er..., "coil scale"). It had a totally different appearance and featured a wide-angle illuminated projection screen for the first time. The spring counterforce produced faster indication, and the projection screen eliminated parallax. It was a hit.

Other new Toledo machines appeared on many product fronts. In addition to the Toledo-Triangle Cross-Wrap and the Speed-Pak, the Metrogram package classifier, a new bulk weigher, the Remocom remote batching control, a device for accurately recording weights-in-motion, and a new rackless conveyor dishwasher and line of vertical mixers from Toledo Kitchen Machines were introduced.

The year saw either entirely new or improved Toledo models in retail, standard and custom industrial, food machines, kitchen machines, in fact for every product group.

Not all were successful. The industrial marketing people had an idea to improve the sales of the 2830 Person Weigher. It was adapted to become a "talking" scale. When someone stepped on the platform, a soft voice spoke an eight-second advertising message.

A magnetic tape unit had been installed inside that transmitted 12 different short messages each time someone stepped on the platform, one after the other. The message played through speakers installed at the top front of the cabinet.

Marketing wrote, "The talking scale has unlimited possibilities as an advertising medium. It is designed to be used in practically all places where Person Weighers are now located—department stores, drug stores, supermarkets, restaurants, medical clinics, public buildings, schools, athletic clubs, laundries, car washes—to name a few."

BOB TERRY

Red Miller, Toledo Weights and Measures manager, prepared a tape and tried it out at the Ohio Sealers Association annual convention in Columbus. For the sealers and their wives, Red prepared a tape with 12 different messages about the importance of proper weight to good health. While those attending the convention enjoyed the novelty of the idea, the talking scale did not sell. It was soon dropped.

In October 1957, Americans were stunned when the Soviet Union successfully launched Sputnik. It was the world's first manmade satellite placed into orbit around the earth. U.S. officials were astonished not only by the Soviet first but also by the size of Sputnik. It weighed 184 lb, eight times heavier than the satellite the U.S. hoped to launch next year. It marked the beginning of the space race.

Harris McIntosh had already expanded the company with several acquisitions and wanted to continue that growth. "Early this year we decided to further diversify our activities," McIntosh said. "We cast around for the most likely marriage prospect. It was obvious to us that such an acquisition should not be in a field that required different technologies and skills—such as the chemical field—but one with much the same activities."

In September 1957, McIntosh announced a merger with the Haughton Elevator Company of Toledo. Many thought it was brought about by the "old boy" network in Toledo since Haughton was another local company, even older than Toledo Scale.

Haughton Elevator was incorporated in 1897 as the successor to a machine shop established shortly after the Civil War. At the time of the merger Haughton manufactured, sold and serviced passenger, freight and residential elevators. Haughton technology produced geared, gearless, hydraulic and screw lift elevators.

Their range of technology served every elevator application including high-speed units for the largest high rise buildings. It was among the first to develop new "operatorless" elevators, then in demand for all new buildings. They were the third largest elevator manufacturer in the U.S.

The merger was viewed in financial circles as one of the most significant actions ever taken in the Toledo business community. Still, the merger posed the question of what relationship a scale had to an elevator. In announcing the merger McIntosh said, "Although scales and elevators are vastly different products, they are very closely related in many respects. Haughton's elevators are electro-mechanical devices and so are many Toledo Scale products. Both companies are in the metal working field. Both make end products. And service is a very important segment of both firms' business."

McIntosh explained that unlike most products, the demand for service is made constant by government regulations for both scales and elevators.

"If a scale becomes inaccurate, it is taken out of service by officials until it's repaired," he explained. "And when periodic government inspections find an elevator that doesn't pass inspection and might be unsafe, it's taken out of service until it's fixed."

The merger was approved in November. The emerging company became Toledo Scale Corporation. Both Toledo Scale and Haughton Elevator continued as operating divisions of Toledo Scale Corporation. Combined annual sales were estimated to be in excess of $40,000,000 for 1957.

Toledo Scale had always been a closed corporation, and never made public its sales or earnings figures. It was said there were only about 100 Toledo Scale shareholders, with most of the stock being concentrated in a few blocks. The merger was effected by an exchange of stock and a new stock was created for Toledo Scale Corporation and offered to the public.

After more than half a century, Toledo Scale became a public company for the first time. Reports showed that 50,000 to 70,000 shares of the new stock were offered "over the counter."

Soon after the new corporation was established, McIntosh published the company's objectives. It was one of the first companies in the nation to publish mission objectives. These objectives read as well today as when they were first published more than 40 years ago:

Objectives

OF TOLEDO SCALE CORPORATION

The basic objectives of this Company are to provide useful products and services to society. In carrying out these objectives we recognize a variety of responsibilities:

1. To Our Customers
To provide them with quality products of increasing and continuing utility at the lowest practical cost, and to make available technical assistance and service for the maintenance of these products.

2. To Our Employees
To provide them with the opportunity for steady work at fair compensation and under good working conditions with opportunity and encouragement to advance themselves.

3. To Our Shareholders
To earn a proper return on their investment commensurate with the risk involved, at the same time protecting the intrinsic value of their investment.

4. To Our Vendors
To give them the opportunity, without bias or prejudice but with understanding and consideration, to supply us, at a reasonable profit to themselves, with the materials and service required to operate our business.

5. To Our Nation and the Communities In Which We Operate
To recognize and embrace our duties and responsibilities as an industrial citizen working for the best interests of our country during times of both peace and war. To share the burdens and

responsibilities of our community life by actively participating in local activities and supporting worthy causes as a corporation, and encouraging our employees to do likewise.

Fortunately, the pursuit of these objectives and the fulfillment of our responsibilities involve fewer differences than at first might be imagined. The common interests of the various groups far exceed the separate or individual ones. One of the prime responsibilities of the Management is to reconcile and balance those diverse interests if and when they occur.

In our efforts to continuously improve our products we must be mindful of the practical economics of our industry, and while continuing to advance our knowledge, skill, and abilities, temper their application to the actual needs and requirements of the customers with emphasis on the utility of the product rather than its theoretical technical superiority.

To accomplish all this, the Company must at all times maintain its fundamental strength measured in terms of people, technical skills, finances, plant and equipment, and above all, its reputation.

Harris McIntosh
PRESIDENT
TOLEDO SCALE CORPORATION

CHAPTER 22

Haughton Elevator

The merger with Haughton prompted the company to name a controller for each division. As a result, Greg Rothe moved up in the finance department to be named controller of the Toledo Scale Division, reporting to Frank Billett, who was promoted to corporate vice president of finance. Billett had been Toledo Scale's controller prior to the merger.

Engineer Don Hall was assigned to work with the Haughton Elevator Division. Haughton had a license agreement with Otis Elevator. The agreement was running out and it became clear that Otis didn't want to renew it. Hall needed to quickly improve on the Otis patents with new technology.

He succeeded in doing this within a few years, often working back and forth between the two divisions of Toledo Scale Corporation. Toledo's culture of invention continued.

In 1969 alone, he registered three elevator patents; one for a plural car elevator system that developed hall car assignments between individual cars and calls for service, another for an elevator motor speed control, and the third for demand memory. By 1973 when he returned exclusively to scale engineering, he had a total of 13 elevator patents issued with Donivan L. Hall listed as the inventor.

Toledo coil scales had a few advantages over traditional pendulum scales, which increased the demand for them. A new Toledo Net Weight Loading System was sold to the Reading Company and installed in their loading facility at the Port Richmond Terminal. It included a scale head connected to the customer's existing levers, a direct digital selector with output to an adding machine and a data input station to identify each railcar.

The dial mechanism consisted of the new Toledo Compensating Coil Balancing Mechanism (yes, a spring) built so the indicator traveled clockwise with loss of weight. The spring mechanism was specified for this installation because it was faster and had greater immunity to damage caused by shock and movement.

S. E. Haines, Port Engineer, said, "Reading needed to speed up unloading ore ships into railroad cars so the ship owners could keep the boats on the move and increase their percentage of carrying time. After the new system was installed, a time study showed the Toledo method improved overall unloading time by 30% over the previous mechanical method." He added, "The Reading buyer told me they had insisted on a Toledo Scale because if anyone could help them Toledo could."

The better-known double pendulum counterforce was still best for the majority of applications. The Colorado Milling & Elevator Company of Denver specified it for their new Toledo automatic bulk weigher, which they used to load flour into railcars accurately. Before the new system was installed, the company was forced to use railroad track scales to determine a legal weight of the flour in the car.

A company spokesman said, "The new Toledo system has saved as much as two days of shipping time between Denver and Albuquerque alone. We don't have to lay over en route anymore to weigh the product on a railroad track scale," he reported. "And the Toledo provides more consistent accuracy since the unit is enclosed and not subject to the elements that normally affect railroad scales."

It was a year in which bulk flour was much in the news. One of Chicago's largest cookie baking firms, the Schulze & Burch Biscuit Company, heaped praise—and flour—on their new Toledo hopper scale. A company official said, "It speeded up our dough-to-trough production operation. What's more, it increased our flexibility on the types of flour we could handle. And it furnished the consistent accuracy we've come to expect from a Toledo."

As testimony to its brand power, the Toledo name was showing up everywhere.

In 1958, a popular Folger cartoon titled "The Girls" appeared in the *Detroit Free Press* and later on the cover of the *Saturday Evening Post*. It showed a stout matron standing on the platform of a Toledo Scale glaring at the dial. The caption read, "And that goes for everybody in Toledo!"

It was a good year for *Saturday Evening Post* covers. Later that year a Norman Rockwell cover painting showed famous jockey Eddie Arcaro weighing in on a Toledo Scale with a race track handicapper peering over his shoulder to check his weight. Once again, it helped keep the Toledo name the best-known scale brand.

The Lionel Corporation was prompted to respond. Lionel produced the famous miniature trains that Santa placed by the thousands under Christmas trees every December 25. Their production manager called because he had lost track of who his local sales representative was due to a recent change in the territory. While he was on the phone he said, "We really appreciate the good service your scales and your service people give us."

It was discovered that Lionel had used Toledo counting and weighing scales for years to control the production of more than 10,000 different components used in manufacturing their train sets. Lionel produced them in varying quantities, some in the millions every year. The production manager said, "How else could we keep track of so many items without your scales? In fact, they're a vital part of our accounting system."

A new weight printer was introduced with much fanfare in 1958. It was designed and developed by engineers Larry Williams and British expatriate Geoff Gray who had been hired for the task several years previously. It replaced the original Printweigh, designed in 1931, which had limited capabilities.

Called the Printweigh "400" the new printer with its mechanical binary disc was a vast improvement. It would print anywhere on an 8-1/2" x 11" form, or on any special weight ticket, or even on a continuous strip. It would print full figures even when unit weights were used by the scale.

It offered up to 12 banks of selective numbering or up to 10 weight symbol keys for positive product ID. Consecutive numbering was offered so no weighment was unaccounted for, and it would print the date and time automatically.

The Printweigh "400" had a "memory" to print weight data even after the load was removed. And it was capable of transmitting all the data to an adding machine or other office machines located remotely. It was an immediate success. The Printweigh "400" was Toledo's standard industrial weight printer through the entire life of mechanical scales.

The Toledo Kitchen Machine Division had added a wide range of new products since it became part of Toledo when McIntosh engineered his first acquisition. It started with peelers and a few commercial dishwashers. Now, 10 years later, it had a wide range of products.

The line now included food waste disposals, vertical mixers, and many varieties of commercial dishwashers to completely serve the restaurant and institutional market. The dishwasher line now covered a full range, with machines capable of washing 150 dishes per hour to more than 14,000 per hour. In 1958, a major addition was added to the Rochester plant for the increased dishwasher line.

In May 1959, Ed Quertinmont moved up to retail sales manager, replacing Bob Schick who returned to Atlanta as region manager. Quertinmont had been Schick's chief assistant as retail product manager since 1955 where he helped launch the troublesome Valueprint prepackaging system. Now he became responsible for the sales and planning for all retail scales and food machines.

Quertinmont was appointed just in time to kick off a major new retail product, the Valuematic prepackaging system. The Valuematic was Toledo's answer to the Hobart 2000 prepackaging system introduced about four years previously. Toledo had been trying to compete against Hobart with the Valueprint without much success. Now they were sure they had a superior product.

The Valuematic was designed with the help of the Batelle Institute of Columbus. It was the first fully electronic computing scale system, using vacuum tube technology in its computer. The Valuematic was larger than the Hobart 2000 since it contained a fast-acting scale, a computer and a printer all in a single unit. It provided a means to tare off the various weights of meat trays.

Now for a large run of the same kind of meat, a user had only to enter a printing plate with the name of the meat, punch in the price per pound, place the wrapped tray package on the scale platform and moments later see a label issued from the integrated printer. The heat-sensitive label dropped onto a heat block, which activated the adhesive. The operator turned over the package and placed it over the heating device, which caused the label to adhere to the package.

To protect against label switching, the label couldn't be removed without tearing the wrapping film. After the package was labeled, it was placed into a collecting bin, which was delivered to the meat case when the entire run had been completed. The Valuematic was fast enough to stay ahead of the fastest operator, even when they learned to apply the label with their right hand as they placed another package on the scale with their left hand.

A large rack installed above the scale held a hundred or so printing plates, each containing the name of a variety of meat. Labels were preprinted with the name and logo of the store. They showed the name of the meat (pork chops, etc.) the weight of the package, the price per pound and total value of the package. Plates were also available with names of produce items for those stores who prepackaged their produce.

Quertinmont arranged for home office service training prior to its introduction. Servicemen were prepared to maintain the Valuematic even before it was introduced to the field. Then he conducted meetings around the country for the sales force. The Valuematic was received with enthusiasm. Finally they had a product to compete head-on with Hobart. A fully electronic, superior product at that.

The Valuematic sold well from the start. Many accessories were developed to speed up product flow. It became obvious, however, that even more automation would be required soon. New stores were growing larger every year. For their high volume stores, the chains wanted a device to apply the label automatically, and fully automatic wrapping machines rather than the semi-automatic type. Quertinmont began to make plans for retail to meet these upcoming needs.

John F. Kennedy won a close race against Richard Nixon for president in 1960. Claims were made that Chicago Mayor Daley manipulated ballots to give Kennedy the small margin of victory. Within months the Bay of Pigs disaster occurred which led to the Cuban Missile Crisis a year later.

Early that year, John Lewis, another English expatriate, came to the home office as manager of marketing research. Lewis had joined Toledo in 1954 when he initially came to the United States after a messy divorce. He first became a sales representative in Washington, D.C. Soon learning the ins and outs of selling to the government, he was named the manager of government sales.

John Lewis had been a mathematics professor in England. Later he was associated with the Avery Scale Company, where he learned how to make and market scales. He was highly intelligent, sophisticated and urbane, reminding many of the late English actor, George Sanders.

Lewis liked to talk, yet was always correct in his demeanor. He wore his suit coat even in the hottest weather, with his handkerchief stored and sticking out of his coat sleeve in the manner of an English gentleman.

Within a few years Lewis would become the scale division's industrial marketing manager, replacing John McLellan who moved to New York as region manager.

John Lewis was a scholar. Soon after becoming industrial marketing manager, he spoke to the Institute of Electrical and Electronic Engineers. His title, "The History of Weighing." His script read in part:

"As the main purpose of this talk is to take a look at 10,000 years of weighing progress, let's take a look backward:

The progress of civilization can be related to the extent that man has used some form of measurement. Probably the oldest form of measurement is by weight. Archaeologists have found primitive weighing balances in Egyptian tombs dating back to 8,000 BC. They consisted simply of a piece of wood, suspended in the middle by a leather thong. Two flat pieces were hung on either end by the same means.

A few centuries later, in the land of Sumer near the Persian Gulf, a complete system of balances and standard weights were used for trading in metals and agricultural products. This early system spread to India, China and then into Europe. The weight units of this early system were still in use up to the Renaissance, several centuries before Columbus sailed for America.

Ancient Greece, too, had its system of weights and measures. Archimedes, a famous Greek philosopher and mathematician, actually saved himself from being beheaded by using his rapidly acquired knowledge of weighing principals. King Hieron of Greece commissioned Archimedes to prove the goldsmith who fabricated his new crown hadn't diluted the gold and silver in the crown.

The King gave Archimedes 24 hours to come up with a method to test the goldsmith's honesty…and if he failed he would be beheaded.

Naturally, Archimedes was a bit stressed. He went home to relax in a warm bath. As he watched the water rise in the tub as he sat down, inspiration struck. He rushed from the bath into the street nude shouting 'Eureka!' (I have found it!)

Archimedes balanced the finished crown in one pan and the specified content of gold and silver in the other pan, first in the air and secondly with both arms submerged in water.

He had discovered the principle named after him, which states that a body surrounded by a fluid is buoyed up by a force equal to the weight of the displaced fluid. Fortunately for the goldsmith, the balance was achieved in water and both their lives were spared.

Through all ancient history the coinage was based on the weight of gold or precious metal each coin contained. Designations of weight and money were often interchangeable. The shekel of Egyptian and Biblical history was originally a measure of weight. Applied to precious metal it became the name of a coin, which weighed one shekel.

At any rate, 4,500 years rolled by before the slightest of improvements was made to the Egyptian balance. The Romans developed the steelyard which was suspended near the load end and had a movable weight which could be placed in notches across the longer end. Each notch represented a greater weight in the scale pan. The Roman steelyard remained unchanged for almost 19 centuries. During this time it developed only in its ability to handle larger and larger loads. In fact it was used for weighing carts, the forerunner of today's motor trick scale.

Towards the end of the 19th century, scales were coming into use for retail trade, designed to be placed on the counter top. They used springs to counterbalance the load with some form of indicator across the dial. These spring scales were hopelessly unreliable and, of course, the consumer nearly always lost out.

At this point, in 1901, a man named Henry Theobald became interested in a scale, which was balanced by raising a pendulum higher and higher as the load on the platform increased. No springs were used. It produced a true weight since it balanced weight against weight. Thus Theobald's slogan, 'No Springs—Honest Weight'".

Lewis continued bringing the history up to the moment load cells and electronic scales were coming into use. His talk was quite successful and he was asked to repeat it many times before other groups.

That same year, Frank Instone was named general sales manager, replacing George McKenna who abruptly left the company. Instone had joined Toledo Scale in 1957 as manager of custom products.

Prior to Toledo, he was with St. Regis Paper Company in Chicago, in charge of sales and engineering on scales and other equipment. Earlier he was with Richardson Scale Company, where he headed the development of special scales and material handling equipment. He quickly made his presence felt throughout the field.

Tall and thin with a penetrating look, Instone had a strong personality. He moved fast to put his own team in place. One of his first moves was to appoint engineer Geoff Gray as advertising manager. Instone had worked with Gray in custom engineering and had a high regard for his design sense and communication skills.

Instone's scale experience was entirely industrial. He realized how important retail would be in his new job. For retail guidance he sought out Jack Dee, Toledo's top performing salesman. Within weeks, Instone became the one to greet Dee on his monthly visits to Toledo with his new orders.

Instone would come out of his office and greet Dee in the Customer Order Center, a large open office area just outside his own office. Dee was Jewish, and Instone would publicly lean down and greet the much shorter Dee with a kiss on the cheek, which he understood to be a gesture of high respect in Jewish culture.

The two would usually have drinks, dinner and party together the night Dee was in town. Instone learned fast…to understand retail and keep large orders flowing, court Jack Dee.

A few months later the Customer Order Center learned that Dee had had an exceptional month and planned to bring in an extra large number of orders. Tom Siegler, Gary Wilkins and Joe LaConey from the COC decided it was worth extra attention. They arranged to rent a large red carpet and had it laid temporarily along the hall past Instone's office…the path Dee walked to reach them with his orders.

When Dee walked in along the carpet the staff rose and applauded. He was only momentarily speechless. "This can't be for me," he said. "Come on, who's it for…who deserves the red carpet treatment? I wanna meet him!"

"Who else but you, Jack," Instone said as he left his office to greet him. "There's only one Jack Dee." Obviously delighted, this was that rare occasion when Dee was upstaged. He spent little time negotiating for special treatment as was his usual habit.

McIntosh next made a move to strengthen top management and give him more time for corporate duties, which now included the Haughton Elevator Division. He recruited Richard Moss from outside the company, naming him to the new position of general manager of the Toledo Scale Division, and a vice president of Toledo Scale Corporation. He was given responsibility for the entire scale operation.

Dick Moss was a steel man. He came to Toledo from Lukens Steel in Pennsylvania, and for several years was general manager of E. W. Bliss in Canton, Ohio. He also had been an executive at the Sheffield Division of Bendix Aviation Corporation.

Moss looked the executive, with a strong bearing. He had a deep, rich, well-modulated voice, which commanded attention. He soon toured the country to get acquainted with field people, accompanying sales training program teams on their travels.

CHAPTER 23

More Systems

By 1961, the increased capabilities of the Printweigh 400 opened up many unique new markets. One was sold to Armour, the large Chicago meat packer, which had established a joint research project with an Oklahoma rancher for bull development designed to improve beef cattle.

Toledo scales with Printweigh 400 printers provided weight checks for feed conversion testing of 20 sire groups. A push of a button sent a given amount of different special feeds to different pens. The system was automatic. Printweigh records kept track of the weight gains of the different bulls in the tests.

Retail sales increased as well. At Tujunga, California, a new Shop Easy supermarket opened with 23 Toledo scales and food machines installed. Included were six checkstand scales, 12 hanging scales in the produce department, and in an open-view meat department customers saw a receiving scale, a complete Valuematic wrapping system, and a Toledo steak machine, among others. The store was typical of new supermarkets with a full range of Toledo products.

In the early 60s, Toledo had established an operation in Utah called Toledo Defense Systems with Bill Susor as chief engineer. Susor supervised the design of an automatic batching plant for Thiokol Chemical to manufacture solid rocket fuel. The fuel was very volatile. The blending part of the plant was built to operate remotely without people in attendance because of the real risk of explosion.

Toledo Systems began to develop many successful automation systems that made a mark in the early '60s. A Center of Gravity (CG) unit was developed for Aerojet General especially for the Minuteman missile. Many other successful automation systems came in the '60s...to manufacture rubber, glass, beer and more.

In April 1961, Frank Instone, Bob Bell and Bob Bradley were each named vice president...Instone for Toledo Scale Division sales, Bell for engineering and Bradley for engineering at Haughton Elevator.

Later that year, the Andersons of Maumee, Ohio, began operating what was reported to be the only truly automatic grain elevator known in the world. The heart of the huge structure was an automatic bulk grain weighing system designed and installed by Toledo Scale.

Robert Anderson, a partner in the firm, said, "When we learned that Toledo Scale could supply a 60,000 bushel-per-hour continuous grain weighing system capable of meeting or exceeding grain accuracy tolerances, plus automatic recording and control, we realized we had found the basis upon which to build the grain elevator."

The system required only three men to operate it...a coordinator, a weighman, and a basement beltman. Also involved were Toledo Board of Trade inspectors and stevedores. Basic accuracy of the scale weighed each 50,000 lb draft to an accuracy of 1/12th of a bushel. Technology had advanced.

The space race escalated. On February 20, 1962, John Glenn became the first American to orbit the earth. Glenn's Mercury spacecraft, The Friendship 7, made three orbits 99 miles above the earth.

A month later, Geoff Gray was named advertising manager of the Toledo Scale Division. Born in London, Gray was educated at colleges in Bristol, England, which awarded him a Certificate in Mechanical Engineering. He worked for the Bristol Aeroplane Company as chief engineer and designer for prominent aircraft and chemical processing equipment before coming to the U.S.

On November 22, 1963, the nation and the world were shocked when America's popular young president, John F. Kennedy, was shot and killed by Lee Harvey Oswald in Dallas.

Just 99 minutes after Kennedy's death, Vice President Lyndon Johnson was sworn in as the 36th President of the United States aboard Air Force One as it stood on the runway at Love Field. The plane then bore the body of the slain president and the 55-year-old new president to Washington, D.C.

Two days later millions watched on television as Jack Ruby unloaded his pistol into Oswald in the basement of the Dallas jail, killing him instantly. And on November 25, the world watched the funeral ceremony and wept as Kennedy was buried in Arlington Cemetery.

Also in 1963, *Toledo System* magazine wrote a story which showed how far we've come as a nation since Theobald sold the idea of establishing Honest Weight weights and measures laws. It was about the single one-pound platinum weight at the U.S. Bureau of Standards in Washington against which all weights in the country are checked. It read:

"The little platinum cylinder is the most tenderly cared for piece of metal in the country. About 1-1/2 inches high, it's kept in a platinum lined niche in a quartz plate, mounted on a special brass platform. Three glass bells are placed over it…the second and third each a little larger. The whole thing is kept in an air-tight cabinet which itself is stored inside a vault with double steel doors.

This one-pound weight is actually rated in kilograms. It's officially considered to be 46.35% of a kilogram. Many people forget that, as far as weight is concerned, the United States has been legally on the metric system since 1866, when we signed an international agreement to that effect.

Periodically the one-pound weight is brought out and tenderly placed on a special scale. Master weights used by weight inspectors from each state are then checked against it. Later, in each state capitol, local city and county master weights are checked against the state weights.

Once every ten years the master weight cylinder gets a check-up of its own. It's sent to be compared with the International Prototype

Kilogram that's housed in a vault in Sevres, France. To get it there, it's wrapped in a chamois, then put in a metal box wrapped in felt, then repeated through five layers of felt and five boxes.

In Sevres, the cylinder gets a steam bath, an alcohol bath, then rinsed in distilled water and allowed to air dry. Next it's placed on one of the most delicate scales in the world inside a special weighing room. There master metrologists determine once again that our master weight has never lost or gained weight.

This means that all certified scales everywhere in the country can be traced to this single one-pound weight in Washington, which in turn is traced to the master weight in France."

Theobald would have loved the story.

Weight information became more visible with another new Toledo product made possible by the Printweigh "400" since it could transmit weight data to remote locations. Large "scoreboard" readouts with digit sizes up to 14 inches were developed so weights could be read as far as 300 to 400 feet away.

One of the first uses of Toledo scoreboards was in livestock auctions. Animals were often auctioned in lots of as many as a dozen animals and the scoreboard indicated the weight of the entire lot. The weight of a single animal could also be shown on the scoreboard. Whether the bidding was to be for a lot or a single animal, the indicated weight was kept on the scoreboard until the bidding was over.

The meat packing industry was going through many changes in the '60s. Synthetics had greatly reduced the demand—and the price—of many animal by-products, especially hides. This year fewer than 30% of the shoes sold in the U.S. had leather soles.

In the 1920s, the price of a green hide was 156% of the price of cattle on the hoof. Now hide prices were averaging only 58% of live cattle costs. From a commodity that was once worth more than the average price of meat, hides were now bringing half the meat prices. Figures on tallow and other by-products followed much the same trend.

A thousand pound steer that cost $262.50 at the stockyards yielded about 97% of its market value from carcass beef, variety meats and edible organs, which together weighed about 630 pounds. The hide, which averaged 78 pounds, yielded only about 2%. Of the remaining 292 pounds only about 1% yielded any return. The packers were forced to change old habits. They needed closer controls…which meant more weight control throughout the plant.

To better serve the industry, Joe Nies was moved from St. Louis to Chicago as meat packing industry manager. Chicago was still the nation's center for meat packing. Nies had been the St. Louis regional sales engineer where he worked with area meat plants and became an expert on changing meat industry needs.

From Chicago, he regularly advised home office marketing people on what new or different scales the industry required.

Toledo next hired Paul McGiverin who had been with Wilson Meat Packing Company. For years, McGiverin had been Wilson's authority on scales and Toledo's contact to check out prototypes of new scales for the industry. He had a wide knowledge of both the meat packing industry and scales.

Soon after McGiverin was hired, Toledo obtained a contract to do an extensive weighing survey of an older Swift Meat Packing Company plant in Kansas City, Kansas. This Swift plant was seven stories high. Beef cattle were kept in large holding pens near the plant. Every day those scheduled for slaughter were herded onto a long ramp that wound back-and-forth, and driven up to the seventh floor.

The cattle entered the top floor one at a time. Next each one was driven onto a scale and held in place with a device that squeezed them so they had to hold still. An operator checked the weight, loaded a large hypodermic needle with an amount of tenderizing fluid based on weight and injected it into the neck of the cow.

Cattle were a bit upset at this treatment and often moved off the scale bellowing. Swift marketed the tenderized cuts from these cattle under the brand name, "ProTen Beef."

This took place just before the creature was slaughtered. The animal had to live at least a minute before being slaughtered so the tenderizer had enough time to circulate through his system…and not more than five minutes or the meat could be mushy. So between one and five minutes after being injected with the tenderizer, the animal was stunned, a hook put into a hind leg, then raised onto a powered conveyor line and his throat was cut. Blood was collected in a trough below the line.

After the hide was removed, the cattle were cut into halves, then smaller sections. The sections were dropped into slots that took them down one floor where they were further divided and dropped down another floor where they were divided again. On the bottom floor they were packed ready for shipping.

Toledo Scale's Industrial Marketing Manager assigned the author, then an industrial marketing specialist, to team with McGiverin on the Swift survey. Terry and McGiverin spent more than two weeks in the plant. An executive from Swift's home office in Chicago was part of the team. A local Swift plant employee pushed a cart with test weights from scale to scale for them.

Together they checked all of the hundreds of scales in the plant, recording the location, serial number, model and capacity of each. The checks were not only for accuracy and reliability, but also to determine if they were used for the proper application. They discovered that the majority of scales had been used in the plant for decades. They all had been badly maintained and misused.

For the accuracy checks, test weights were placed in the center of the platform and McGiverin recorded the indicated weight for each quadrant on the dial. Then they performed a "shift test". This was an accuracy check when the weights were placed on each of the four corners of the platform and checked again at each quadrant.

Early in the second week, McGiverin yelled, "Bob, come look at this one!" He had been walking ahead and reached the scale first. When Terry looked at it he saw what had attracted McGiverin's attention. It was an old Toledo bench scale mounted on a rusted, leaning stand with water standing in the dial head about a third of the way up from the bottom of the dial.

The serial number showed the scale was built prior to the first World War. It was over 50-years-old.

Terry said, "What the hell, Paul. Let's check it anyway."

McGiverin put the first test weight in the center of the platform. The indicator was in the water all the way but chattered to a reading in the first quadrant. When it stopped, it showed the scale was reading right on the money. He put the second test weight on the platform. The indicator chattered until it was out of the water, then snapped instantly to a reading in the second quadrant.

There was clearly no oil in the dashpot to control and steady the indicator. Yet once again it showed the scale was right on.

"I don't believe this!" Terry exclaimed. McGiverin just smiled and continued the tests. When they were complete, the tests showed the scale was within 1% accuracy all the way. It was accurate in all quadrants and on all corners of the platform.

"How can that be?" Terry asked.

"All these old Toledos stay remarkably accurate," McGiverin said, "even when they're badly maintained and abused like this one. Now you know why the meat packing industry buys Toledos."

When they were finished, they saw that the majority of scales in the plant had not been maintained, were still accurate to within about 2%, and were incorrectly applied with 250 lb and 500 lb capacity scales routinely assigned to weigh cuts of ten pounds or less.

While McGiverin felt right at home, this had been Terry's first visit to a meat packing plant. He saw that workers faced cold, wet, smelly and dangerous conditions every day. Terry also saw all the parts that were ground up to make hot dogs. He couldn't eat a hot dog for almost a year.

Back home in Toledo, Terry and McGiverin took about a month to complete their report. Then they took it back to Kansas City and, along with the Swift executive who had been part of the team, presented it to the plant manager.

The discussion covered every scale individually. The report showed that this Swift plant badly needed about 50 new scales, extensive service on hundreds more, and a shakeup in the maintenance department.

The plant manager glanced at the Swift executive who was on the team as each flaw was uncovered. He nodded agreement every time. Terry had visions of a large order, but it was not to be. Swift decided to do some minimum maintenance, then phase out the old plant. They would run it for another year or two, then tear it down. But after the survey, Toledo Scale was perceived as the prime weighing authority by the Swift Packing Company. As time passed, good orders did result.

Not long after, Terry was sent to Greensboro, North Carolina to call on a Holly Farms operation. Holly Farms was a large company that raised, slaughtered, packaged and distributed case-ready chicken throughout much of the Eastern U.S. They used the Valuematic prepackaging scale to weigh and price the trayed packages with their own branded Holly Farms label.

While Holly Farms was loyal to Toledo, they claimed that they had been experiencing some troubles with the Valuematic. Terry was sent to see what could be done to fix any problems and keep them happy. It was a missionary call more than anything else.

Holly Farms was one of the first true "chicken factories" in the nation. They did everything themselves. They raised their own chicken feed, hatched their own chicks, raised them until they were six weeks old, sent them to their own processing plant, processed them, packaged, weighed and labeled them and shipped the packages in their own refrigerated trucks directly to individual supermarkets.

Six weeks was the optimum age for slaughter since they had gained almost all their normal weight by then. The feet of the chickens never touched the ground in their brief lives.

The large processing plant was incredibly efficient. Chickens ready for processing were hung on a moving conveyor line by their feet. The line took them to a station where they were beheaded and bled, then moved to what resembled an automatic car wash station where they first went through a steam bath and rotating devices which removed their feathers. Next the remaining small feathers were removed by hand...then the chickens were manually eviscerated and visually inspected.

Further down the line a worker removed one wing. The next worker removed the other wing. The next another part, and so on until the chicken had been completely cut apart. Each individual part was placed on its own line…breasts, wings, thighs, etc. Later the parts were assembled on retail trays containing various retail mixes of parts.

Some were packaged as legs and thighs, some only breasts, etc. When a package was identified as a whole chicken it did indeed contain all the parts of a chicken but each part was almost certainly from a different chicken.

Next, each trayed package was wrapped and sent over one of the Valuematic scales which weighed it, multiplied the weight by the entered price per pound, calculated the value, and printed and applied a retail Holly Farms label. Then the packages were refrigerated.

Their case-ready trayed packages of chicken were not quite frozen when they were shipped. The packages were "chill packed" to a temperature of between 28° and 30° F. They didn't want to freeze them because when chicken had been frozen, the bones turned an unappetizing dark color when cooked.

Holly Farms helped to convert chicken from a commodity to a brand, unlike red meat, which was—and still is—a commodity. It was very convenient for their supermarket customers since Holly Farms chicken was delivered ready to be displayed in the store's refrigerated retail cases. And their prices were good. The efficiency of their operation helped drive down the price of chicken.

Before the advent of chicken factories like Holly Farms, Purdue and Tyson, chicken was quite costly. It was usually reserved for Sunday dinner. "A chicken in every pot," was the politicians cry.

Even though Holly Farms' workers in the processing plant faced cold, wet, smelly and dangerous conditions, the same as workers in meat packing houses, Terry was impressed by what he saw. The operation was cleaner and far more efficient. It took some time for him to determine what the problem was. The Valuematics performed as expected under the heavy use conditions and were serviced promptly when they acted up.

It seemed as if the plant manager simply needed some personal attention. Terry discovered that he was a huge fan of stock car racing, then becoming increasingly popular in the Southeast. He kept talking about Holly Farms sponsorship of their own stock car. Once Terry mentioned he would take back the idea of supporting stock car racing, the problem went away.

Toledo Scale really had no interest in sponsoring stock car racing so nothing came of it. Yet there was no more talk of problems at Holly Farms.

Corporate controller Frank Billett retired at the end of 1963. Billett had started with the company in 1922. He had worked with Theobald, Bennett and McIntosh during his career. Self-taught, Billett became a master of corporate finance. He was a member of the corporation's board of directors and on the boards of both the Canadian and Mexican affiliates. And Billet himself was ultimately promoted to Vice President, Finance.

Billett was replaced as corporate controller by Greg Rothe, division controller of Toledo Scale.

International operations had grown dramatically since World War II. They handled all of Toledo's global dealings, including foreign subsidiaries and licensees in Australia, Brazil, Germany, Mexico, Italy and Belgium. Global activities were led by International Operations Vice President Frank Parmelee and his Assistant Manager, Ted Metcalf. The Export Office was headed by Paul Greene.

At *Toledo do Brasil*, a line of industrial scales was manufactured in São Paulo. *Toledo-Werk*, the factory in Cologne, not only manufactured scales but was the largest scale facility in Europe.

Toledo de Mexico did some assembly work and had offices in Mexico City, Guadalajara, and Monterey to handle sales and service of all types of scales and food machines. *Toledo-Berkel Australia, Pty. Ltd.* had been a licensee before World War II and had been acquired in the mid 60s. *Toledo Italiana* had headquarters in Milan with sub-offices in Naples, Turin and Venice. They sold and serviced scales and did some partial assembly.

Toledo was represented in Belgium by *Toledo-Copaba*, with facilities in Brussels. It was an engineering, sales, service and assembly operation with business extending into the Netherlands and Luxembourg.

Like McIntosh, Frank Parmelee was a graduate of Yale. He started in the service school and later worked in retail assembly. He was a credit correspondent and had both retail and industrial field selling experience before first becoming Export Manager, then Vice President, International.

Assistant International Operations Manager Ted Metcalf started as an attorney in the legal department in 1947, specializing in international law. After a special assignment as credit manager, he joined the international department. Metcalf was also assistant secretary and assistant treasurer of Toledo Scale Corporation.

Paul Greene, Manager of the Export Office, had an assignment in Antwerp, Belgium just prior to the 1930's Depression in Toledo's assembly and sales operation there. When the world-wide Depression reduced activities in Belgium, Greene returned to Toledo in the export department.

Greene's export office covered products manufactured in Toledo and exported overseas through some 50 foreign distributors. Export accounted for about 10% of Toledo Scale product bookings. About 75% of exports were industrial scales. The French distributor was the largest foreign distributor, employing more than 125 people selling and servicing Toledo scales. Made-in-Toledo scale products went to 72 different countries, including some in which Toledo did not have a distributor.

Formerly, a foreign distributors' servicemen were brought to Toledo for training. Though this was still done for more sophisticated equipment, Toledo service training centers had been established by now in Mexico City, Bogota, São Paulo, Cologne and Milan.

The Dutch ship PRINS WILLEM VAN ORANGE stopped in the Port of Toledo in 1963 to pick up a cargo of rubber, refrigerators, auto parts, and Toledo Scales before getting up steam for Glasgow and LeHavre. A look at the scales in the cargo showed the slogans "Peso Exacto", "Poids Honnête", and "Pesagens Exactas", showing they stood for "Honest Weight" just about anywhere in the world.

Toledo Scale had indeed become a global company.

CHAPTER 24

Sales Meetings Resume

Electrical engineer Bill Susor was promoted to assistant research manager. He returned to Toledo from Utah where he had been chief engineer of Toledo's defense systems for three years. A brilliant engineer, Susor also taught electronics part time at Toledo University where he had received his degree in electrical engineering. He soon acquired many patents for the company on both weighing equipment and elevator controls.

In the mid '60s Toledo's Model 1070 Bench Scale with a magnified, non-parallax chart and ball bearing pivots was developed by engineer Larry Williams. From it, the 1080 computing scale was developed with the magnified, illuminated non-parallax chart, which evolved into the current line of retail load cell scales with digital readouts.

Because of the clear advantages of a magnified, illuminated, non-parallax chart, engineer Fred Carroll was assigned the task of designing the same advantages into the industrial scale line. He developed a method of magnifying an analog chart to display half inch high digits alongside every graduation in a backlit window about 2-1/2" x 4" in the middle of the scale dial. It was the forerunner of today's digital indication on industrial scales.

It wasn't easy. Carroll had been working on a combination of lenses to magnify and project weight indication to an illuminated window in the center of the scale head. He ran into trouble. The lens combinations always seemed to cause the projected indication to zoom up or down in size. To work in a scale they would have to remain precisely the same size whatever the weight.

Carroll was determined to solve the problem. He took a variety of lenses home and began experimenting with them in his basement. In time, he found a combination that worked. He confirmed it back at the plant and designed a projected indication that used his "anti-zoom" lens.

Marketing was excited about its potential. Not only was a digital weight displayed a half inch apart at every graduation, the graduations themselves were about an eighth of an inch wide. This meant that the user could easily interpolate between graduations if he chose. If the indication was about half way between 852 and 853 on a 1000 lb scale, he could call it 852-1/2 lb.

This was virtually impossible on a standard dial scale where the graduation lines were thin, close together, and marked with a small digital number only at every five graduations. Verilux had a large digital number at every one.

Industrial marketing manager John Lewis named it Verilux, combining the Latin word for truth, "veritas," with the one for light, "lux," and added the model number. Verilux "711" sold well. It projected a genuine non-parallax indication. In the center of the dial head users saw illuminated half-inch high digits displayed in a window which were easy to read from quite a distance.

Marketing produced a 16 mm sales promotion motion picture that told the Verilux story, featuring Fred Carroll's discovery. It included details on the work he did on his own time in his basement. Continuous loop eight mm copies of the movie were made and used in portable projectors. One projector and two copies of the movie were distributed to each region. The region manager scheduled it throughout his region so each salesmen could carry it into a prospect's office.

An early use of Verilux was to help doctors accurately monitor the weight of kidney patients during dialysis treatment with an "artificial kidney" at the Veterans Administration Hospital in Washington, DC. Although the artificial kidney originated in Holland in about 1941, only recently had the procedure reached what doctors considered to be the practical stage.

Toledo representative Jim Masseron worked with Dr. Ervin A. Gombos, chief of the hemodialysis center at the hospital. A modified portable scale with Verilux indication was installed to weigh a hospital bed with a patient in it to constantly monitor the patient's weight loss while he was on the artificial kidney.

"We have found the constant monitoring of the patient's weight while on the artificial kidney to be most helpful in controlling the rate of removal of fluid," Dr. Gombos said. "The large individually numbered graduations of the Verilux scale facilitate such observation."

"Patients had to often spend two days—ten to twelve hours at a time—each week under treatment," Dr. Gombos explained. "Extreme sensitivity was demanded of this weighing-dialysis system since the average amount of fluid removed per hour was only around 120 grams."

Thus the Toledo Verilux remained on guard during the patient's long stay for treatment to protect against any excessive fluid withdrawal. While this Verilux weighing-dialysis system was a use with perhaps the most human interest, Verilux "711" was a hit everywhere.

The company's stock had been traded over-the-counter since 1958. Now in 1964, management concluded it was ready for the big time. Sales were $65.5 million in 1963. Toledo Scale wanted to broaden its list of investors to include institutional investors and endowment funds, which were limited by law, or policy to listed securities.

So on July 24, 1964, Toledo Scale Corporation stock made its debut on the New York Stock Exchange with the ticker symbol TDS. It opened at 29-1/2 and rose to 29-7/8 by mid-afternoon. In a listing ceremony with exchange president Keith Funston, Harris McIntosh bought the first 100 shares.

In November 1964, Frank Instone called Clarence Weinandy to his office. Weinandy was the supervisor of promotions and displays in the advertising department. He was a company veteran, having been with the company since starting as a 17-year-old youth in 1926.

He was an army officer during WWII specializing in logistics. Within the company Weinandy was known for his ability to deal with minutiae…able to handle a large number of details at the same time.

Instone said, "Clarence, we're going to resume a full blown 100% Club. Three months from now, in February, we're going to have a three day meeting honoring all salesmen who made 100% of their quota in 1964."

Weinandy knew the company had not done this since Bennett's last meeting on Rattlesnake Island during the Depression. Since then only the 100% Club officers and directors—a total of 11 men—had been invited to attend a recognition meeting at company expense…always in Toledo. Weinandy had been handling the logistics for these Toledo 100% Club meetings. Now he knew there could be as many as several hundred people attending the meeting in February 1965.

Instone explained, "I've arranged with the Maritz organization to handle all transportation for the men, and to book a hotel for us. The meeting will be held at the Hotel Roosevelt in New Orleans the week prior to Mardi Gras. I want you to handle everything else…every detail of the schedule."

Weinandy flew to New Orleans to case the Roosevelt Hotel. He arranged for meeting rooms for the various activities, talked to the chef and set up the menu for all three days, and plotted the flow of traffic. For seminars, the retail salesmen required separate meeting rooms from the industrial salesmen. At other times the entire sales force would be together for general meetings and entertainment.

Back in Toledo, Weinandy met separately with the retail, industrial and systems sales managers. He gave them each a schematic layout of the hotel seminar rooms and determined how much time each would need. Then he wrote a complete schedule…from arrival time of the men until their departure.

The meeting went smoothly. There was one glitch that was noticed only by the industrial team. They had made their presentation on the first day and had risen early on the second day to help the retail team set up for their presentation. Waiting for the auditorium to be opened they noticed a dozen or so 100% Club members make their way one or two at a time into the hotel from the street.

They had spent the entire night carousing on Bourbon Street. The retail team had unfortunately built their presentation around 35 mm slides. When the lights were dimmed, these revelers went right to sleep.

In spite of this, the meeting was a major success. On the last night after the entertainment, Weinandy was sitting on the steps of the stage with his head in his hands coming down from the stress. Instone saw him there, came up to him and said, "Clarence, you did a superb job. Call your wife and have her come down here for a couple of days."

Weinandy called his wife, Jeanne. The next morning a Maritz man came to her door in Toledo, pinned an orchid corsage on her coat and escorted her to the plane. Weinandy said, "We had two glorious days seeing New Orleans. Then we had to come down to earth and come home."

Soon after, many executive changes were made. Wes Jenkins was hired as general sales manager by Frank Instone, by then the vice president of sales. Jenkins came from Friden Calculator Company and was well known to Toledo because he bought branded postal scales for Friden from Toledo. Before Friden, he had been vice president of sales for Marchant Calculator Company.

As a young man, Jenkins had been a professional musician during the big band era. He played the sax in Jack Teagarden's band until the big band era slowly disappeared and the group disbanded.

Not long after, Dick Moss became executive vice president of the corporation, Greg Rothe was named a corporate vice president, and Frank Instone was named vice president and general manager of the Toledo Scale Division, replacing Moss.

Meanwhile, Don Hall had been reading about how Japanese steel companies were importing scrap steel from the U.S., making finished steel out of it and shipping it back to the U.S. profitably.

He discovered they were using new steel-making technology that produced steel at much less cost than the blast furnaces used in the U.S. The steel in Japan was made in a Basic Oxygen Furnace, which could make steel at about half the cost of a blast furnace. Hall concluded that Toledo Scale could design a superior BOF system. He talked it over with Dick Moss. Moss was a steel man before coming to Toledo. He liked the idea and gave Hall the go ahead. Working jointly with Bob Pelke from the University of Michigan, Hall co-authored a paper titled, "A Systematic Approach to the Design of a Control System for the Basic Oxygen Steelmaking Process".

The paper resulted in a Toledo BOF control system design. In addition to the necessary scales, the system included a control center, a computer and a spectrometer. It could translate steel specifications into command signals, control the vital inputs and present a complete record of the steel produced. It would cut the cost of making steel in half.

Hall's team included Harry Droulliard and Roger Williams. They were sure they had a big winner. "We were gonna set the world on fire," Hall said. "We learned a big lesson, though…making a better mousetrap doesn't do it."

Hall discovered that steel people had no real incentive to adopt BOF technology. Their incentives were based on making small, incremental improvements in blast furnace production. They were paid well to improve existing plants, not build new ones. They had no incentive to throw out the old hardware and build totally new steelmaking plants even if it would cut production costs in half.

As time passed, more and more foreign steel was imported from the Far East and Europe. American steel companies saw their markets shrink drastically. Labor costs in American steel mills were higher, of course. With their lower labor costs coupled with more efficient technology, foreign steelmakers could easily absorb the high cost of shipping heavy steel across oceans and still beat American prices.

Blast furnaces shut down all over the nation. By the time U.S. steel makers concluded they had to build new BOF plants, it was almost too late. Toledo had abandoned the BOF project in the meantime. In spite of its great promise, no BOF plants were ever built using Toledo's "better mousetrap".

In the fall of 1965, Clarence Weinandy was told by Instone to plan the complete program for the next 100% Club meeting. This task was clearly going to be his for a long time since he had done such a good job in New Orleans. The company wanted it to be held near Toledo in the spring of 1966.

In downtown Detroit, the new Ponchartrain Hotel was promoting its facilities. It had a sawtooth construction that allowed each room to have an attractive view.

After visiting the Ponchartrain, Weinandy proposed it to Instone who liked the idea. He began to work out the details. Again Maritz would handle all travel arrangements. Since the Ponchartrain Hotel was only about 50 miles from the plant, Weinandy had an easier time planning, scheduling and handling the logistics involved in moving equipment.

On the last day of the meeting, Weinandy arranged for the entire group to be transported over the river to Windsor for a night club dinner and show. The show starred the actor Pat O'Brien who had played Knute Rockne in a motion picture about the legendary Notre Dame coach. In his show, O'Brien reprised Rockne's famous "Win one for the Gipper" half-time speech from the movie.

In one of his early roles, the Gipper was played by Ronald Reagan. Again, the 100% Club meeting was a success.

Geoff Gray moved from advertising manager to manager of training. He was a skilled public speaker, having polished his skills as an active member of a Toastmaster's club. His wry wit and delightful British accent made it a joy to listen to him and helped make him one of the most successful training managers in the company's history. Gray was replaced as advertising manager by Dick Herron.

After 18 months in this job, Gray was named General Sales Manager of the Toledo Scale Company of Canada. He moved to the Canadian headquarters in Windsor, Ontario to take on this latest assignment.

Gray was replaced as training manager by Ed Quertinmont, who in turn was replaced as retail marketing manager by John Carver. John McLellan returned to the home office as manager, field operations. He had been the New York region manager. McLellan replaced Harvey Sanford who retired. At the same time Tom Siegler was named manager of the Customer Order Center. Bill Susor became manager of systems engineering. Earlier he had been chief engineer for Toledo Systems Western operations in Utah.

Susor didn't stay long in systems engineering. He was given a special assignment leading a team to update the Valuematic pre-packaging scale. Its large size in a single assembly was a problem, and its vacuum tube technology was rapidly becoming obsolete. Susor was a brilliant electronics engineer. He taught electronics in the evening at Toledo University. He designed the new Valuematic replacement in three separate components...a scale, a printer, and a solid-state computer.

Susor explained to the marketing people how it worked in a unique way. Pointing to a transistor in the computer, he would say, "This fella knows when the scale settles, reads the weight and talks to the printer." Pointing to another component he continued, "And this fella reads the price-per-pound and also talks to the printer. Those fellas talk real fast and the printer has all the information almost instantly."

He had a way of explaining solid-state electronics that made it relatively easy to understand.

Called the Valuematic II, the new system included an exclusive feature called Price-Rite. The operator placed small, individual Price-Rite tabs in the printing plate that contained the name of the product. These tabs read the price-per-pound electronically which greatly reduced the chance for an incorrect price being dialed into the scale. Price-Rite tabs were left in the printing plate until the price changed.

Management and marketing people were invited to see the prototype. The three components were attractively finished in black vinyl with aluminum trim, and the name TOLEDO appeared on the scale component in the same way the name appeared on all products.

When McIntosh saw it, he made a cogent remark. He said, "You know, this doesn't really look very much like a scale anymore. For the first time we have a scale that doesn't look like a scale. People might say 'It's a Toledo…what?' Maybe it would be a good idea to add the word 'scale' to the name."

So for the first time the word "scale" was added to the brand name on the scale because it didn't look like a scale. It was identified as TOLEDO SCALE *Valuematic II.*

The new solid-state Valuematic II was introduced via 13 regional meetings during August and September 1966. To prepare for the introduction, marketing produced a continuous-loop movie to use with the company's 13 Fairchild portable projectors so it could be shown in a customer's office.

It showed the Valuematic II used as a stand-alone, in a semiautomatic wrapping/labeling system, and with the new Toledo/ Triangle automatic wrapper in a fully automatic weighing/wrapping/labeling system. The movie was titled "Sequel to Success". And a success the Valuematic II proved to be.

Quertinmont sent retail marketing specialist Bob Terry to Chicago to work with Dee for a few days. He was sent to make calls with Dee and determine what kind of new or different scales and food machines were needed.

Quertinmont didn't want the popularity of the Valuematic II to overshadow other retail scales and food machines in the minds of Toledo customers. Dee welcomed the visit. He used home office visits to show his customers how important they were to Toledo management.

Terry was sitting in Dee's office when Dee's assistant sales manager, Mort Sernovicz, strolled in. Sernovicz tended to talk out of the side of his mouth as if he was passing on confidential information. "Jack," he said, "I thought you should know…Rocco's got a Sanitary scale in his big store on Michigan. He says he's trying it out."

Dee snapped around. "No shit! How do you know?"

"I saw it on the counter. I took that Guardian scale out there like you told me. Rocco wouldn't let me bring it in. He says he's gonna try out the Sanitary."

Dee swung around abruptly and picked up his phone. He dialed a number from memory and waited impatiently until it was answered.

"Rocco? Jack Dee. Listen, I heard you got a Sanitary scale in your store…" He paused a moment to listen. "I don't give a shit about that!" he said. "Now, here's what's gonna happen…I'm gonna send Mort right back out there with that Toledo Guardian Duplex, and I want that GAW-DAM SANITARY off the counter and OUTA SIGHT before he gets there!"

Dee slammed down the phone, turned and resumed discussing plans for the day with Terry as if nothing had happened. Near the end of the day, after they had returned to the office, Terry saw Sernovicz and spoke to him. "Mort, when you got to that store was the Sanitary scale gone?"

"Oh, sure," Sernovicz said, sounding surprised as if it should have been taken for granted. "Oh, sure. I took the Guardian in and set it up right where the Sanitary was. No problem."

Terry couldn't understand what he had seen. How could Jack Dee get away with talking to a customer like that? When he returned to Toledo, he discussed it with others in retail marketing. They all knew that Dee had made quite a bit of money over the years and owned stock in some of his customer's operations.

When a store needed remodeling, sometimes he would trade new equipment for stock. They thought he was even on the board of some of the chains he had invested in. But at the end, they concluded that wasn't it.

Terry summed up what they believed. "You know, Jack never quits selling, always in his own way. He just knows his customers so well, he knows which ones he can bully and which ones call for the velvet glove approach. It's as simple as that." They all shook their heads.

Later that year a major retail trade show was held in Las Vegas. Toledo's retail sales managers from around the country worked the show with home office people since many of their customers were expected to be there. Of course, Jack Dee was one of them.

The evening before the show opened, a meeting was held for the 20 or so people who were going to take turns working the show. It was intended to explain which products were featured in the booth and how everyone was to explain them. After the meeting there was a social hour with drinks and snacks. Once the crowd loosened up, Dee yelled to get their attention. He acted a little smashed.

"We're in Las Vegas," he said, "the gambling capital of the world. I feel like making a little bet." He picked up one of the large serving trays about 30" in diameter that had been left in the room. He put a glass of water in the middle of the tray, then took one of the linen napkins and laid it on the floor in front of him with the peak pointing upward.

"Here's the bet," he said. "I'll bet anyone even money that I can balance this tray with the glass of water on my head, put my hands behind my back, lean down and pick up the napkin with my teeth…and not spill a drop!" He pulled out a roll of bills. "Come on, I'll take all bets."

It sounded impossible and everyone laughed. One said, "Okay Jack, what's the catch?" Dee replied, "There's no catch…I'll do exactly what I said or you win. If the tray falls or the water spills, you win. Hell, even if I use my hands to stop it from falling, you win. Now, who wants some of the action?"

In a few minutes Dee had covered about a dozen bets. Terry noticed that Ed Quertinmont didn't bet. He just smiled, watching. When all the bets were covered, Dee placed the glass of water in the middle of the tray and carefully balanced it on his bald head. He didn't act so smashed any longer.

Slowly he lowered himself to his knees. The tray seemed to be leaning slightly backwards already. Very slowly he tipped his bald head forward and leaned towards the napkin. The tray's center of gravity changed slightly on Dee's head and now appeared to be leaning a bit forward. He picked up the napkin with his teeth, slowly raised his head and stood up, never using his hands.

The group applauded. Dee collected his bets amongst much laughter. Later Quertinmont said he didn't bet because he had seen Dee do this several times before, successful four times out of five.

The show opened the next day. Toledo's booth was in a prime location right inside the entrance. It was the first booth visitors saw. To take advantage of the good position and generate additional interest, the company had purchased an oval race track with small electric cars operated by hand-held controls.

The race track was set up just inside the booth for visitors to try their luck racing each other and win a prize. Since it was only going to be used this once for this show, visitors could also sign up for a drawing to win the whole thing and have it shipped home.

Toledo hired a model to sign-up visitors for the drawing. Show management had a book containing head shot photos of available models. A modest looking brunette was chosen during setup before the show opened. When she showed up for work in a miniskirt the day it opened, she turned out to be well over six feet tall, her long exposed legs especially stunning. She spoke with a charming British accent.

She explained that she was indeed British and had taken a job in Paris in the Lido show appearing there. The Lido show featured topless models and she was one of them. When a Las Vegas casino brought the entire Lido show to town from Paris she came with it.

Dee was challenged. He was a bit beyond middle age, short and bald. She was young, tall and voluptuous. If fact she was more than a foot taller than he was. Still, when they both had a spare moment he would stand close, look up and hit on her. She would simply look down and smile.

When she was busy signing in visitors, Dee would use any spare moment to sell home office people the idea that certain products needed improvement. Standing by the steak machine, he said to one, "You know, the company would be better off to throw that thing into the GAW-DAM MAW-MEE RIVER! It's not worth…"

At that moment one of his Chicago customers came in the booth. Without catching his breath Dee grabbed him by the arm and said, "I'm glad you came by, Maury. I've been wanting to show you this great steak machine 'cause it will really increase your profits. Come here, let me show you…" He extolled its virtues to his customer with the same verve and enthusiasm he used to complain about it to Toledo marketing people.

Just before the trade show closed for the day, the model's young, handsome 6'6" tall boyfriend showed up to escort her home. Dee organized a group to take in the Lido show that night.

Dee acted the same with both home office people and the model for the next three days until the tradeshow ended. He would complain to them about products, and hit on her every chance he got. She continued to smile down at him, not really paying much attention. Everyone enjoyed watching him. They agreed: No matter how bad the odds, Dee just never quit selling.

Everyone went back to work. And the legend grew.

Selling retail scales and food machines was unique everywhere. Perhaps New York was the most unusual. Bob Terry was sent to New York City to call on customers with Russ Barracca, the retail sales manager. They entered a small meat market together.

Barracca explained to Terry that the customer had been trying out a Toledo steak machine for several months and he wanted to close the sale today. The owner saw them come in.

He said, "Barracca you sonofabitch, I been waiting for you." Gesturing towards the steak machine he shouted, "Get that piece of shit outa here!"

Barracca acted stunned for a moment, then went into action. Tearing off his coat he grabbed a butcher knife off the counter and lifted up his shirt in back. He offered the knife to his customer. "Just a minute…just a minute goddammit, if you're gonna stab me in the back, DO IT RIGHT fer chrissake!"

The customer backed away from the knife. "Here! take the goddam knife and stab me right in the middle of the back! Go ahead! After all the time I let you use that machine that's what you're doing…"

They yelled and insulted each other for another five minutes, then began to settle down. Ten minutes later they were buddies again.

Barracca walked out with a signed order. When Terry asked him about the experience he said, "Hell, that wasn't unusual...it's often like that here in New York. It's just the nature of the business here." Retail salesmen often dealt with store owners and managers who were often unschooled, learning the food retailing business by working their way up. They would be suspicious of any salesman, never really believing that the price quoted to them was the lowest they could get, if they only kept fighting.

On the other hand, industrial salesmen usually dealt with people in the industry that were far more sophisticated and knowledgeable, often with technical degrees. Some of these industrial salesmen became truly ingenious.

One of the best of these was Erich Wolf, Toledo's district manager in Riverside, California. Born in Yugoslavia, Wolf moved with his family to Hungary at the age of 10. As Jews, the Wolfs became caught up in the horrors of the Holocaust. Erich was separated from his family. He was tattooed on the forearm with a number and sent to a concentration camp. He survived two years of imprisonment.

After the war, Wolf managed to join the thousands emigrating from Europe to America. He was sent to Milwaukee, arriving at the age of 21. "I was approached by George Ormsbee, Toledo's former district manager in Milwaukee," Wolf said. "He offered me the chance to work for Toledo. I was very familiar with the name 'Toledo' because the company had models throughout Europe. I knew I would enjoy working for Toledo, but I also heard a lot about California. I told Mr. Ormsbee I would happily accept his offer if he could find me a job with Toledo in California."

Ormsbee came through. In a few weeks Wolf was in Riverside, California, with a job as a serviceman for a Toledo distributorship. In six months he was Service Manager. He next became a partner in the distributorship, a regional sales engineer (directly employed by Toledo for the first time), district industrial sales manager, and in 1966 district manager.

Wolf was an innovator. Early on, he acquired a solid reputation as a man who didn't see problems, only solutions. His region manager Bill Lowe said, "The man has a fantastic mind. When others give up, Erich just goes right ahead and finds the solution, proves the theory, or adapts the part."

Wolf developed a method of counting coins by weight and sold it to the El Cortez casino in Las Vegas. They were so grateful for his help, they presented him with a clock they had made ringed with a variety of coins. He pioneered coin counting scales, now manufactured and sold to casinos everywhere.

Wolf adapted Toledo's first "in-motion" truck scale from a standard truck scale and installed it at the Beaumont-Banning weighing station near Los Angeles. The driver could weigh his load while continuing to move over the scale if he did not exceed five mph.

Wolf always used existing parts, which was a key to his popularity in home office manufacturing circles. Toledo's first 100-foot long platform scale was installed at the Riverside plant of the California Cement Company. With Wolf's suggestions, again using standard parts, the scale was completely assembled at the Toledo plant before being shipped to Riverside.

Wolf designed a new concept counting scale. Previously, the ratio method was used (e.g. one item weighed two oz, so a dozen would weigh one lb eight oz). Wolf said, "The scale is actually a dumb animal. Like a computer, it knows what you tell it. By placing a sample on the platform, I established its own factor. A total count is achieved by digital means. Thanks to the cooperation of Home Office Engineering, the idea proved feasible and was built by Toledo."

At 100% Club sales meetings, Wolf was always surrounded by other Toledo salesmen who were seeking his ideas on how he might solve a problem they had. He often had a solution for them. His friends began to call him an "Imagineer", a term coined by the late Walt Disney.

Erich Wolf remained humble all through his career. He said, "The ideas and innovations I've been able to come up with are possible only with the trust and cooperation of engineering personnel and management at the home office. My thanks to them for their encouragement."

CHAPTER 25

"I've sold the company."

On Palm Sunday, 1966, a weather disaster hit Toledo…a violent tornado roared through the area. It bounced up and down damaging many area homes until it reached the factory building on Telegraph Road. It roared through the south end of the building, blowing out much of the wall and destroying all the garages just south of the plant, which had been built at the time the main plant was built in 1939. At the same time the tornado's vacuum sucked in a large part of the far north wall.

Since it was a Sunday, only a guard was on duty and he escaped injury. Had it happened on a work day there would certainly have been many casualties and probably some deaths. In North Toledo several deaths were caused by the same tornado when it moved on and struck that area.

The tornado could have wiped out production for months…perhaps years. Damage came very near to the Chart Room at the south end of the plant where all the master charts were stored. Had they been destroyed, the company would have been out of production for a long time.

People who came to work Monday morning were sent home, but production was disrupted for only a few days. Both the south and north walls were quickly rebuilt. The windows of the second floor offices of the marketing departments at the south end had been blown out too. Papers left in the offices the previous Friday were simply missing.

Terry had fallen behind in his work and had a stack of corre-spondence four inches high in his in-basket on Friday when he left work. The whole stack was missing when he returned to work. He worried about it. Some of it had to be important, he thought, and he didn't know who had written to him or what he could do about it.

Several weeks passed and he heard from no one. Then several months. Nobody complained that he had never responded. Terry said, "It's pretty obvious…people generate a lot of paper that clearly doesn't mean much. The correspondence couldn't been very im-portant after all."

The tornado became the excuse for everything that went wrong for about a year afterwards. If a delivery was missed, it was because of the tornado. If a department fell behind, it was because of the tor-nado. It was a convenient excuse for anyone who needed an excuse.

Almost immediately after the tornado, a new addition to re-pair the main plant began. The Chart Room's brush with disaster caused it to be relocated in a reinforced area. A heavily protected room was included for all the master charts. The area included a clean-room environment for micro-charts, which were needed for an expanding line of sophisticated products. A number of other departments were relocated or enlarged as well.

The addition included a new, modern air-conditioned cafete-ria with a unique type of arrangement to speed up food service and shorten waiting time. The old Hickory House which had offered food service since the plant first opened was converted to offices for the Toledo Scale Federal Credit Union.

The garages were not rebuilt. For the first time in about 25 years top management people had to leave their cars outside in the elements like everyone else.

Meanwhile, Toledo scales began to appear more often in many Hollywood movies and television shows produced on the West Coast. Toledo had lent scales for props at no cost to Hollywood studios for many years, but now requests increased.

A California firm named Commercial Studio Rentals reversed the old system in which some manufacturers paid a public rela-

tions firm to promote products in movies and television. Toledo
never did this. The firm rented the props at a modest cost to the
studios. The manufacturer provided the products free to get widespread free exposure.

The company was founded by Fred Kline, long-time Hollywood public relations expert. "I did some quiet research," Kline
said, "and found that there was a big market for product props. I
found that many companies would gladly supply their products
to get them used as props on top television shows and movies."
His firm became a single source for producers to find authentic
props by arranging to rent them for a small fee to studios.

"Since the studios don't have to chase all over for different props,
they're quite willing to pay a small fee," Kline explained. "Many producers feel real products lend the set a highly desirable authenticity."

Toledo Scale became one of Kline's suppliers. In just a few months
Toledo scales had been briefly loaned by the Los Angeles office to
appear on *The Andy Griffith Show, Gomer Pyle, U.S.M.C.* and other
top-rated television shows. The Toledo name was always easy to identify. Much invaluable publicity resulted. The Toledo brand name became even further entrenched in the minds of the public.

Hollywood wasn't the only place that made movies. Thousands of industrial 16 mm motion pictures were being made in
the nation during the '60s. Toledo Scale had made several just in
recent years. Among the first was to tell the story of Verilux 711.
Then came "Sequel to Success" introducing the Valuematic II.
Continuous loop 8 mm copies of both movies were made and used
in portable projectors . . . one for each region.

Next came "Checkpoint Charlie", a film written and produced
by Bernard J. Stanton, a sales promotion specialist in Toledo Systems. The film illustrated the variety of uses for Toledo's
checkweigher system. It illustrated the quick, accurate weight inspection of small packages going over the checkweigher in-motion
at several hundred packages per minute.

"Checkpoint Charlie" won an international film competition.
It was awarded a first-place gold medal at the Ipac-Ima Exhibition

in Milan, Italy. Ipac-Ima was a major international exhibition dedicated to material handling, food processing and packaging equipment. "Checkpoint Charlie" was in competition with 18 films from six countries.

The medal was presented to Bernie Stanton by Vice President, International Frank Parmelee in Parmelee's office. An earlier award ceremony was held at the U.S. Trade Center in Milan. Representatives of Toledo Italiana accepted the award on Stanton's behalf and forwarded the gold medal to Parmelee. Stanton discovered the medal was real 18 carat gold.

Thoughts turned to the next 100% Club meeting, planned for April 1967. Weinandy had been hearing about Pheasant Run, a new resort on Fox River a bit west of Chicago's O'Hare airport. With his wife Jeanne, he went there to inspect it. He liked what he saw.

Pheasant Run was meeting-oriented. It featured an enclosed replica of Bourbon Street, reminiscent of the successful New Orleans meeting. Along the street were little shops, boutiques and grills. And the resort featured professional stage plays every other night…ideal entertainment right on the site. About 200 Toledo salesmen would attend, including 19 from Canada who were invited for the first time.

Weinandy told Instone, "It looks ideal. The men can be kept together day and night. No reason to go out on the town." After two successful meetings, management had a lot of confidence in Weinandy. They agreed with his choice.

It proved to be a popular one with everyone…except the golfers. Since it was held in early spring, only the hardiest enthusiasts played golf, and then for only nine holes.

Weinandy had his third consecutive 100% Club meeting under his belt.

In the spring of 1967, Frank Parmelee convinced McIntosh that a technical expert should visit the European affiliates. Parmelee was concerned that Toledo was falling behind. They chose Don Hall to make the trip. Hall said, "They told me to go over there and see what the hell was wrong." At the same time he was to see what European competitors were doing.

Hall first visited the huge Hanover Fair in Germany. All European scale companies exhibited in Hanover. During his three days there, he was able to pick up valuable technical information on a dozen or so scale competitors. Next he visited the Toledo operations in Cologne, Brussels and Zurich. He discovered all the affiliates had problems, many caused by the fact that European accuracy standards were higher than in the U.S. and were not met by standard scales shipped over there.

While in Zurich, arrangements were made for Hall to visit the research laboratories of Mettler Instrument A.G., the first documented contact between Mettler and Toledo Scale at Mettler's headquarters. Mettler's assistant sales manager A. Spoerri, and assistant research director E. Grunder spent about half a day with him. Discussions centered around the possibility of Mettler supplying a low capacity electrical output scale to Toledo for use in automatic counting.

Hall's report made many recommendations to solve the problems at the Toledo affiliates. And about his Mettler visit he said, "The Mettler people were most gracious, although extremely constrained." The discussions were held in a new building housing the research facility along with the sales department. "This association is significant since it's in line with other evidence of the strong influence—almost domination—exercised by the technical side of European weighing firms," he wrote.

"Prior to my visit I was informed that Mettler was preparing to enter the checkweighing or automatic filling business," Hall said. "There was no evidence of this in the facility I visited…but this is not of great significance since my tour was carefully directed. Mettler is without question well qualified to enter either of these fields if they choose. It would be consistent with their present product line."

In August 1967, Toledo Scale was honored by Chevrolet for 30 years of contributions to the All-American Soap Box Derby. Special ceremonies were held in Akron in front of a sellout crowd of 70,000 spectators, prior to the final runoff. The ceremonies

recognized that Toledo had weighed-in all of the Derby participants at all the finals in Akron and most local derbies around the
world for 30 years.

During the ceremonies Pete Estes, Chevrolet General Manager, presented a plaque to Toledo Scale's General Manager Frank
Instone. Toledo made friends in high places. Pete Estes became the
president of General Motors Corporation a few years later.

Some time previously, Geoff Gray was replaced as advertising
manager by Dick Herron. Early in 1967, Herron was given a special public relations assignment with a separate budget to fund it.
He was told that the objective was to raise the awareness about the
company in the marketplace with emphasis on the financial community.

To handle the assignment, Toledo Scale's agency hired two
skilled public relations people…one who specialized in financial
public relations.

Toledo management thought that their stock was undervalued. They wanted to do something to raise its trading price. Many
other undervalued companies had been successful in boosting the
value of their stock through financial public relations activities.

Since many U.S. companies were going through mergers at
the time, those Toledo employees who were aware of the effort
speculated that Toledo was preparing to seek a major acquisition
by merging a large, compatible company into Toledo Scale.

In mid-year the public relations assignment was abruptly canceled and the budget withdrawn. It appeared that management's
objectives had changed. Since not too many employees were aware
of the effort in the first place, no unusual internal speculation took
place. Dick Herron resigned to become advertising manager for
Toledo Edison, and Bob Terry was named to replace him.

On a Sunday afternoon in the early fall of 1967, Ted Metcalf
got a phone call from Greg Rothe. "Ted," Rothe said, "I want you
to be at the plant at 7 p.m. tonight for an important meeting. Just
go on in to the main conference room."

"What's it all about, Greg?"

"I can't tell you. Just be there. It's important."

Metcalf and Rothe had become good friends, and Metcalf was somewhat surprised that Rothe's message was so terse. He arrived at the conference room a few minutes early. A small group of the company's top executives were already there…all with bigger jobs than his.

Metcalf figured he was there to represent his boss, Frank Parmelee, who was out of the country.

Sharply at 7 p.m. McIntosh stood and walked to the head of the room. "I have some important news," he said, "and I wanted you to hear it directly from me." He paused.

"I've sold the company," he said quietly.

There was a hush. "Toledo Scale will be merged into the Reliance Electric Company of Cleveland through an exchange of stock," he said. "All company managers and supervisors will be called to the cafeteria at nine tomorrow morning. We'll tell them all about it then."

"I've determined that none of my children are interested in the business," he said. "There's really no one in the family who wants to learn this job, and we have to be sure the company's future is in solid hands for all our sakes. My family. Your families. All our employees and their families. Everyone. So without considering any conglomerates, we went looking for a merger."

McIntosh paused and wiped his eyes. Metcalf saw that he was wiping away tears. "And we've determined that Reliance is a solid, well-managed company. Though it's not nearly as well known as we are, it's about twice our size in terms of annual sales. Reliance had sales of over $172 million in their fiscal year that just ended October 31. We had sales of $88 million last year."

Gesturing to Rothe he said, "Greg here helped us narrow the possibilities and find Reliance. Now, we'll answer questions."

After McIntosh and Rothe answered several questions about Reliance, the group broke up and walked slowly to their individual cars in deep thought.

Early the next morning the blockbuster announcement was made in the cafeteria to company managers and supervisors, but the news had already been printed in the morning paper. Toledo Scale would be merged into the Reliance Electric Company of Cleveland.

Employees whispered to each other. "Who is Reliance Electric?," they asked. Instone talked about "synergy", how one and one can equal three. It was the first time most people in the meeting had ever heard the word. To them, the important thing was that Toledo Scale would no longer be independent…it would become a division of Reliance Electric, a little-known company, even if twice as large.

The merger marked the end of Toledo Scale as a locally owned and operated independent company, one of Toledo's top ten employers. And many predicted that it marked the beginning of the end of Toledo Scale in Toledo, Ohio.

Almost immediately a rumor went through the organization that Harris McIntosh had changed his mind about seeking to acquire another company. The story was his wife, Betty, wanted him to retire…and she was sure that if a major company was acquired, her husband would not want to retire for many more years. He was already 63-years-old.

The story claimed that she wanted to take a slow, leisurely trip around the world with him very soon…so he could learn how to relax and enjoy the remaining years of their lives together. They both loved to travel and had made many good friends on their visits to company offices overseas.

They could certainly afford it. And, as the daughter of W. W. Knight, Sr., it was said she encouraged family members who controlled large blocks of Toledo Scale stock to be on her side in her discussions with her husband.

So instead of moving ahead to seek another company, McIntosh asked Toledo Scale's controller, Greg Rothe, to find a compatible company that might want to acquire Toledo. No conglomerates were to be considered. Talks were held with several candidates…but when Rothe talked to Reliance, they appeared to be the most compatible since they had a number of common customers with Toledo.

After the merger Greg Rothe was the first to leave and find a new job, knowing that Reliance needed only one corporate controller. He successfully completed his assignment…aware that he would work himself out of a job in the process.

A year or so before they merged with Toledo Scale, Reliance had funded a half-million-dollar advertising and financial public relations campaign using the slogan, "For Fresh Ideas in Automation". Their stock began to trade at a higher price. In September 1967 Reliance acquired Dodge Manufacturing Company of Mishawaka, Indiana, which generated more interest in Reliance within the financial community.

Reliance stock rose again. During the same time frame, the price of Toledo Scale stock remained static.

This prompted some to observe that Reliance had acquired Toledo Scale for not too much more than the half-million-dollar cost of the campaign…saying they got a really good deal for a company the size of Toledo Scale. It had returned a good profit on sales of $88 million in the year prior to the merger.

In *The Blade* story that reported on the merger, it stated that compatibility was the key word that prompted it. Toledo was heavily involved in the competitive electronics industry, which demands a costly research and development program.

"It's increasingly difficult for most companies to keep up to date and cover a broad spectrum of technology without a large business to support it," McIntosh said. "Reliance is doing R&D work in areas similar to that being done at Toledo Scale. Together the two firms can step up this program on a more economical basis."

Hugh Luke, Reliance president, visualized the two operations fitting together to produce packaged systems. "Pressure is on industry to automate 'batch' operations due to increases in material and labor costs, which means there's more demand for greater precision and faster production," he said. "Toledo Scale has wider experience than Reliance in international markets, and this also could be a road to expansion of the overall operation."

Reliance products were manufactured overseas by jointly-owned companies in Mexico, Japan, Switzerland and Australia, and by a Belgian licensee. They also had a Swiss partner, Schindler A.G., a leading European manufacturer of elevators, who together with Reliance owned and operated Schindler-Reliance Electronic A.G.

The Reliance board of directors was expanded to 14 members with the addition of Harris McIntosh, H. L. Thompson, Jr., and W. W. Knight, Jr., McIntosh's brother-in-law. The Knight family was a major shareholder in Toledo Scale. All three had been directors of Toledo Scale.

The merger called for Toledo Scale to maintain its corporate identity with its present management. It would operate as TOLEDO SCALE Division of Reliance Electric Company. Haughton Elevator was to remain an operating division of Toledo Scale.

Clarence Weinandy began to plan for the 1968 100% Club meeting. He had learned to do it early since the best were often booked well in advance. He and his wife Jeanne searched out possible locations in Charleston, South Carolina, Clearwater, Florida, and St. Louis, Missouri.

He found the ideal spot at the Jack Tar Hotel in Clearwater and booked it on the spot. The hotel had a large theatre-like auditorium, ideal for the general meeting. Again he arranged for all the required meeting rooms for the various activities, set up the menu for all three days, and plotted the flow of traffic. He was ready for 1968.

CHAPTER 26

Strike!

Toledo's labor contract with the UAW expired within a few months of the merger. The union began tough negotiations with the new Reliance negotiating team. No longer were McIntosh and Gosser available to work it out between themselves as they had in the past. The negotiations soon failed. When it became clear the negotiations were failing—and failing badly—the union called a strike.

The strike began March 14, 1968. It was bitter and occasionally violent. The union set up picket lines. The number of pickets were not limited…there were often many, mostly near the entrance to the parking lot. Management employees crossed the lines and kept working. Rumors were rampant along the line.

The union installed a primitive barrier arm across the entrance to the driveway and stopped every car in and out, glaring at the driver to let it be known that they knew the individuals who were crossing the line.

The cafeteria had been closed when the strike began. Instone ordered Terry to have the advertising department set up their 16 mm movie camera on a tripod in a cafeteria window, which overlooked the driveway entrance area.

Terry was told to have the camera manned by department people every morning, noon and afternoon during the times management employees were entering or leaving the parking lot…and photograph every scene that looked like trouble could start. A schedule was set up in the advertising department to man the camera.

The union came to believe that management employees were taking parts out of the plant in the trunks of their cars every evening when they went home. They thought management ordered this so several remote operations could continue to make scales and supply replacement parts to the field. In case this was true, they wanted to put a stop to it.

Shortly after the strike began, the line of cars leaving the plant was especially slow moving. The pickets left the barrier down and asked each driver to open his trunk for inspection. If the driver refused to get out of his car and open his trunk they left the barrier down.

The driver had a choice...open his trunk, or drive through the closed barrier past pickets who were holding logs to throw under the wheels, and carrying bricks and chunks of concrete. The pickets appeared ready for action.

The intimidation worked. Every driver soon came to automatically get out of his car and open his trunk every time he left the parking lot...even for lunch. Nothing was ever found in the trunk of any car. Still, the inspection continued for months. Every car continued to be stopped at the barrier, to enter the parking lot as well. The driver was scrutinized by a picket. After his inspection the picket would saunter to the barrier, slowly raise it. The driver was permitted to pass while other pickets stood near ready to throw something. This continued day after day, week after week.

It couldn't last. Returning from lunch one day, Bob Bradley apparently decided he wasn't going to take any more of this nonsense. Bradley was normally calm, even-tempered and quiet spoken. He had been head of the company's engineering department until moving to international operations as their chief engineer.

Mumbling as he turned towards the gate, he abruptly speeded up and attempted to smash through the barrier. The strikers had a few seconds to react as Bradley accelerated. One threw a large log under a front wheel as others smashed his windshield, door windows and the car body with their concrete blocks and bricks. The car continued through the barrier pushing the log ahead of it until it stopped inside the property about 50 feet past the now broken bar.

He abandoned the car along the driveway to the parking lot. It was a mess. It looked like it had been hit by a truck. Bradley got out on the driver's side, apparently unhurt. He walked around his car checking the damage as the strikers yelled and cursed at him from the gate area. In a daze, he walked into the plant, then to his office in the international department.

The police had been called and arrived en masse. First they asked the strikers what had happened, working to calm them down. The police then called for Bradley who returned to his car to answer their questions. The officer taking his statement asked him. "Didn't you think something like this might happen? You could have been seriously hurt. What made you do it?"

Still in a bit of a daze, Bradley thought about his answer. "I don't know," he said. "Really I don't. Suddenly a feeling came over me…the hell with them, I've had enough of their crap. I just did it on the spur of the moment. I just wanted to get back to work, that's all. The hell with them."

John Portwood, a company attorney, had been trying to get the court to limit the number of pickets. Now with the Bradley violence he thought he had a good chance to get an injunction. After talking to Bradley, he asked Terry, "Did your camera operator get it on film?"

"I'm pretty sure he did," Terry said. "He had the camera running all the time…but everything happened so fast…"

"Well, get the film processed right away," Portwood told him. "I need it for court in the morning…I've got an emergency court time scheduled and I'm going for an injunction."

The film was processed that evening. It showed the whole scene clearly. Terry and the camera operator were told to bring it to court by 10 a.m. the next morning with a projector in case they needed to show it to the judge. But Portwood got his injunction without the need to show the film. No one outside top management ever saw it.

The number of pickets was limited by the injunction…but not as limited as Portwood had requested. A large number were permitted. The judge refused to consider the barrier issue. The strikers repaired their barrier and continued to stop every car. Nothing changed. Yet people on both sides seemed to avoid doing anything that would provide an excuse for more violence. The strike continued.

The Toledo Scale strike was only a tiny example of a period of violence that hit the nation. The times themselves were violent.

Two major tragedies affected the country during the months of the strike. First, on April 4, Dr. Martin Luther King was slain in Memphis. Race riots broke out all over the U.S. Then only two months later on June 6, Robert Kennedy was assassinated in Los Angeles while campaigning for president. The country mourned them both, worried about the spread of violence.

During the strike, a replacement was named for McIntosh. Bob Metzger was named Group Vice President of the Toledo Group, which included Toledo Scale, Haughton Elevator and Toledo Kitchen Machines. He came from Columbus, Indiana where he had been manager of the Reliance Master Electric Division. He was a graduate of MIT and had served in several Reliance executive positions.

At the same time Frank Parmelee was appointed general manager of Reliance Electric International, a new division. This recognized that Parmelee was the most experienced international executive in the combined companies. He reported directly to Reliance President Hugh Luke. Ted Metcalf replaced Parmelee as General Manager of Toledo Scale's International Operations.

Shortly after the merger, Toledo's engineering staff, led by Bob Bell, met with Reliance engineering executives in Cleveland. Not long after this meeting, Bill Howe, vice president of engineering for Reliance, called Toledo engineer Don Hall on the phone. "Don, what do you plan to do in the future?" Hall replied, "I'd like to stay right here, with Toledo."

About a week later Howe arranged a breakfast meeting in Toledo with Hall. Howe said, "Don, Bob won't be in this morning…he left the company. How would you like to be his replacement?" Hall learned for the first time that his boss, Bob Bell, had left at Howe's instigation.

Hall was pleased to accept. He had been a Toledo engineer for 13 years. Most recently he had directed research and development engineering. With his wide ranging elevator and scale engineering experience he was a logical candidate. The appointment was a popular one. For one thing, a Toledo Scale engineer had been promoted to the job instead of a Reliance engineer.

Meanwhile the thought of going ahead with the previously scheduled 100% Club sales meeting at Clearwater, Florida, had to be faced. Weinandy had booked it the previous year. Hundreds of Toledo salesmen from around the U.S. and Canada had earned a trip to Florida.

Yet these were commissioned salesmen with nothing to sell as long as the strike continued. Their income was drastically cut. After everything was considered it was decided to go ahead with the 100% Club meeting even if it was filled with gloomy, unhappy salesmen.

Rather than attempt to introduce improved products or conduct sales seminars, Jenkins agreed with the idea proposed by advertising manager Terry to build an entertaining program. A Chicago producer was hired. He wrote a script that was a take-off on a Broadway musical complete with music and dancing.

It told the story of the troubles faced by the first female Toledo sales representative, a fanciful thought at the time. No one there would have believed there would be several bright, attractive females actually employed by the company as sales representatives within the next five years.

The producer hired three professional actors for the starring roles and worked with a group of home office marketing people to fill out the other roles. The play proved to be a hit. The leaders of the 100% Club declared it made the meeting a success by taking their minds off their troubles. They began to share ideas on how they could buy and refurbish used scales to serve the urgent needs of their customers until new scales would be available again.

Golf, fishing and other sports activities cheered them up. Management talks reassured them that every effort was being made to settle the strike quickly, and they went home from Florida feeling better than when they had arrived. Not long after the meeting, Weinandy began to look for a location for the 1969 meeting.

He had obtained promotional material on the Bahamas and checked out several options, finally booking the meeting in the Grand Bahama Resort and Country Club on Grand Bahama Island.

Jenkins was willing to consider the Bahamas because of his confidence in Weinandy. He also believed something special would be needed to counter the negative feelings caused by the lingering strike. Weinandy gave notice that he planned to retire to Cape Coral, Florida at the end of July 1968 with the understanding that he would assist in the 1969 100% Club meeting from his Florida home.

Jenkins announced the location for the next meeting well in advance as the strike continued to provide the extra incentive the 1969 meeting in the Bahamas would generate.

The strike continued. It lasted through the spring and summer. In the middle of July, company and union officials joined in asking Toledo's Labor-Management-Citizens Committee to mediate the negotiations. Walter Murphy, UAW regional director, termed the move "a last resort" effort. The session failed but the parties agreed to try again in late July.

Then on August 7, a tentative agreement was reached. The union ratified the agreement the following Saturday. After almost five months the barrier across the driveway came down and the strike was over.

The violent period in America was not yet over, however. Within weeks of the strike settlement, protesters shouted their disdain for the 1968 Democratic National Convention in Chicago with protests over the Vietnam War.

At Mayor Richard Daley's request, the governor ordered over 5,000 Illinois National Guardsmen to round-the-clock duty to head off threats of "tumult, riot, or mob disorder". The nation watched on television as Chicago police bludgeoned, beat and maced the protesters outside the convention center.

Amid the tear gas and blood, over 100 people were injured including children, the elderly, and members of the press who were watching when police turned on the crowd. Daley was blamed for the police violence. Millions of Americans witnessed the violence in the streets and on the convention floor on television. Hubert Humphrey won the nomination for president on a platform supporting the war. His candidacy was however seriously wounded when Senator Ribicoff, a fellow democrat, objected on television to Mayor Daley's "Gestapo tactics" against the protesters.

When the settlement had finally ended the strike at Toledo Scale, Dick Moss wrote the lead in *Toledo System* magazine. It was headed by a 1907 Henry Adams quote: "At best, the renewal of broken relations is a nervous matter."

Moss wrote, "For the past few days, the greeting 'welcome back' has echoed throughout our plant. Old friends, so recently divided by issues, are carefully renewing old relationships. The time, then, is one of healing...of beginning to work together in peace and friendship towards a common goal."

"For now our thoughts must turn to those upon whom we all depend...our customers. Our relations with many good customers have been damaged. This damage can only be assuaged by the ability to supply traditional Toledo Scale quality products as swiftly as possible. Please help, because to survive, we must be able to say to customers, too—'welcome back'".

Next, Metzger named Reliance executive Mel Zeitz controller of the Toledo Scale Group. Like Metzger, Zeitz came from Columbus, Indiana where he had been controller of the Reliance Master Division. He had reported to Metzger there.

Toledo management people had the feeling that Hugh Luke tended to blame the existing management for the strike. Whether or not this was true, Dick Moss resigned soon after. He remained in Toledo and became an executive recruiter, having acquired a franchise from one of the large firms that specialized in recruiting top executives for large companies.

Luke gave McIntosh one more troubling task while he was still available. McIntosh invited Instone to lunch at the Toledo Club. He insisted they order a drink. When the drinks were served and lunch ordered, Instone asked, "What can I do for you, Harris?"

McIntosh grimaced. "Frank, I have to ask you for your resignation."

Instone paused a moment. "You got it," he replied.

After returning from lunch, Instone packed up his personal belongings and was out of his office by mid-afternoon. The news swept through the building.

Reliance had taken over completely.

McIntosh had vacated his office in the plant for Bob Metzger. He rented an office in the National Bank Building in downtown Toledo for personal business but was rarely seen by anyone.

When his many friends within the company approached him about a retirement party or ceremony to mark the end of his more than 20 years of Toledo Scale leadership, he refused to have anything to do with it. He was firm—no retirement party for him—saying that he simply wouldn't attend.

He appeared to take his lead from the farewell speech General Douglas MacArthur made before the U.S. Congress after he was fired by President Truman. MacArthur closed his speech with his famous remark, "Old soldiers never die, they just fade away."

By his own firm choice, Harris McIntosh did indeed choose to simply "fade away".

PART IV

et al.

"I am the only child of parents who weighed, measured and priced everything; for whom could not be weighed, measured and priced had no existence."
Charles Dickens, 1857, "Little Dorrit"

CHAPTER 27

Leadership Changes Again

Employee apprehension over the leadership changes at the Toledo Scale Division remained even as business continued to grow and new products were developed. Reliance continued to bring in their own people as top managers.

The product marketing department was reorganized as Gloer Helman was transferred from Reliance as General Product Manager. The marketing managers of custom, standard industrial and retail reported to him.

Parmelee encouraged Don Hall to return to Europe in 1969 to see what progress had been made in the European affiliates since his last trip two years before. Metzger approved the trip. Metzger's career was strictly in managing U.S. plant operations.

He had no international experience. As a result, he arranged to meet Hall in Brussels to show him around Europe and introduce him to the people running the various Toledo affiliates. With Metzger in tow, Hall saw that the affiliates had adopted many of the recommendations he had detailed in his 1967 report.

1969 marked the real surge of electronic products at Toledo Scale. The first completely successful electronic digital indicator, the Model 8130, was developed by Roger Williams early in the year. It provided outstanding zero stability and established Toledo's leadership position in electronic scales and indicators. More electronic scales and instruments quickly followed.

Don Hall used Toledo industrial designer Cecil Blank to design the 8130. Blank continued his design work for Toledo including almost all of Toledo's first series of electronic instruments.

Fundamental changes in several basic industries had taken place. One of the most notable was the beef packing industry, sparked by the success of chicken factories. The founders of Iowa Beef Packers, Currier Holman and A. D. Anderson, stated their philosophy:

"IBP is not just another slaughterer," they wrote, "it is a complete beef factory. It is involved not just in the slaughter of beef, but also in the marketing and distribution of beef. IBP's goal is to eliminate gross waste in the present system and to recover part of these high costs as profit. It is somewhat ironic that in order to bring about these efficiencies in beef production today, we must rebuild an industry and reshape its economic pattern."

Centralized cutting and packaging became a reality for the company after completion of the world's largest beef-producing plant. This development, which resulted in extraordinary profits for IBP, was the result of identifying and solving many problems, among them the one of proper weight control.

IBP's problem was to get both packaged beef and beef carcasses weighed in-motion as quickly and accurately as possible. They had to get the beef packaged and sent to the stores as quickly as possible to maintain freshness. To do this, the meat had to be processed at high speed on an assembly line basis. This immediately ruled out any hand weighing methods that would slow down the prepackaging process.

Toledo Scale's Systems Division developed the Expressweigh, which solved IBP's problem. It provided random weight package handling, instant in-motion weighing and data recording. Weight data was recorded in a fraction of a second after an item reached the scale.

At the Dakota City plant, boxes of vacuum-packed cuts such as tenderloins, sirloins and briskets moved across the Toledo balanced belt conveyors in-motion at a top speed of 20 boxes per minute. Weight and product identification was recorded remotely.

A code pattern established at the packing station was scanned by photo-eyes and recorded the product ID.

Using the Toledo Expressweigh system, which weighed, recorded, and tabulated vacuum-packed sub-primal cuts at a rate of 20 boxes per minute, permitted IBP to handle over 1000 boxes of meat per hour.

IBP also handled beef carcasses, which required accurate weighing of all hanging beef sent out. Toledo installed four Expressweigh overhead track scale systems, two for production and two for shipping, with data recording taking place automatically.

The systems had classification circuitry so the operator could establish weight zones. The carcasses were automatically switched onto one of three lines: light, medium or heavy. The sorting system was also used to grade beef into prime, choice, or good categories.

The systems handled about 1000 items per hour. The two shipping systems fed their stored data into adding machines that provided a record of individual weight with grade designation and weight class. IBP led the way to modern beef handling systems.

The market for beer was expanding also. All three of the largest brewers had nearly reached their capacity. Toledo Scale's System Division participated in a big way in fabricating equipment for the increasing number of breweries. Toledo Systems was a producer of control systems and batching panels, for not only the brewing industry, but other industries as well.

Most of Toledo Systems business came through engineering and construction firms since most brewers preferred to let them do the design, procurement and construction of the entire project. These consultants in turn chose Toledo Systems.

The same Toledo project engineers were involved with every new or expanded brewery. They quickly learned to "talk the language" when formulating control sequences. Not only could they interpret and execute specifications, but also offer solid contributions to the project. Their product knowledge and specialization, combined with automation, made Toledo Scale specialists in the brewing industry.

Others became specialists in the glass and rubber batching industries. Full computer control of the weighing process through the use of mini-computers and microprocessors began. Technology had been advancing rapidly since the end of World War II.

This became clearer in March 1969, when the French-British Concorde made its first flight. Relatively soon it began to cross the Atlantic in three and a half hours at twice the speed of sound.

Technology showed its most dramatic advance in July when Neil Armstrong and Buzz Aldrin descended from the Apollo 11 Lunar Module to walk on the surface of the moon. Much of the world watched the momentous event on television as Neil Armstrong took "a small step for man, a giant leap for mankind". The TV audience was estimated at 600 million people, one-fifth of the Earth's population.

Advances in technology had brought the U.S. space program a long way since 1961, when President Kennedy pledged that the United States would place a man on the moon and bring him safely back before the end of the decade.

But it wasn't just the well-publicized breakthroughs in space technology that made space exploration feasible. At the same time, fantastic discoveries were made in lightweight, rehydratable foods carried aboard Apollo 11 for the astronaut's meals.

The rehydratable foods had to be reconstituted with water to eat. They were weighed out on Toledo Laboratory Computagram scales, sensitive to 1/2 a gram in exacting amounts, then molded into bars to be quick frozen. After the frozen bars were removed from the molds, they were freeze dried to remove all moisture without changing the shape, color or taste.

A Toledo High Sensitivity Person Weigher was also used in the space program. It was built for the NASA Manned Spacecraft Center in Houston, Texas. Rigorous training, environmental experiments and other demanding performances could have a number of effects on astronauts in the manned space projects.

One variable is weight, and fluctuations were so critical that Toledo built a Person Weigher for Houston with a capacity of 150 kg, accurate to plus or minus 15 grams. In a small way, Toledo Scale helped the Apollo program reach the moon.

Sales were not overlooked. In 1968 the location of the upcoming December 100% Club meeting had been announced by Wes Jenkins. Clarence Weinandy had researched it prior to his retirement. It would be on Grand Bahama Island at the Grand Bahama Hotel and Country Club.

Jenkins, Field Operations Manager John McLellan and Bob Terry personally visited the location to check it out since it would be the first 100% Club meeting held outside the United States. Clarence Weinandy flew over from his home in Cape Coral to join them.

By October, the incentive provided by a meeting in the Bahamas was working. October 1969, was the greatest single sales month in Toledo Scale history. A total of 347 orders for both industrial and retail products was processed by the Customer Order Center with the dollar volume setting a new record.

Customer Order Center Manager Tom Siegler said, "The race to qualify for the 100% Club trip to the Bahamas plus the neck and neck contest of three sales regions for the President's Cup stimulated this tremendous surge of business. Verna Miller, who registers industrial orders, and Virginia Konecny, who does the same for retail, did a great job keeping up."

Reliance management became convinced that the Toledo industrial sales force had to be converted to all engineers, the same as the Reliance sales force. The Toledo Group created a new post and named Bob Terry as Manager, Management and Development to assure the availability of qualified technical manpower for all three divisions— Toledo Scale, Haughton Elevator and Reliance International.

The program included recruiting management level personnel for sales, engineering, financial and service operations to achieve a broader and stronger marketing and management organization for the Toledo Group.

Since Reliance sales people were salaried, it was announced that the Toledo industrial sales force would also become salaried, as engineers were hired to replace commissioned industrial salesmen. The technology explosion would require engineers to sell technical products. No change was contemplated for retail sales-men. Retail would remain commissioned.

From the beginning of Toledo Scale in 1901, industrial sales-men had been compensated on a commissioned basis. Many made a large amount of money with their commissions. It was believed, however, that engineers would not accept a commission arrange-ment, another reason for the change.

As word got out about the change, many of the top industrial salesmen resigned, seeing that their compensation would be re-duced. Most of them quickly found commissioned jobs with com-petitive scale companies.

A recession the following year put a stop to the recruiting. The post of Manager, Management and Development was eliminated and Terry was first given a special assignment to develop an entirely new industrial catalog, then again was named advertising manager.

Manfred Mundelius, Toledo's manager of marketing services, found it impossible to comprehend all the changes. Fred Mundelius had a fascinating background. He was born and raised in Nazi Germany and was about 13-years-old at the end of World War II. He had been a "Hitler Youth" as required by German law.

Mundelius had been raised by his mother alone after his fa-ther had been killed in a mine accident when he was a little boy. Towards the end of the war, his mother rented a house in the Black Forest to avoid the bombing.

When Patton's Third Army invaded Germany and swept through the area, Mundelius and his mother were abruptly kicked out of the house by Patton's staff. The famous General used the house as his headquarters for a day or two, then moved on.

Mundelius said, "It turned out to be the best thing that hap-pened to us during the war. When Patton and his staff moved out, we moved back in. We discovered that they had left quantities of food and other supplies in the house. My mother somehow made the food last for months."

After the war, the American government established a pro-gram under the Marshall Plan that permitted qualified German youth to be educated in the United States. Highly intelligent, Mundelius met the standards for the program.

He was invited to live in Green Bay, Wisconsin, in the home of a man who was the publisher of the Green Bay newspaper and had become a three-star General in the American Army during the war. He became part of the family and finished high school in Green Bay. After high school, the family sent him to Lawrence College in nearby Appleton, the General's alma mater. Mundelius went on to earn an MBA from the prestigious University of Chicago before joining Toledo Scale as market research manager. Later he was promoted to manager of marketing services.

In spite of all the changes that Mundelius thought were wrong, industrial scale sales held up. A big, friendly, bear of a man, he propounded his theory for why they held up to all that would listen. "You know," he said, "Even if Toledo Scale hired someone whose only job was to destroy the company, he would fail! The Toledo brand name is so strong, so powerful, by God, he would fail!"

Mundelius was recruited away to the Foremost Insurance Company in Grand Rapids, Michigan. In turn he recruited several other executives to Foremost, including Toledo's training manager, Bill McDonagh. Mundelius was replaced as marketing services manager by Ed Harrigan who had been with Owens Corning Fiberglas in sales and marketing.

John Landis was named Vice President of Marketing. Landis was another Reliance executive reassigned to the Toledo Scale Division. Then Wes Jenkins abruptly resigned, perhaps due to all the changes in the industrial selling organization he had no control over.

An experienced Reliance sales manager, Bill Prettyman, was brought in as general sales manager to replace Jenkins.

Bob Metzger concluded that Toledo Scale should go out of the food machine business after looking closely at the cost and profitability numbers. He told Quertinmont that Toledo would make an announcement they were going to discontinue making and selling all food machines.

Quertinmont was taken aback. "Bob, you can't do that," he said. "You can start to phase out food machines on a gradual basis, but if you announce that Toledo is going out of the food machine business, the whole industry is going to read that as if we're going out of the entire retail business. The impact on our scale business will be tremendous."

Metzger replied, "Well, we're not making any money on food machines, Ed. I'm just going to have to do it." He made the announcement, telling the field and all customers that Toledo was abandoning the food machine business and would discontinue production in the next few months when the inventory was gone.

Quertinmont immediately resigned. Retail scale sales plummeted, just as he had predicted. He quickly found a new job as sales manager for Bettcher Industries in Vermilion, Ohio, a manufacturer of high-quality meat processing equipment. Quertinmont had known the Bettchers for years. They were glad to get him. No one had as much industry knowledge.

Even more changes came soon. Reliance sold Toledo's Kitchen Machines Division to McGraw Edison since it didn't fit into the vision of automation.

General sales manager Bill Prettyman was not happy with his job. Even though they were both trained by Reliance, Prettyman appeared to have several differences of opinion with his boss, Landis. Whatever the reason, he resigned.

Don Boudinot, the Toledo Scale Division region manager in Detroit, was transferred to the home office as Prettyman's replacement.

Retail scale sales were a major problem. Boudinot talked to the people left in retail marketing to get their ideas on what could be done. He concluded the company needed to get Quertinmont back if they were to have any chance of solving their problems.

He said to retail marketing specialist Mel Mikols, "The first thing I'm going to do is talk to Ed Quertinmont and bring him back here as retail marketing manager." Don Boudinot had been the Buffalo district manager that caused Quertinmont to resign the first time over 20 years previously when he changed

Quertinmont's customers into house accounts. Now he took the opposite action, determined to bring him back.

Boudinot called Quertinmont. "Ed, what would it take to get you to come back?"

Quertinmont hesitated. After thinking it over he told Boudinot it would take three things the company probably wouldn't want to do to bring him back. "First," he said, "I must be treated as if I never left with no break in company service or pension."

"OK. What are the other two?" Boudinot asked.

"The others will be tougher for them," Quertinmont said. "Second, Metzger must agree to rescind the announcement about going out of the food machine business. He must agree to stay in the business. And third, the company must make a commitment to try to buy Wrapping Machinery Company."

Quertinmont knew that Hobart was the company Toledo had to compete against. And Hobart not only had an excellent complete line of food machines, they had recently bought Corley-Miller Wrapping Machine Company which filled out their automatic scale line with automatic labelers and wrappers.

Wrapping Machinery Company manufactured a high quality line of automatic labelers and meat wrappers under the trade name "Superwrapper" in Franksville, Wisconsin, a suburb of Milwaukee. If Quertinmont was going to come back and be successful, he knew he had to have the tools to compete with Hobart across the board. And Wrapping Machinery Company was the best bet.

Boudinot reported the conversation to Metzger, who in turn took the terms to Hugh Luke. They agreed to meet all three of Quertinmont's conditions. His length of service would be the same as if he never left, and Metzger did indeed rescind his announcement that Toledo would go out of the food machine business. In fact, he said that Toledo would be in the food machine business to stay.

Quertinmont rejoined the company for the second time in his career.

Not long after, Luke came over from Cleveland and spoke to Quertinmont. "Ed, we met the first two of the commitments we made to you," he said. "Now, what can we do to get the third one started?"

"Well, we're going to have to somehow make an approach to Wrapping Machinery Company."

"We don't want to make a direct approach on an acquisition," Luke said. "Here's what I suggest…let's get that law firm out of Chicago that specializes in acquisitions to approach them for us."

The law firm made the approach without identifying who was interested in buying them. They discovered that the management of Wrapping Machinery had recently come to the conclusion that they needed to affiliate with an automatic scale company if they were going to be able to compete effectively in the future. Hobart's acquisition of Corley-Miller had them worried.

Toledo Scale was identified to the Wrapping Machinery owners who agreed to a meeting. Luke and Quertinmont flew to Milwaukee in the Reliance company aircraft. They met with Wrapping Machinery president and majority owner Bill Stremke, and sales manager Vic Palmer. Negotiations were completed successfully and Wrapping Machinery Company became a part of the Toledo Scale Division.

With *Superwrapper* labelers and wrappers, Quertinmont now had the tools he needed to fit the Valuematic II into a complete, company manufactured, high-quality wrapping/weighing/labeling system. And management publicly stated that Toledo was in the food machine business to stay. He began to repair the damage in the marketplace.

In the early 1970s, a rumor went through the Toledo division headquarters that Reliance Electric was seriously thinking of changing Toledo Scale's name to Reliance. At the time, ad manager Terry obtained approval for a major research firm to conduct a study to determine what comes to the public's mind when the name of a city is mentioned.

The cities selected for the study were Akron, Atlanta, Cleveland, Los Angeles, Milwaukee, Pittsburgh, Rochester, Seattle, and Toledo. Many of these had what seemed to be an obvious connection to a given product or company.

Twelve cities other than those nine being studied were selected in which two questions were asked. More than 100 adults in each of the twelve locations were chosen at random in a shopping mall to provide the answers.

The questions were: "What is the first thing that comes to mind when you hear the word (city name)? Second, what company or product comes to mind that you associate with this city? In only three cities was there much of an association with anything. About Milwaukee, 86% answered "beer". About Toledo, 82% answered "scales". About Akron, 57% answered "rubber". While two of these cities were identified with a product, the only association with a given company was Toledo with scales.

For the other cities, more than four out of five answered "nothing". About Atlanta only 10% answered "Coca-Cola". About Los Angeles 15% answered "airplanes" (people thought movies were being made in Hollywood...not Los Angeles). And about Cleveland— home of Reliance Electric—only a combined 12% answered "Browns" or "Indians". Over 80% answered "nothing" about Cleveland.

Study results were sent to the advertising manager at Reliance headquarters in Cleveland and the rumors stopped.

Technology continued to advance rapidly. The advent of the microprocessor in the early '70s made greatly increased reliability possible. Toledo Scale was the first scale company to employ the Intel® MCS-4, using it in its 8200 series retail counter scales. Actually, Toledo was among the first half-dozen of Intel's customers.

Toledo engineers immediately saw the potential of this new technology. This led to the microprocessor playing a major role somewhere in the manufacture and performance of every electronic scale.

At a technical advisory board meeting in March 1971, a brief review of Toledo electronic computing scales was presented. The original Valuematic was conceived in 1954, marketed in 1960, and discontinued in 1966.

Its replacement was the Valuematic II, conceived in 1963 and marketed in 1966. And the third generation, the 8300, was con-

ceived in 1970 and marketed in late 1971. The 8200 counter
scale was conceived in 1970 and marketed in early 1971.

With electronics everything was happening faster. Products
were becoming obsolete much more rapidly. Investments in research and development projects had almost doubled in only eight
years, from about $400,000 in 1963 to about $750,000 in 1971.

Top management of the Toledo Group changed again. While
swimming in the ocean on vacation, Bob Metzger came into the
range of a large Portuguese man-of-war, a jellyfish with long, poi-
sonous tentacles. He was seriously poisoned over large parts of his
body. Recovery was slow.

He couldn't work and the prognosis was for a long recovery. Reliance decided to put him on extended sick leave and replace him.

Tony DiVincenzo became head of the Toledo Group. He had
been the manager of the Reliance custom plant in Cleveland before his assignment in Toledo. He was of average height, bald, with
a dark complexion. While soft spoken, DiVincenzo was a firm leader
with equally firm opinions on how things should be done. He
took charge immediately.

A Reliance area sales manager, Ben Dillon, was named General Product Manager, replacing Gloer Helman who "resigned to
pursue other interests". Like Prettyman before him, Helman was a
Reliance manager who was apparently not happy being in the
Toledo operation.

Dillon took right to the scale business. He proved to be a
popular and effective manager, soon becoming responsible for
marketing Toledo products world wide.

General sales manager Don Boudinot preferred working in
the field rather than the home office. He returned to Detroit as
region manager, and Don Zelazny, another Reliance sales manager, transferred to Toledo to replace Boudinot.

This was also the year that singer-songwriter Randy Sparks,
founder of the New Cristy Minstrels, found himself stuck in Toledo on a weekend between gigs. All the downtown movie theaters, night clubs and other action had moved to the suburbs. The

downtown area was dead. Sparks found nothing to do on his first visit to Toledo. His impression of the city was negative. This experience prompted him to write the song, "Saturday Night In Toledo, Ohio." The lyrics were not kind to the city's image. Popular singer John Denver performed the song at his first appearance on Johnny Carson's "Tonight" show. He recorded the song and it became a novelty hit for him. Mayor Harry Kessler was publicly outraged but most Toledoans enjoyed the satire.

Sparks knew little about the city and trusted his memory to write the second verse, which included: *"Ah, but let's not forget that the folks of Toledo unselfishly gave us the scales, 'No Springs—Honest Weight' was the promise they made, so smile and be thankful next time you get weighed…"*

Randy Sparks later became a popular guest of the city, singing the song he composed and adding updated lyrics. He even received the keys to the city from a later mayor, Donna Owens, in front of a huge, enthusiastic crowd on the city's riverfront during a Riverfest celebration.

CHAPTER 28

"Over a million dollars a year!"

The new 8400 digital electronic candy scale was completed in 1974. For the first time Toledo had a candy scale that displayed large, vacuum-fluorescent digits for the weight, the price-per-pound and the total value on both sides of the counter.

It was designed to replace mechanical fan-type candy scales with a price of $87 each. Yet the 8400 carried a suggested list price many times higher.

Ed Quertinmont took it first to Sears headquarters in Chicago. Sears and many other customers had used the $87 mechanical fan computing candy scale for decades. The first model was introduced in 1905 and it hadn't changed much since. Quertinmont knew he had to convince Sears that the new 8400 was worth a great deal more than what they were used to paying for a candy scale. He pondered—how could he convince them it was good value?

The evening before his scheduled presentation he and his wife, Ruby, checked into Chicago's Weston Hotel. He paced their room thinking about the approach he would take as Ruby watched. He knew the features cold. No mistakes reading the wrong column on a fan scale. But features didn't sell scales: benefits did. What was the real benefit? How would it pay for itself?

About 7 p.m. Quertinmont had an idea. As it happened, it was very similar to the idea Theobald had over 60 years before when he told salesmen to reweigh groceries that had been weighed on a spring scale and were bagged, ready to be delivered to a merchant's customers.

A nearby Sears store was open until 9 p.m. Quertinmont walked over to the store and bought seven different kinds of candy. "Give me 75 cents worth of that, and a dollar's worth of that, and I'll take a dollar and a quarter's worth of that…" until he had seven separate bags each with the different cost amount he had requested.

He watched the scale carefully, knowing the clerk would be careful to give him full value—and perhaps a bit more—if he watched.

He explained to the clerk that he was doing a survey and would like her to write the price per pound and the weights on the sales slip which had the value he had requested printed on it, then she was to staple the individual sales slips to seal each bag.

The next morning Quertinmont took the unopened bags of candy with him to Sears. They took him to a large meeting room with a chalkboard at the front, which contained a large number of chairs set up auditorium style. Much to his surprise there were about 50 people, including most of Sears merchandising vice presidents, in the room for his presentation…a much larger group than he had expected.

He began his presentation by showing the scale and discussing its digital electronic features.

Then he said, "I have something else to show you but I need your help. Last night I bought these seven bags of candy at your store down the street. I asked the clerk to write the price per pound and the weight on the slip that showed the price I paid."

He went to the blackboard and wrote two columns. "I don't know any more about what's going to happen here than you do," he said. "The bags were stapled shut when I bought them last night."

Then he pointed to a man in the audience. "Give me a hand, will you? What I'd like you to do is this…open this bag of candy and hand the sales slip to me. Notice the price per pound written on the slip and enter it on the keyboard. Now, look at the new scale…it's at zero? Fine. Now just pour the candy into the scoop.

The weight and price are shown immediately. Let's just write the price per pound, weight and total price on the blackboard."

He repeated this with a different member of the audience until the seven bags had been opened and priced by the new candy scale, writing the weight, price per pound and total price into the right hand column on the blackboard each time.

He said, "Now I need one final volunteer," pointing at another man in the audience. "Here, check all these sales slips, tell me what they say and I'll write it on the blackboard in the left hand column."

When he was through he added up both columns. At his request the audience agreed with his addition. "Well, look," he said. "I paid a total of $2.06 less for these seven bags of candy than I would have paid if they had been priced on the new Toledo 8400 Candy Scale the way you just priced them here. This means that Sears lost $2.06 on me...on just one customer."

Quertinmont began to calculate with a pencil and paper. "Let's say that you average 200 individual candy transactions a day over one fan scale. That's what?...You lose a bit over 29 cents every time you keep using it instead of the new 8400, or about $58 every day. At this rate the 8400 would pay for itself in about eighteen days. And that's just one scale for one day. Multiply your daily loss for each fan scale you have times the number of scales you have in all your stores, then times the number of days you're open...what do you suppose Sears is losing in an year's time?"

Just then a voice from the back of the room spoke up. "I'll tell you how much we're losing in an year. Over a *million dollars*, that's how much!"

During the discussion that followed Quertinmont learned that Sears was selling about $87 million dollars worth of candy every year. He was overwhelmed at the volume. At the time, Toledo Scale's entire volume for every product in their line added up to only about $50 million annually...and Sears sold $87 million in just candy alone! He knew then he had won an order.

Sears put a hold on the first 500 scales manufactured at the volume price Quertinmont offered. They never made it easy, however. Quertinmont had to leave the new scale with them. Sears gave it to their engineering department who took it apart and estimated the cost of every part that went into it. They added the estimated cost of required labor, tooling and assembly, added a small mark up…and made a counter offer that was much less than Toledo's asking price.

Quertinmont gave it a lot of thought. He had to counter the lower price Sears offered. He met with their purchasing manager. "Well, your estimates are too low of course, but I could lower the price if you meet some other conditions," he said.

"What conditions?"

"For one thing, you'd have to pay for and take ownership of all 500 scales all at once. It costs a lot to make and deliver them to you one, five or ten at a time, the way you insist we do it now, and you don't pay for them until we deliver them. I expect you didn't factor in that cost?"

"Okay, perhaps not. Anything else?"

"You'd have to agree to buy, maintain, store and deliver your own stock of loaner scales. Now when you want a loaner you just call for one and we deliver it free. This adds to our cost too."

"Are you through?"

"Not yet," Quertinmont continued, "when you want them serviced you have to agree to send them back to the factory and wait for service. Now you want our service people to be on call to take care of them in your stores. If you send them back to our factory we could close down our service operation and save that cost too."

Sears purchasing agent quarreled over each of these conditions but Quertinmont was firm. Finally the buyer said, "Okay, I guess we overlooked some costs. You made your case. You have the order for 500 new candy scales at your price."

This first purchase represented an order for more than half a million dollars. Sears ordered more 8400 candy scales later. The sale of all retail digital electronic scales escalated.

In addition to the new candy scale, many other new electronic products hit the market that year. Included were an electronic parts counting scale, a digital retail computing scale, the Bridgemaster truck scale, the 500 series electronic printer, and load cell railroad scales.

As the mid '70s neared, high volume load cells for retail scales were being manufactured by Toledo in capacities of 15, 25, 50 and 100 lb as well as higher capacity cells for vehicle scales and industry.

Load cells were becoming vital to the manufacture of scales. The operation in the white room in the Toledo plant couldn't keep up. A decision was made to build a new plant dedicated to the manufacture of load cells. After examining many options, a decision was made to build the plant in Spartanburg, South Carolina.

The state had been losing its population of young people for lack of jobs. They were moving out of South Carolina to other states where the jobs were. As a result, South Carolina established many incentives for companies to locate plants in the state that would result in jobs for its citizens.

In addition to tax incentives, South Carolina offered to train any new employees at state expense to manufacture load cells for Toledo Scale in a new plant located in the state. In other words, they would see to it that the company had as many qualified employees available for hire as it would need.

The plant was built in a rural setting with a great view near major intersections on the edge of Spartanburg…yet it was built largely without windows to better control heating and cooling costs. The pastoral view was lost to the workers except when they arrived for work and left for home.

Not long after the Spartanburg plant was completed, small assembly operations were established in both Worthington and Westerville, Ohio, both suburbs of Columbus. Reliance management had become enamored of the culture and labor climate in the Columbus area. Both operations grew rapidly.

About this time, Reliance president Hugh Luke moved up to chairman of the board. He was replaced as president by B. Charles Ames who had been a McKenzie consultant until becoming president of Reliance Electric Company.

All the new electronic products were featured in a national sales meeting held at a resort complex in Innsbruck, Florida. Called TelStar '74, the meeting was planned by Harrigan and Terry, and led by Landis and Zelazny. A panel of outside executives told the group what they expected from a scale company and answered questions from the floor. The advertising department's Tom Miller had prepared several dramatic slide-sound-motion picture programs for the meeting that used a new, programmed three-screen rear-projection technique.

The guest speaker for the main banquet was Captain Dick Merrill from Eastern Air Lines. Now 80-years-old, Merrill had been a senior captain for Eastern until he was forced to retire at the age of 67 when the FAA's "60 and out" rule went into effect for airline pilots who flew passengers.

Next to Lindbergh, Merrill had been the most famous American pilot during the '30s, '40s and '50s. He had been the pilot on the world's first round-trip commercial flight across the Atlantic in the mid '30s. Merrill had flown Dwight Eisenhower's chartered airplane during his 1952 campaign for the presidency, and later a new corporate jet around the world with popular radio and television star, Arthur Godfrey.

Eastern kept Merrill on the payroll in public relations because he was a gifted speaker as well as an aviation pioneer. Speaking informally without notes, he exuded a special charm. His stories of early adventures and how weight control plays such an important part in aviation captivated the group. Several hundred Toledomen gave him a standing ovation.

Tom Miller had been taking hundreds of photos throughout the four days of the meeting. To close the meeting, he stayed up all night and prepared another three-screen rear-projection slide program that showed all that had been taking place during the past four days. While the new electronic products were the stars of TelStar '74, Captain Merrill's talk and Miller's shows were the biggest hits.

After TelStar '74, disagreements between DiVincenzo and
Landis became obvious. Landis huddled with Harrigan on approaches they would jointly recommend. The recommendations
appeared to fly in the face of DiVincenzo's policies. It was rumored that Landis and Harrigan then went over DiVincenzo's head
to Reliance president Chuck Ames to complain about DiVincenzo's
leadership.

If true, it was the wrong thing to do. Ames called DiVincenzo.
Almost immediately both Landis and Harrigan "resigned". Once
again there was a conflict in top management. This time it was
settled quickly by DiVincenzo personally.

There was a far more important resignation in the nation at about
the same time. On August 8, 1974, President Richard Nixon, faced
with impeachment in Congress, announced he would resign. Nixon
was the first American president in history to ever resign the office.

He was succeeded by Vice President Gerald Ford. The previous
year Ford had been nominated by Nixon to replace Vice President
Spiro Agnew who resigned in disgrace. Ford's nomination was approved by both houses of Congress under the recently adopted 25th
Amendment. Thus he became the only man ever to hold the office of
president without ever having his name appear on a general election
ballot for the office of president or vice president.

In early 1975, DiVincenzo announced a change that threw a
scare into everybody in Toledo…the engineering department in its
entirety would be moved to the Columbus, Ohio area in the next few
months. The company had a presence in the Columbus area since
1969 with a leased electronics plant that employed five people. Toledo had already established an electronic plant in Westerville. As
Reliance became more impressed with the growing Columbus area
operation, the cost of doing business in Toledo kept increasing.

A decision had been made to develop small, specialized plants
for future growth. Central Ohio was chosen because the company
believed the region had the best available talent and non-union
wage rates. Toledo engineering would be better able to tap this
talent from a Columbus area location.

Later in the year DiVincenzo dropped the bomb...he announced that the headquarters for the Toledo Scale Division would also be moved to the Columbus area. Soon he revealed that a new building had been leased for the headquarters on West Wilson Bridge Road in Worthington, a Columbus suburb. Virtually all management employees, supervisors and some selected staff people were invited to move their homes to the area at company expense. Plans began to have the move completed by August 1, 1976.

Not long after Reliance announced that Toledo Scale was going to move both their engineering and headquarters out of Toledo to the Columbus, Ohio area, Ed Quertinmont ran into Harris McIntosh at the Toledo airport.

Quertinmont was catching a plane for New York. McIntosh was bound for Boston and saw him across the lobby. He walked over and tapped Quertinmont on the shoulder. "How are you, Ed?"

Quertinmont turned around, pleased to see him. "I'm fine, Mr. McIntosh, how are you?"

"Well, okay, but sometimes I'm not so sure. I just can't believe..." His lips began to quiver as he paused. "I never would have believed when I sold Toledo Scale to Reliance—I never would have believed they would move it out of Toledo! I just can't talk about it."

Obviously moved, McIntosh shook hands and walked away to catch his flight. It was the last time Quertinmont ever saw him.

Six years later Harris McIntosh died in his Perrysburg home at the age of 78. He was buried in Cayuga, New York, his birthplace. Among his many community service activities he had been a trustee of The Toledo Hospital for years and had served as board president. Today there is a Harris McIntosh building named in his memory on the campus of the Toledo Hospital.

In late 1975, Allen Briston, general manager of Toledo Scale of Canada, and his district manager in Montreal, Jacques Laplante, visited Toledo headquarters with some big news.

Zelazny and Terry met them. Briston said, "Jacques has made a tentative deal with the Olympic organizing committee in

Montreal for Toledo Scale to be named the 'Official Supplier of Scales for the 21st Olympic Games' that will be held in Montreal next year. They agreed to our proposal. We came down here to tell you the details and get final company approval."

"Hey, that's exciting!" Terry exclaimed. Zelazny said, "Tell us about it, Jacques."

Laplante explained that he had been approached by the Montreal Olympic organizing committee to submit a proposal to supply the scales. "I talked it over with Allen," Laplante said. "If we were selected, we could use the special Montreal Olympic logo and refer to ourselves as the 'Official Supplier of Scales for the 21st Olympic Games' in our advertising. We needed to attest that Toledo manufactured all of the types of scales the Olympics would need, and I've determined that we do."

"What about the cost?" Zelazny asked. "Don't they get a lot of money for Olympic endorsements?"

"Well, we agreed to loan them all the scales if they would pay the service costs of about $20,000 to set them up and keep them serviced all through the games," Laplante said. "They agreed. So they pay us."

Toledo Scale's selection as official scale supplier was different from many other official suppliers who have paid for the right to use an Olympic connection in their advertising and promotion. The official scale supplier and firms involved in producing timing and measurement devices had been put in a special category by the Montreal Olympic committee because they were necessary in carrying out the games.

The agreement was finalized. It was Toledo's first connection with the Olympics since the company was chosen to supply the scales for the 1932 Winter Olympics at Lake Placid, New York.

Toledo supplied 63 scales for the 1976 Montreal Olympic Games. Toledo scales were used officially, in one or more capacities, in more than half of the 21 events in these Summer Olympics.

They were used in all events where weight was any kind of a factor. Many were used to weigh participants where weight is an obvious factor, such as boxing, wrestling and weightlifting. Others were used in less obvious areas where weight is seldom thought of as being involved.

In the shooting competition, every bullet was weighed on a Toledo scale. Specially outfitted Toledo scales were used to weigh the yachts for this competition...as well as the sails, mast, and lines. In the more familiar track and field events, every shot, discus, javelin and hammer were weighed. Each and every basketball, soccer and water polo ball was weighed to make sure they met Olympic standards. In the cycling competition, the racing bikes were weighed and classified. Rowing shells and kayaks had to be officially weighed too.

Toledo also furnished 40 Person Weigher scales for use in dormitories and training areas in the Olympic Village. The athletes used them to assure themselves their weight hadn't changed since arriving in Montreal.

They also helped those athletes who chose to adjust their weights by hitting the sauna or eating that extra pizza to compete in different weight categories. Some wrestlers, for example, wrestled both above and below 220 pounds, depending on the event.

If there was an American hero in the Montreal Olympics, it was Bruce Jenner of San Jose State, winner of the decathlon. He topped his fellow decathletes by more than 200 points.

But the clear star in Montreal was a tiny girl from Romania. Nadia Comaneci was only 14-years-old, barely five feet tall and weighed 83 pounds. Her initial exercise on the uneven bars drew the first perfect ten in history. She next scored three perfect tens on her way to a gold on the balance beam. Nadia Comaneci captured three gold medals as she whirled her way into the hearts of millions of television viewers.

To help make the Montreal Olympics special for the sales force, Zelazny established an incentive program in which sales people won free tickets and trips to the games.

The 1976 Summer Olympics marked a major renewal of the company's Olympic involvement. Except for the 1980 Olympic

Games in Moscow which were boycotted by the United States,
West Germany and Japan, Toledo Scale has been the official scale
supplier…including the 1996 Centennial Olympics in Atlanta.

1976 also marked the company's 75th anniversary. In the
spring, Don Zelazny challenged Terry and his advertising department to recommend something special for the 100% Club sales
meeting to mark the event. Of course it had to stay within budget.
The 1974 meeting in Innsbruck had been a major success for
Zelazny and he wanted this anniversary meeting to be even better.

Terry discussed ideas with Ken Cooper, the manager of the
Toledo Trust travel agency. The travel agent reported that many
European locations had special incentives to attract convention
business. The best incentives were offered by Spain.

Their infamous dictator, Francisco Franco, had died the previous year. Before his death, he named Prince Juan Carlos de Borbon
his heir. Now Juan Carlos was King, and the new King wanted to
encourage visitors to see a different Spain.

Terry said to Cooper, "Let's think about holding the meeting in
Toledo, Spain. After all, it's the city name that Toledo, Ohio adopted.
So it's the name Toledo Scale adopted too." Toledo, Ohio and Toledo,
Spain had just resumed their "sister city" relationship first established
in the 1930s, but put on hold during the Franco regime.

Cooper checked into the idea. He discovered that Toledo, Spain
didn't have the facilities to handle a group estimated to total over
200 people. Madrid, however, had plenty of facilities and was only
about an hour's drive from Toledo. So they planned for the major
part of the meeting to be in Madrid, with a full day planned for a
drive to Toledo via motor coach.

The cost numbers held up…by flying people to two central
locations in the U.S. and chartering two long range aircraft for the
trip to Madrid, the meeting could be held at even less cost than
any location in the United States.

Terry presented the idea to Zelazny. "I like it!" he said. "This
would indeed outshine TelStar '74. Let me see if I can get an OK
from the boss for a trip to check it out."

Zelazny obtained approval to look at the facilities in Spain. Zelazny, Terry and Cooper flew to Madrid where they found a good choice of hotels large enough and with excellent rates, each eager to host the meeting.

They drove south to Toledo, which they found to be an ancient, medieval, walled city where nothing had really changed since Columbus left there to discover America. They visited a steel foundry where world famous Toledo swords were still being made by hand and for which Toledo, Ohio's newspaper, *The Blade,* was named.

They visited Toledo's magnificent, gothic cathedral completed in 1492…the year in which Queen Isabella commissioned Columbus to seek a new route to India from this very city, then the seat of the Spanish throne. And the studio home in which El Greco produced the bulk of his famous paintings.

They located a beautiful restaurant surrounded by olive trees that overlooked the city from a hill outside, large enough to handle the group for a classic Spanish mid-day meal.

On the flight home Zelazny said, "I think we have all our ducks in a row now. When we get home let's write it out in a proposal. Then check first with Ben Dillon. DiVincenzo has a lot of confidence in Ben. If we can get his endorsement we stand a better chance of selling it to Tony."

Dillon looked the proposal over carefully. He said, "I'm a bit concerned about putting the entire sales force on only two chartered airplanes. If one went down over the ocean we'll lose half our work force. But that's really a remote possibility…and the insurance in the plan looks like it covers the dangers adequately. Other than that, it's a good plan. I'll endorse it."

DiVincenzo talked it over thoroughly with Dillon, Zelazny and Terry. "If all of you think this is the way to go, I'll go along," he said, "but I have to take it to Ames and Luke. We need an OK from corporate before we go any further."

A week later he walked into Zelazny's office. "I'm sorry, Don…Spain is out. Luke and Ames don't want this division to be the first to have a glamorous overseas meeting. He was afraid the

Reliance sales organization would feel slighted. See if you can find a U.S. spot for the meeting."

Disappointed, Zelazny took the news to Terry. The search for a meeting location resumed. Soon one was found and booked for a September meeting near Brunswick, Georgia. The meeting would take place a month after Toledo Scale headquarters had made the move to Worthington.

Meanwhile the headquarters move was progressing. The leased building in Worthington was available for occupancy by June. A number of people had already moved their homes and began working in the building.

For those who still lived in Toledo and had not yet completed the sale of their homes, the company leased an aircraft to fly them down to the Ohio State University airport on Monday morning and then fly them back to Toledo on Friday evening.

By the end of July, the executive offices on the second floor offices in the Toledo plant were virtually empty. One of the last to leave the offices was Terry, who had resigned to go into the advertising agency business in Toledo.

The factory was still operating but at less capacity. The Toledo plant made mechanical scales, which were gradually being replaced in the marketplace by the electronic scales now being manufactured by Toledo Scale in the Columbus area.

Food machine manufacturing was moved to Franksville, Wisconsin, the plant acquired when Toledo bought Superwrapper. This plant did a good job making labelers and wrapping machines, but had trouble manufacturing the food machines transferred from the Toledo plant. Soon there were many complaints about poor quality and unreliable performance.

Toledo plant employment continued to shrink.

CHAPTER 29

Patents and Innovations

Meanwhile, Toledo continued to market mechanical scales as top of the line. In spite of their success with many electronic products, they were slow to embrace pure electronics for the full line. They had a large investment in tooling and facilities to produce mechanical scales. The market, however, was moving to electronic scales.

Tony DiVincenzo retired. Management of the Toledo Scale Division was then split between Ben Dillon and Al Schiff. Dillon became responsible for sales, marketing and engineering and Schiff, who had been national service manager, was responsible for everything else, including service. Dillon and Schiff were not compatible. Leadership problems resulted.

Still, other inventions continued to be developed at Toledo Scale. The company was way ahead in patenting inventions. By 1978, Don Hall alone held 19 patents for electronic scales as well as patents for elevator innovations while he was on loan to Haughton Elevator.

"In the late 1960s and early '70s, three others and I worked on a new system for supervising elevator cars to most efficiently handle traffic which resulted in the patents," Hall said. "It's a unique system that's still used for high rise elevators."

For Toledo Scale, Hall's patents are related to the application of load cells in electronic scales. "Around 1969, Toledo Scale made the decision to move from mechanical scales to electronic scales," he recalled. "We sponsored and led the charge into electronic weighing. If we hadn't done it, I don't think we'd be in business today—or, at least, we wouldn't be what we are."

Chuck Loshbaugh, a research scientist at the Worthington plant, patented a device for the deli scale that made the indication more stable. The digital indicator would blink from one number to another because it couldn't decide which it was. One of Loshbaugh's patents was for the unique way he improved the digital indicator controls so it wouldn't blink.

"Roger Williams, our engineering manager for electronic products and Chuck Loshbaugh hold a total of 51 U.S. patents, plus many foreign ones." Hall said. "And some of the new patents on the load cells are the result of work done by Dr. George Oetjen who is presently in Germany setting up a research, development and engineering function there." Oetjen was an engineer in Toledo's German operation.

The Cap-Check Load Cell was developed by Oetjen in the late '70s. The Cap-Check's inherent ability to withstand side loads generated by vehicles starting and stopping eliminated the need for check rods, often a source of scale error.

At the time, Loshbaugh held 28 U.S. patents generally dealing with innovations for electronic scales. In many cases, patents were issued to more than one person when there were co-inventors.

Roger Williams and Loshbaugh shared patents for many of Toledo Scale's inventions. Many of the patents were very subtle or very technical in nature, but they resulted in Toledo Scale making a better product than its competition, and often at a lower cost.

A very unusual Toledo Scale order was booked in 1978. Tom Lloyd, a pharmaceutical industry specialist, sold a $400,000 Toledo system in 1971 that did not include a single scale. He was working with Sterling Drug on a tentative proposal for $20,000 worth of scales for a drug dispensing system…and converted it into a $400,000 order for a security system.

After the technical details of his scale proposal were finalized, Lloyd explained that Toledo Scale people went out to dinner with the customer. "After ordering dinner, one of Sterling's engineers leaned over and said to me how excited he was about the two new computer systems they had ordered."

"I told him I knew about our system," Lloyd said, "but what was the other?"

He learned that it was for a security system from IBM, a giant in the field. Sterling had a large inventory of narcotics and other dangerous drugs. They needed tight security to prevent theft by employees or outsiders.

"I felt there wasn't that much difference between the weighing systems we build and the controlled access system Sterling had in mind," Lloyd said. "What's the difference between a computer system where we capture data from a scale and a computer system that captures data from a card that's inserted in a reader at a door? Functionally, it's the same."

Toledo engineers designed an innovative security system in which each of Sterling's employees was assigned a badge the size of a credit card. Special codes were imbedded in the plastic card. Each card contained a code, which indicated a particular level of access.

Lloyd explained, "A 'level one' person can go through door A, but if a 'level two' comes along he can't get through door A but can pass through door B and every other door he was approved to enter."

Card readers at each door transmitted the code to the computer. The computer instantly checked its memory to see if the card is valid and the employee had clearance for the area he was trying to enter.

"In a very secure area, such as the narcotics vault, there are floor to ceiling turnstiles that only one person can pass through. The computer also takes a look at such things as how long the door stays open, what area the person has left, and so forth," Lloyd explained. "If there are any abnormal occurrences, they're recorded on a terminal at the guard station. A guard could then take his own corrective action. Our Toledo Scale system had some clear advantages over IBM."

Lloyd commented, "But the interesting part of the project is that we started out trying to get a $20,000 scale order and were having a tough time getting it. So rather than selling just hardware, we sold a solution to our customer's problem. That solution was worth $400,000 to us. We also sold a maintenance contract with it, and spare parts over the next three years for another $100,000."

Tom Lloyd sold a solution to a customer's problem. Much like Theobald had advised over 70 years previously.

Reliance Electric sold their electric motors and related control products through distributors. These were pure distributors in that they bought the products from Reliance and sold them with a mark-up. Toledo had a selling organization they called distributors...but they were really agents.

Scales were sent to them on consignment and the company was not paid until the scales were sold. Part of the Toledo deal was that their distributors—unlike Reliance distributors—would handle only Toledo products...no competitors.

Toledo's arrangement had bothered Reliance from the beginning. Now they issued instructions to change it...after all, if Toledo distributors paid for the scales when they ordered them, it would increase cash flow significantly.

Traditional Toledo distributors were not happy with the new arrangement. To show their displeasure at being forced to become pure distributors, many signed up to handle competitive scales along with the Toledo line.

This decision helped spark a new, competitive scale company.

CHAPTER 30

Masstron Scale Company

Many new scale companies entered the marketplace with electronic scales that usually had more capability and cost less than Toledo scales. Toledo's Mechanical scales were losing market share to them. Ben Dillon had been talking with management about these concerns but nothing was being done about it. Many speculated that this was the main reason he resigned in 1977 and founded Masstron Scale Company.

He also thought that many existing Toledo distributors would welcome a new entry in the marketplace since they were still unhappy with the new pure distributorship arrangement forced upon them by Toledo.

These factors pointed to an opportunity for him. Electronic scales were being rapidly accepted in the marketplace, and he saw the real possibility of very quickly establishing a distributor organization for his scales with people who already knew and respected him. And the joint leadership at Toledo was constantly frustrating.

Dillon structured his new company to manufacture only products that were purely electronic. He would measure mass electronically…thus the name Masstron. His original intention was to produce a scale for a market niche where competitors were weak…electronic floor scales.

One of his first moves was to call Terry at his agency in Toledo. Dillon needed graphics and print material for everything a new company required: stationery, all business forms, a logo, literature for his first product, ads, and more. Terry's business partner, graphic designer Jan Robie, designed all of these, including the Masstron logo in a stylized capital M shaped like a scale balance.

Dillon chose an industrial shade of orange for his second color. Reliance had been using a bright orange on some electrical products. While at Reliance, Dillon became fond of orange because it helped him identify a Reliance product from a distance when he walked through a factory.

Dillon especially admired the shade of orange on his riding lawn mower. He wanted just that shade. Robie determined the color was really PMS Warm Red. She designed the logo and all other elements using this as the second color. The color did the job. It did indeed help identify a Masstron scale from a distance. A bit later it caused some consternation at Toledo Scale.

As a matter of principle, Dillon refused to recruit Toledo Scale employees. Yet many sought him out on their own. When they took the initiative and applied for a job, Dillon felt free to hire them...and did hire many of them. The same was true of Toledo Scale distributors...Dillon did not recruit them directly. Instead, he advertised for distributors in a scale trade journal. Many Toledo distributors answered the ad. They were still unhappy with the pure distributor arrangement Toledo forced on them.

Dillon knew them all personally and they knew him. He knew which ones did a good job and paid their bills. He signed up the best of those who applied as Masstron distributors. This immediately gave him a highly qualified national sales organization composed of people who liked and respected him.

Masstron's first product was Liftmate®, a pure electronic floor scale with an electronic indicator. It was designed to weigh lift trucks and their loads. It was delivered completely assembled, to be flush mounted in a shallow pit or surface mounted. The platform could be lifted out of its frame without disconnecting anything. The scale frame made its own concrete pouring form. It was a quick hit.

He leased a small office from the city of Columbus on Doubletree across from the Busch brewery. It was in a modern industrial building in northern Columbus and included an assembly area. His first products were assembled there. However, in a short time, the city notified him that he had to vacate his leased space. The city exercised their right to the space. He had to move. This time he purchased a building on Schrock a block or so west of the large Busch brewery complex, and there Masstron thrived.

Toledo Scale engineer Bill Susor had resigned and joined Masstron, buying in with an equity position. Susor was a brilliant engineer. He had become a good friend with Dillon while both worked at Toledo Scale. As they worked together at Masstron, he became Dillon's best friend.

Not long after, Allen Briston, Toledo's general manager in Canada, also resigned to form Masstron Scale Ltd. in Burlington, Ontario.

Soon Masstron had systems capability. The young company acquired a systems-oriented firm founded by Larry Anderson and Bill Pickard, both ex-Toledo employees. The firm quickly became a force in heavy capacity scales and systems in both the U.S. and Canada.

Susor designed a new truck scale using an innovative new concept. Named the Masstron Truckmate®, it pioneered pitless electronic modular truck scales. A Truckmate could be surface or flush mounted with its foundation, saving on expensive pits. It included Centerlign™, a patented self-aligning, self-centering load cell assembly that assured only vertical forces were transmitted to the load cells.

The first Truckmate was installed at a Sohigro facility in Piqua, Ohio that stored liquid anhydrous ammonia. The facility filled large containers and trucks with this highly corrosive fertilizer for delivery to farmers.

When any of the anhydrous ammonia was spilled on an existing pit-type truck scales in the filling process, gravity led it down to the levers or load cells and they quickly corroded, greatly reducing scale life.

The Truckmate was built with corrosion protection. Yet one of the most important design features had the platform installed several inches above the concrete slab foundation. This made it easy for the operator to use a fire hose to hose away the corrosive chemicals both on top of the platform and underneath it. The scale's useful life was vastly increased. Sohigro soon ordered dozens more. Word swiftly got around. The Truckmate became Masstron's breakthrough product.

While living in Toledo, "the glass capital of the world", Dillon noticed the trucks used to deliver very large panes of glass. They included an inverted V on the truck bed. The panes of glass were leaned up against the inverted V and held in place. The back end of the truck had a small crane permanently installed. The crane could lift a large pane of glass off the truck and place it in position to be installed.

Dillon determined the cranes were made in a small shop in nearby Swanton. He visited them to see if their cranes could handle the weight of the largest truck scale module…something less than 6,000 lb. They could.

He ordered a Freightliner and a trailer with the inverted V installed, with a crane on the back end. Now he could deliver a complete 70' long truck scale made up of four 17-1/2' modules, lift them off the truck and place them directly in position on the concrete foundation slab. Dillon trained his truck driver to install and calibrate his scales. Soon he acquired a second truck with the same configuration.

Competitors had to rent a crane locally to individually install all the components of their truck scales. They usually took three days or more to install the scale at a high rental cost for the crane and operator.

Now, once simple concrete foundations and approaches were in place, a Masstron truck scale could often be completely installed in less than a day. His scale delivery innovation permitted him to install a Masstron Truckmate faster and at much less cost than any other truck scale…one more competitive advantage.

Toledo grain industry manager Tom Quertinmont, Ed Quertinmont's son, was another who had left Toledo and joined Masstron. Dillon assigned him all the marketing communications responsibilities he no longer had time to handle himself, plus some marketing responsibilities.

While still with Toledo Scale, Tom Quertinmont sat in on a presentation made to Toledo management by Richardson-Smith, a well respected design firm in suburban Columbus. The firm had been retained to recommend design changes to Toledo's industrial product line.

"We all were impressed with their presentation at first," Tom Quertinmont said. They had researched all of Toledo's major competitors. It was going well for them...until they showed their artist's renditions of their recommendations. "The designs all recommended and showed orange as the second color. All of us in the room glanced around and looked at each other sheepishly. Finally someone told them, 'I'm sorry, we can't use orange. Masstron is using that color and it would look like we're imitating them.'"

Richardson-Smith had researched all the big names in the business but no one had told them about the small new upstart about a mile away. Their second choice, a bright green, was accepted by Toledo.

Masstron growth was rapid. The product line grew with many new and innovative heavy capacity scales and instruments. Within a few years it had taken a large part of Toledo's heavy capacity market away from them...along with many of their best people.

Masstron developed strong relationships with their customers, employees and vendors. One of their most popular activities was hosting a "brats and beer" party inside the Schrock Road plant during annual televised Ohio-Michigan football games.

Large screen TV sets were scattered throughout the plant for the football fans. A beer truck that dispensed cold draft beer was rented from the nearby brewery and parked inside where it was convenient for everyone to replenish their glass.

Chuck Handford, a friend who was also a Masstron distributor in Columbus, cooked beer-soaked bratwurst and hot "Bahama Mamas" over a large charcoal fire. The brats were a Columbus fixture, made popular by the celebrated German Village in near-downtown Columbus.

Limburger cheese on rye bread appealed to a surprising number of men even as their wives turned up their noses and sniffed their disapproval. Potato salad and other delectables rounded out the repast. Several hundred customers, vendors and friends greatly enjoyed the annual event.

The Buckeyes-Wolverines brats and beer bash continued for several years until Masstron once again had to move because increased truck scale and other heavy capacity scale business required even more space. The next move was to a much larger plant that Dillon purchased. This plant was about a block away, on the corner of Huntley and Schrock. The new plant was better able to manufacture the large modules, which employed modern new manufacturing methods.

Then…disaster. Masstron had installed a system for a coal mine operator in the Appalachian mountains of Southeastern Kentucky. The system experienced some technical difficulties. The coal mine operator sent his company airplane—a light twin—to Columbus to pick up Bill Susor and Bill Pickard. On a Saturday morning, they were flown to the Kentucky site to check the installation.

Susor had taken some flying lessons when he was in Utah. He loved to fly and welcomed the trip. Pickard did not. He was always apprehensive about flying.

The weather was marginal with scattered, low-hanging clouds and some lingering fog as they approached the Kentucky airport near the mine. The airport was surrounded by small mountains.

The pilot made his approach to the runway. He apparently concluded the runway was not clearly in sight, and executed a missed approach. He hit the throttles to climb out on instruments. Soon after establishing a normal climb rate, the aircraft entered a cloud. Moments later, it smashed into a mountain very near the top.

All on board—Susor, Pickard and the pilot—were killed instantly. The aircraft was scattered all over the mountain top.

Dillon was notified. He immediately got into his car and drove to the site. When he arrived hours later, it became his sad duty to identify the bodies. It was not easy, and it broke him up. In an instant, he had lost his best friend and partner, and a young friend he liked and admired. He was devastated.

Grief and shock struck everyone in the small company. Little real work was accomplished for some time.

Friends then rallied around. Masstron's small engineering staff had been decimated with the death of Susor and Pickard. They needed help. A friend, Toledo Scale senior engineer Fred Weihs, told Dillon that his son Mark might be an answer. He said, "Mark is a good electronics man with his own small consulting and engineering firm. Why don't you see if he can help you?"

He could. The small firm led by Mark Weihs consulted with Masstron for the next several years. It was able to successfully finish most of the incomplete projects started by Susor, and add some innovative new products to the line as well.

Everyone pitched in to recover from the blow, and Masstron continued its steady growth. Yet to most, it just wasn't as much fun anymore.

CHAPTER 31

Exxon Buys Reliance

After Ben Dillon had left Toledo to start Masstron, Al Schiff remained the leading executive at the Toledo Scale Division. His solo tenure was brief. Reliance soon transferred Pete Tsivitse to Toledo Scale, naming him vice president of the group. Later David Patterson joined him from Reliance as general manager of weighing and controls.

Once again, Toledo Scale decided to get out of the food machine business. They began to phase them out. Food machines made in Franksville still were unprofitable…and still had quality problems.

On top of this, litigation against all kinds of manufactured equipment accelerated in the U.S., especially food machines from all manufacturers. Whenever a worker got hurt, whether it was his own fault or not, he easily found a contingency lawyer who would sue for damages. Often the lawyer would seek out the worker.

Insurance carriers habitually settled no matter the circumstances. Then they would raise their rates drastically. Since Toledo was getting out of the food machine business anyway, Reliance decided to eliminate the litigation problem by buying back every meat saw, chopper, slicer, steak machine…every food machine Toledo ever made…then junk them. Quertinmont said, "They spent millions".

Toledo Scale made an agreement with the Biro Manufacturing Company, a top manufacturer of similar food processing equipment, to trade in Toledo food machines on an equivalent Biro product, then buy the trade-in from Biro and junk it.

Biro was also experiencing serious litigation problems, but all they made was food processing equipment. They had no fall-back line, so they stayed in the business determined to fight. Over the next several years, Toledo bought many Toledo brand food machine trade-ins from Biro and junked them all.

This meant that Hobart, with both scales and food machines, was now a more complete product supplier to the supermarket industry. They quickly came to dominate this retail marketplace.

Then in early 1979, Reliance abruptly announced that they had sold the Haughton Elevator Division to Schindler Elevator A.G. of Switzerland. Schindler was Reliance's Swiss partner in a joint company, Schindler-Reliance Electronics A.G. It was the last piece left of the Toledo Scale Corporation that McIntosh had put together.

In late 1979, a major change took place at Reliance Electric. Some months before, Reliance had announced the development of a new electric motor that was declared to be extremely energy efficient, requiring much less electricity to operate.

The announcement attracted the attention of Exxon, the giant oil company. Exxon made an attractive tender offer for Reliance largely based on the development of the energy efficient motor. The offer was accepted and Reliance was acquired by Exxon. Now it was Reliance's turn.

Exxon soon discovered that the energy efficient electric motor didn't perform as announced. Exxon replaced many Reliance executives. They started by naming their own John Morley as president and CEO of Reliance Electric. History repeated itself...just as Reliance replaced Toledo Scale top executives, Exxon replaced Reliance top executives.

In 1977, Reliance had acquired Kato Engineering of North Mankato, Minnesota, a manufacturer of AC generators. Among the management changes Morley made was to assign another Exxon executive, Steve Perry, to run Kato as plant manager. Perry was soon to run Toledo Scale.

The 1980s saw the digital era explode, with satellites hundreds of miles in space sending back sharp images, and compact discs reproducing music with outstanding clarity.

In 1981, engineering in the weighing and controls group was reorganized into four operating departments at four separate locations. Development and customer order responsibility for light industrial products was shifted to Spartanburg, South Carolina.

Retail product engineering was assigned to the Worthington, Ohio plant, wrapping and labeling to Franksville, Wisconsin, and heavy industrial products to the small Toledo operation. Leo Niese remained in Toledo as the project engineer.

Niese had worked in the Toledo plant for 26 years. His engineering department was located in the former Systems area at the back end of the plant. Much of the Toledo plant was unused since most electronic scales were now being manufactured in Columbus area plants. However, a few mechanical bench, portable and heavy capacity scales were still being produced in Toledo.

In 1981, Reliance CEO Morley negotiated to acquire Hi-Speed Checkweigher Company, Inc. of Ithaca, New York, for Toledo Scale. Toledo had manufactured checkweighers as early as 1951 but its checkweigher line was incomplete and never very profitable. Meanwhile Hi-Speed had been quite successful.

Hi-Speed was founded in 1953 by Charles Pettis. He, along with Victor Del Rosso, defined the checkweigher industry and what it has become. Hi-Speed had established itself as the leader in checkweighers.

As early as 1957, the company developed a high-speed line divider for cans that divided at an unprecedented rate of 1100 cans per minute. In 1968, their patented Magnetic Flow Director was introduced. 1974 saw the introduction of microprocessor controls as well as the random Weigh Price Labeler utilizing Intel's first microprocessor.

An in-motion checkweigher doesn't provide an actual weight reading, it simply checks package weights within a small, preset weight range. Speeds over a line can be over 1000 packages per minute. They're used to assure that the package contains at least as much product as is printed on the package to avoid short-weight claims. At the same time it tells packaging line people if they're giving away too much extra product which quickly adds to extra cost.

Hi-Speed kept their own identity. Yet it put Toledo Scale in the checkweigher business with the leading brand.

The following year research engineering was brought together in a new Engineering Center built as an addition to the Worthington plant. "We've consolidated our advanced engineering and added some very sophisticated computer-aided tools," said Don Hall, group engineering manager. "We now have what I believe is the finest research and development facility for scales and weighing systems in the U.S."

Hall pointed out that of the Center's 68 employees, 34 are advanced development engineers. "There's a lot of outstanding talent among our engineers; many have 20 to 25 years of experience in scale technology," he said. "Three engineers hold Ph.Ds. Many are the holders of the nearly 100 patents issued for Toledo Scale's innovative products."

"Before the advent of electronic weighing, Toledo Scale had three or four major competitors," Hall explained. "Now we have two or three dozen that are nibbling away at our traditional business. If we can't quickly produce new and better products we stand to lose some of our market share. This new Engineering Center is a solid investment that will enhance our competitive edge in the scale market."

One of the first new developments to come out of the Engineering Center was the DigiTOL® POWERCELL® load cell, with a built-in microprocessor that output weight data in digital form. This patented development eliminated problems that often resulted from the low voltage signals common to all analog load cells.

DigiTOL POWERCELL load cells continuously monitored scale "history" automatically correcting for errors caused by the effect of temperature changes, creep and nonlinearity. Its built-in diagnostics continuously monitored the performance of the scale. Toledo Scale's DigiTOL technology was a major advance in scale performance, accuracy and reliability.

Back in Toledo, Ohio, Reliance sold the entire 550,000 square foot Telegraph Road plant and its 70-acre site to Willis-Day Properties for $2.1 million. Willis-Day planned to use the plant for light manufacturing and warehousing.

Toledo rented the old Systems area at the back end of the
original plant from Willis-Day and employed a much reduced
manufacturing force to produce mechanical scales and electronic
scale understructures for use with electronic indicators. The old
Systems area had recently been renovated by Reliance.

An Open House for employees and their families was held on
Sunday, July 10, 1983. Overlooked was the fact that this date
happened to be the exact 82nd anniversary of Toledo Scale. A small
booklet was given to each visitor with a welcome by Joel Wise, the
plant manager.

In the booklet, Wise wrote, "The renovation of our plant was
a direct commitment from our parent company, Reliance Electric,
to stay in the Toledo community."

Little did he know. Less than a year later Reliance announced
they would phase out all operations in Toledo. The work done in
Toledo was moved to Windsor, Ontario, and Spartanburg, South
Carolina. The last 140 Toledo Scale employees in Toledo lost their
jobs.

As luck would have it, the move out of the plant was made just
in time. On Sunday, July 7, 1985, nine months after Reliance
moved the Toledo Scale operation completely out, a raging fire
completely destroyed the former Toledo Scale plant.

Now called the Willis-Day Business Center, the warehouse
complex had about ten tenants. One of the tenants, the Purex
Corporation, had bleach bottles containing chlorine in one section of the building. The fire created a risk of releasing chlorine gas
into the air.

At least 600 people were evacuated from the area as the wind
spread the chemical fumes as far as a mile north. A total of 74
firemen and police were treated at two local hospitals for smoke
inhalation and eye irritation.

The fire drew every available fire unit in the city. The Red
Cross set up an emergency shelter at Washington Junior High
School. It took three days to put the fire completely out. The fire
chief predicted the loss would be "several million dollars".

Arson was suspected. The only part of the plant that was saved was the old Systems area at the back that Toledo Scale had rented. The entire half-mile long plant facing Telegraph Road was reduced to a pile of rubble. The building that Theobald had so long dreamed of, and that Bennett had so proudly built in 1939, was no more.

CHAPTER 32

Toledo Buys Masstron—Ciba-Geigy Buys Toledo

Meanwhile, Exxon finally took a closer look at Toledo Scale, which they had acquired as part of Reliance Electric. Toledo's performance had been slipping. They were losing share to Masstron and others. The result was to bring Steve Perry in from Kato Engineering as Toledo Scale's general manager. Morley had placed him at Kato several years previously. It proved to be an excellent move.

Don Hall first met his new boss when he picked up Steve Perry and Bill Hendrix at the Columbus airport for Perry's first visit. They went out to dinner and became acquainted. The next day, Hall introduced Perry around. Hall's first impression was positive…and the impression lasted throughout Perry's tenure at Toledo Scale. Hall said, "He was the best general manager I ever worked for."

One of Perry's first moves was to establish a program for 1985 he called "Focus on Commitment". It created an awareness of the group's commitment to the values of credibility, teamwork, quality, and details…one each quarter. The program was supported by graphic design that tied all the elements together along with a short, quarterly video in which Perry spoke on each topic. The program resulted in improved work performance throughout the group.

Perry soon became aware of the market share—and top employees—Toledo Scale had lost and continued to lose to Masstron. He determined to do something about it.

Perry quietly opened negotiations with Dillon to buy Masstron. Concerned that the vast buying power of Exxon could be used against him, Dillon listened. And he still suffered some trauma from the plane crash that took Susor and Pickard. Perry and Dillon reached an agreement. Toledo Scale acquired Masstron in 1985 and made it their heavy-capacity arm. As part of the agreement, Dillon agreed to stay and run the operation for three more years. All ex-Toledo employees who had resigned to join Masstron had their length of service treated as if they had never left Toledo Scale, which could positively affect their future pensions.

Several Masstron employees returned to Toledo in better jobs than when they had left. Tom Quertinmont, for example, soon became Toledo's manager of marketing communications, the job he had been doing successfully at Masstron.

In December 1986, Exxon sold Reliance Electric to its management in a highly leveraged buyout. Reliance became independent again. About two years later, Reliance president Morley announced they were investigating the potential sale of Toledo Scale to reduce the company's large debt. It went on the block.

Reliance had never been very successful in managing their Toledo Scale property. Now identified again as Toledo Scale Corporation, Toledo employees were worried about who might buy the company…and what affect it would have on their lives. Would it be a corporate raider who would milk it for its assets? Would it be a foreign company who would install a vastly different culture?

The answer came in December 1988. Reliance Electric president John Morley announced they had reached an agreement to sell Toledo Scale Corporation to Ciba-Geigy, the giant Swiss pharmaceutical and chemical company. Reliance sold all the assets of Toledo Scale to Ciba-Geigy except for the Brazilian operation, which they sold at the same time to interests in Brazil.

Ciba-Geigy merged Toledo Scale's industrial and retail capabilities with Mettler Instrumente AG, another Swiss company they had purchased in 1981 and operated as a subsidiary. Mettler manufactured laboratory balances and instruments.

Ciba-Geigy had kept the Mettler name for the subsidiary rather than change it to Ciba-Geigy. They were concerned that their chemical and pharmaceutical competitors who used the lab equipment that Mettler manufactured wouldn't buy products that carried a Ciba-Geigy brand name since it was the name of a major competitor.

Mettler was a well-known brand name in Europe. Mettler had marketed their balances and instruments in the U.S. to laboratories and the scientific community since shortly after the firm was founded in 1945 at the end of World War II. Yet it was a little-known brand in the U.S. outside of laboratories.

Though Mettler was slightly larger overall, it was much smaller in the United States when compared to Toledo Scale. In the U.S. it looked like the minnow had swallowed the whale. Still, most Toledo Scale employees breathed a sigh of relief. Mettler was, after all, involved with weighing.

The only asset Ciba-Geigy did not buy for Mettler was the Brazilian operation. Reliance sold it to Ricardo Haegler interests in Brazil. The Haegler family had been associated with Toledo Scale since 1940, first as a distributor. Later Toledo built a manufacturing plant in São Paulo, which was managed by the Haeglers. The Brazilian plant produced Toledo mechanical scales for years for Latin America. Later they made them for the U.S. market as well, as mechanical scale sales shrunk in the U.S.

Ricardo Haegler acquired full rights to the Toledo Scale operation in Brazil including the existing plant and the right to use the Toledo Scale name. Even today, a small market remains for the mechanical scale line, mostly in Latin America. A few Toledo mechanical scales—and parts for all of them—are still being produced by the independent firm, *Toledo Do Brasil*, in Sao Paulo.

The sale was closed on February 15, 1989. That same day Toledo Scale Corporation's new Board of Directors was announced. The board was composed of William Recker and Richard Duch from Mettler's U.S. operation, Steve Perry of Toledo Scale, Dr. Hermann Vodicka and Friedrich Ort from Mettler Switzerland.

Hermann Vodicka was president of the combined companies. Steve Perry was named president of the U.S. company reporting to Vodicka. Ben Dillon was named vice president and general manager of heavy capacity weighing and systems, and John Robechek vice president and general manager of light capacity weighing and components.

Steve Perry's excellent leadership at Toledo Scale had caught the attention of high-level management recruiters. A year or two later, he was recruited away. Ben Dillon was named president of the U.S. operation to replace Perry, and John Robechek was named Executive Vice President.

Dillon proved to be a popular and successful leader. He watched the bottom line closely. When an executive would suggest that his operation take on a task he didn't believe worth doing he would say, "I'm not going to pay for that". And he didn't.

He had a way of quickly getting to the heart of a matter. When he met with anyone who lacked support information, Dillon could somehow tell. He would stare for a moment, then exclaim, "Bullshit!"

Dillon's natural impatience caused him to follow the MBWA rule…Management By Walking Around. At one time or another, virtually every manager and supervisor in the company was surprised when Dillon would show up and ask an unexpected question. If he tried to dance around an answer, he would get the stare, followed by, "Bullshit!"

There was never any malice. It was just his way of letting someone know the answer couldn't be supported and he knew it. Yet he remained well liked and popular with everyone, all the way down to the workers on the production floor.

He became well known for his favorite expletive, even in Switzerland. Yet everyone who worked with him soon learned it was a very good idea to have their act together when they met with him.

Dillon presided at a monthly Product Development Steering Committee meeting where the progress of new products was discussed. Every department was represented. If progress was lacking, discussions to iron out problems were thorough, serious and complete. However, when Dillon was pleased with the progress, he would begin to tease people. Everybody got their turn. But he often enjoyed teasing Robechek, especially about his being a Harvard man since he knew Robechek was shy about it.

At one meeting, he was in rare form. When a subject came up he would turn to Robechek and regularly ask, "What do you think about that, Harvard?"

Dillon had to leave that meeting early for another appointment. When he left the conference room, everyone looked at each other with a smile and shook their heads. Ken Peters turned to Robechek and said, "He's a piece of work, isn't he?" They all enjoyed working with him.

Hermann Vodicka was Dillon's boss. Vodicka headed the combined companies and ran Mettler's European operation as well. Since both Mettler and Toledo had well established identities in Europe, Vodicka put the two names together in Europe, calling it METTLER TOLEDO. The U.S. company kept the Toledo Scale identity using the signature, "TOLEDO Scales & Systems".

In the United States, Toledo Scale was by far the best-known scale brand name. The U.S. management did not want to lose the marketing power of the biggest brand name in the industry. They believed that their powerful brand name was worth a fortune. Toledo "owned" the scale category. At the same time they recognized there should be a clear, visible connection with Mettler. Consequently, they recommended the identity be changed to TOLEDO SCALE, a Mettler Toledo Company.

The recommendation was rejected by the Swiss owners.

Vodicka announced a single brand global strategy. Toledo Scale would become METTLER TOLEDO, as would every other group with a separate identity...with one exception.

The only exception was the Ohaus Corporation, fully owned by Mettler Toledo. Ohaus manufactures and markets balances and scales from their headquarters in Florham Park, New Jersey. Since Ohaus balances competed in the marketplace with Mettler balances, Vodicka chose not to change their name.

Ohaus balances and scales are still manufactured and sold under the Ohaus brand name with no visible public connection to Mettler Toledo. A few Ohaus brand products are manufactured for them in Mettler Toledo's Worthington, Ohio plant alongside Mettler Toledo brand products.

Toledo Scale had been an international company since the Theobald era early in the century, with operations in most major parts of the world...including Australia, Canada, much of Europe, Mexico, South and Central America and the People's Republic of China. With Mettler's greater strength in Europe, Africa, the Near East and Pacific Rim, the combination became even more global in scope.

Mettler Toledo now had manufacturing plants in seven nations around the world, with sales and service companies in eleven more. These sales and service companies were complemented by established trading alliances with general agents in many parts of the world.

To serve these wider markets the company was organized in two parts. Mettler-Toledo GmbH with headquarters in Greifensee, Switzerland, served Europe, Africa, the Near East and the Pacific Rim. Mettler-Toledo, Inc. served all the Americas and Australia out of Worthington, Ohio.

In 1992 at Vodicka's order, the Toledo Scale name was officially changed to METTLER TOLEDO all over the world...including the United States. Thus Ben Dillon became the last president of Toledo Scale Corporation...and overnight became the first president of Mettler-Toledo, Inc.

For the first time since it was founded in 1901, Toledo Scale lost its separate, highly recognized brand identity...a valuable identity it had carried for more than nine-tenths of the 20th century.

After 91 years, the powerful Toledo Scale brand name and identity were officially ordered to be dropped by its new Swiss owners.

CHAPTER 33

"Toledo Scale doesn't exist any more!"

U.S. management followed instructions. They did their best to use the new name everywhere. No budget was provided to support the name change, which made the task even more difficult. It simply began to appear in all company communications. A "sidebar" was added to trade journal product ads in 1992 and '93 to help explain the change in names. The marketing communications efforts began to make slow progress in establishing the new identity.

At Mettler-Toledo, Inc., Leo Champlin in the law department kept track of company trademarks. He regularly published a list of current trademarks owned by the company. The marketing communications agency noticed that "Honest Weight" was missing from the list. They queried Champlin. His reply stated, "The trademark 'Honest Weight' was abandoned due to non-use in 1993."

This valuable trademark, that for most of the century helped build the company's high public awareness, was simply "abandoned", Champlin wrote.

By 1994, awareness/preference studies showed that the name Mettler Toledo was beginning to be recognized, running in 7th or 8th place among all scale companies. The Toledo name by itself was still way ahead at the top position...the most recognized name by far, even though it hadn't been used for several years. It continued to survive on its own.

Meanwhile, Hermann Vodicka was promoted to a different position within Ciba-Geigy. Robert F. Spoerry was named to replace him as president of Mettler Toledo. As a Mettler executive, Spoerry had been instrumental in the acquisition of Toledo Scale. He continued Vodicka's policies. He continued to endorse the name change and the single-brand strategy. And Spoerry was not happy with the progress being made in the U.S. operation on the identity.

Even after four years, Mettler Toledo's distributors and field organization still were seen to resist the name change. Most did not favor it at all. As independent businessmen, they could be led but not easily dictated to.

Some simply ignored the directive, continuing to identify themselves as Toledo Scale distributors. Their customers knew the Toledo Scale name well, but not the name Mettler. A few distributors continued to use the Honest Weight slogan and the T-balance logo on their service trucks, stationery and invoices. For the most part, it looked as if they were waiting to see what might happen.

Legendary Toledo Scale retail salesman Jack Dee visited the operations in Columbus for the first time since his retirement to California. Almost 90-years-old, Dee was accompanied on his tour by another retiree, his old friend Ed Quertinmont. As they drove up to the Aftermarket facility in Worthington, Dee saw something that powerfully reminded him of his successful career.

A sign on the building read, "Red Carpet Welcome to Jack Dee". The facility was managed by Gary Wilkins who had helped process Jack's orders years previously. Wilkins had arranged for a large red carpet to be laid up the steps to the entranceway. When Dee entered the building, he was greeted with applause by the staff. He was still full of verve and pep, but was clearly moved.

Dee died a few years later, well into his 90s.

Ben Dillon had been wanting to do other things for some time. When he sold Masstron, he had earned enough to be able to afford whatever he wanted to do. But his duties with Toledo Scale didn't give him the time to do them. His job required him to travel all over the world, and he had had enough. So he took early retirement at the end of 1994. Still in his mid 50s, he looked forward to the years ahead.

At the time he sold Masstron to Toledo, Dillon had agreed to
remain three years to help the transition. Before the three years
were up, Perry left and he became president of Toledo Scale which
added more years to his tenure. But now he was eager to move on
with his own agenda.

Dillon was born on a farm near Logansport, Indiana…a farm
that had been homesteaded in 1844 by his maternal great-grand-
father. The farm had been in his family for 150 years, and the
family continued to run it. Dillon loved to work on the
farm…especially with the heavy farm machinery.

He had a fondness for powerful machines. This included those
powerful machines that ran in the Indianapolis 500 every year. He
bought an interest in Tasman Motor Sports, located in nearby
Dublin, Ohio, and became a director of the company. Tasman is
led by veteran racer Steve Horn.

The following May, Tasman had a car in the 1995 Indianapolis 500 that featured a Honda engine…the first one to race at
Indianapolis. The car was very fast. It was leading the race with ten
laps to go and looked like a sure winner. Then a yellow, caution
flag held everyone in position.

When the yellow flag was removed, driver Scott Goodyear ille-
gally sped past the pace car. The resulting penalty cost him the
lead and he lost the race. To be so close, and to lose because of their
driver's error was hard to take. Dillon was devastated, as was the
whole Tasman team.

Within months of joining Tasman Motor Sports, Dillon's team
would have won the Indianapolis 500 but for the mistake of an
over-eager driver. Though a major achievement, it was but small
consolation.

A month before he retired, his friends arranged for a large
retirement party where they called up the ghosts of Dillon's Past,
Present and Future to lightly review his life and career. Several
hundreds of his coworkers and friends attended. Many had traveled far to be there. Affection for him was clearly evident. He retired with a smashing party. A baseball fan all his life, he quoted

Lou Gehrig in his response. "Tonight," he said, "I feel like the luckiest man on the face of the earth."

Executive vice president John Robechek replaced Dillon as president on January 1, 1995. Robechek was eminently qualified by experience, temperament and education. At his request, he had transferred to Toledo Scale from Reliance shortly after the move to Columbus. He possessed an undergraduate degree from Cornell and a prestigious MBA from Harvard. And he had managed many different functions, successful in all of them. He was warm and friendly. The succession went smoothly.

In May, Spoerry attended the 1996 Food Marketing Institute trade show in Chicago where the company had a large display of all their retail equipment. Before the show opened, the company traditionally held a recognition dinner for distributors who were there to work the show and meet their customers. At the dinner, most distributors casually responded to their individual recognition with their habitual mention of "Toledo" or "Toledo Scale" rather than Mettler Toledo.

When he was called upon to speak, Spoerry took strong exception to the Toledo Scale mentions. He is a relatively young top executive, appearing to be in his mid 40s, bespectacled and slightly built. Some claim he displays the awkward appearance and manner of a classic, European college professor.

Quite fluent in English, he's usually soft-spoken. He is not the effective public speaker typical of today's top business executive. But this day he spoke firmly. Prior to launching into his prepared remarks he spontaneously said, "Let me make it clear…you represent *Mettler* Toledo. *Toledo Scale doesn't exist any more!* It hasn't for over four years. I don't want to hear any more about Toledo Scale. It's Mettler Toledo!"

U.S. management, the marketing communications agency, and the MarCom manager, Tom Quertinmont, did all they could to follow the Swiss directives and support the name change. They insisted that everyone use the METTLER TOLEDO signature and elaborate logo. They published and distributed the ways in which they should be used. They eliminated all uses of the Toledo Scale name and corrected those who continued to use it.

In spite of their efforts, they were concerned that Spoerry blamed them for the slow pace at which the Mettler Toledo name was being recognized.

Internal efforts increased. Yet many distributors continued to resist. They saw only disadvantages to their own business. Their customers knew the old name well...not the new one.

In the field they still often presented themselves as representing Toledo Scale...they had no real connection with Mettler lab balances nor did a vast majority of their customers. And in spite of the name, they were not authorized to sell Mettler Toledo balances or instruments.

Paul Werth Associates, a Columbus public relations firm, was given an assignment to conduct a Corporate Image Study for Mettler Toledo. Among the conclusions stated in their December 13, 1995 report they wrote, "There is no evidence to indicate that Mettler Toledo's single brand strategy has taken hold: there is much equity in traditional brand names, especially Toledo Scale. The Mettler Toledo name is confused with Toledo Scale."

It simply wasn't working.

Meanwhile, Ciba-Geigy was cleaning house to prepare for a $27 billion merger with Sandoz AG. The two later combined under the name Novartis. In October Ciba-Geigy announced plans to float Mettler Toledo in a public share offering.

The news sparked a flood of unsolicited offers from prospective buyers. The best offer came from AEA Investors, with headquarters in New York City. AEA Investors is an American investment fund founded in the 1960s as a private investment vehicle for wealthy Americans such as the Rockefellers, Mellons, DuPonts and Harrimans.

AEA Investors specializes in leveraged buyouts of small and medium-sized companies. They discovered that their most useful investors were not the advisors of wealthy families as they had anticipated, but retired large-company chief executives.

These men could come up with the capital needed and lend their talents to the boards of the acquired companies. Sitting on the boards, their management skills could help build acquired companies into industry leaders before reselling them or taking them public.

In April 1996, Ciba-Geigy agreed to sell Mettler Toledo to AEA Investors for $769.2 million. Ownership changed hands on October 15. Named Mettler-Toledo International, Inc., it was now an American-owned company incorporated in Delaware and reporting results in U.S. dollars. Yet headquarters remained in Greifensee, Switzerland.

AEA did indeed choose people from their group of retired chief executives to sit on the board. Phillip Caldwell, former Chairman of Ford Motor Company, was named Chairman of Mettler-Toledo International. Among other prestigious retired chief executives named to sit on the Mettler Toledo board were Reginald Jones, former Chairman of General Electric, and John Macomber, former Chairman of Pfizer. Mettler Toledo president Robert Spoerry was also named to the board.

In early 1997, Spoerry ordered a major change in the U.S. operation. He gave directions for a complete management shakeup and cultural change in the marketing structure to emulate the structure in place in Europe.

What's more, the U.S. lab balance and instrument group would close and sell the valuable, largely empty building in Hightstown, New Jersey, and merge their operations into the Worthington, Ohio headquarters. And since the Worthington building was already too crowded, headquarters would be moved to a new building in Polaris, a suburban area north of Columbus.

In the new structure, management was split into two groups, a Marketing Organization (MO) and a Producing Organization (PO). Retail and industrial POs were established in the Worthington and Columbus plants under the direction of Mettler-Toledo, Inc. president John Robechek, now also titled "Division Head—Mettler Toledo Industrial/Retail-Americas (MTIRA)."

The POs were assigned a global orientation. The scales they produced would be sold all over the world. They had their own marketing groups who were designed to serve not only North American needs but also the needs of global markets. They would work with other POs throughout the world and learn their special needs.

Vice President Ken Peters was named to head the new MO, given the title "General Manager, North American Marketing Organization." At the title suggests, he was made responsible for marketing in North America only...not globally as in the PO's. At the same time the former Canadian company was totally integrated into the North American MO. Assembly operations started in Canada in 1910 and the Toledo Scale Company of Canada had been incorporated as a separate company in 1921.

Peters wrote, "I would like to add some clarity on one specific point. As we have said in earlier announcements, the Canadian business will be totally integrated into the North American Marketing Organization. Therefore you will no longer see a single, separate Canadian Company. Instead you will find that all of the Canadian operations have been absorbed into other functional or business area groups."

In April 1997, 15 individual teams called Delta Teams were established. The team members were told that they should begin designing the new MO and the newest PO in the Worthington plant. Of the 91 people assigned to the separate teams, seven were distributors and only one was not an employee or a distributor.

Jan Robie, president of Mettler Toledo's marketing communications agency, was a member of the Brand Awareness Team. As a contribution to help the company implement their plans, the agency did not bill her time for the countless hours she served on the Delta team.

Several lab group employees who accepted a transfer from New Jersey were assigned to Delta teams as well. It soon became clear that of the almost 60 people in the New Jersey operation, only 11 were willing to relocate to Columbus. Apparently most didn't want to leave their homes in metropolitan New York. Many were coastal types and didn't want to live in "fly-over" country.

Executives from the lab group moved to Columbus since laboratory products were now a part of the industrial MO. There was culture shock all around once they arrived, especially caused by those who were moved into slots in which they had no experience since they were unrelated to the lab business.

Columbus area staff employees were told the organizational structure would start from scratch...even to the point that the headquarters would move to a new suburban building about ten miles away. Everyone would be required to accept a different job than they now held.

This news caused quite a bit of apprehension. What kind of job might they be offered? Would it be something they were already competent to do...or must they learn something entirely new? In spite of the positive spin put on the news, many people worried about their future.

In an attempt to dispel all the rumors and keep everyone advised of the progress being made in the MO and the move to a new headquarters building, Ken Peters set up a toll-free telephone number. Employees were told they could call it and get a freshly recorded message with updated information from Peters every Wednesday.

He recorded a new message every week for several months. The weekly message was intended to reassure people, keeping them current on transfers, new hires, building delays and more.

Current vendors were concerned as well. When any company sweeps through their organization with a new broom this large, vendors were often changed as a matter of course.

In June, the new organizational structures were announced. They were indeed totally different. Now the new jobs were identified but not described since the actual duties were not yet in place. None of the former jobs existed in their old form anymore. People were usually given one or two job options, not really knowing what they would be expected to do.

If they didn't like these options they were told that was all the choices they had. Their previous job didn't exist anymore. The not-so-subtle message appeared to be that they could always re-sign and try to find a job more to their liking.

By January 1998, the new MOs and POs were in place with most of the slots filled. A few important jobs remained. Several people had resigned, yet most slots were filled with internal moves. New hires filled many of the rest. As an example, former market-ing communications manager Tom Quertinmont became part of the industrial MO and a new marketing communications man-ager was hired.

Also in January Robechek announced that sales in 1997 re-sulted in "an excellent year!" He explained that, "For the full year we were 7% ahead of the previous year but 3% behind our goal. I am really proud of what we accomplished together in 1997, and I hope you feel the same way."

The company started healthy in 1998. Still there was concern about what effect the massive structural shakeup would have on sales the rest of the year. As one wag observed, "It's the ultimate example of the Peter Principle...*everybody* has been promoted to their level of incompetence."

Just over a year after buying Mettler Toledo, AEA Investors took the company public. On November 13, 1997, Mettler-To-ledo International, Inc. completed its initial public equity offering in the United States. It sold 6.67 million primary shares at $14 per share. These shares are listed on the New York Stock Exchange under the symbol MTD.

On December 8, 1997, Merrill Lynch published a booklet about Mettler-Toledo International, Inc. titled "The Power of Bal-ance". In their list of Fundamental Highlights they wrote:

- Mettler Toledo is the world's leading supplier of precision weighing instruments.
- Only supplier to operate in all major geographic regions and in all major served markets.
- *Attractive combination of "ivory tower" intellect in lab business and "street smarts" of industrial and retail settings.*

One local reader observed, "I always thought that pimps and drug dealers were the kind of people that were usually credited with 'street smarts'. Now Merrill Lynch seems to have put us in the same category. Their input must have come from the lab people direct from their Swiss 'ivory tower'. But then, Teutonic people have never been known for their humility."

The Blade published a story on December 16 written by senior business writer, Homer Brickey. The headline was, "City name still carries weight on stock exchange". In part, the story read:

"Toledo Scale is back on the Big Board. Oh, it's not exactly called Toledo Scale anymore—it's called Mettler-Toledo International, Inc., and its headquarters are in Switzerland. And for the second time in the last three decades, stock of the Toledo-born company is traded on the New York Stock Exchange.

Toledo Scale made its debut on NYSE on July 24, 1964, with the ticker symbol TDS. In its new incarnation, the Mettler Toledo scale company went on the Big Board November 14, with the ticker symbol MTD. They had sales last year of $850 million. Mettler Toledo styles itself as a U.S. company that happens to have its headquarters in Griefensee, Switzerland. If that sounds a bit confusing, it's only because much has happened to the firm in the last 30 years.

For many years, Toledo Scale was one of Toledo's best known exports and trademarks—ranking right up their with Jeeps and Champion Spark Plugs. Of course, all three trademarks ended up in other hands.

After all that has happened to Toledo Scale and to Mettler Toledo, it's a miracle the name 'Toledo' survives at all. But then again, it's such a grand old name."

By spring, Mettler-Toledo International shares had risen to the low $20s on the New York Stock Exchange. The IPO appeared to be successful. Robert Spoerry was then elected Chairman of the Board of Mettler-Toledo International in March 1998. He continued as the company's president and CEO.

As Chairman, Spoerry replaced Phillip Caldwell who served as Chairman during the time Mettler-Toledo International was being established as a public company. Caldwell wanted to reduce his involvement. He remained a Mettler Toledo Director.

CHAPTER 34

The Antique Scale Market

In the spring of 1998 the company offered a buy-out package to employees who qualified by age and experience…a group that happened to be made up largely of former middle-management employees of Toledo Scale. It appeared that they were not perceived as willing to accept the new culture and a "benevolent genocide" took place for those painted with the Toledo Scale brush.

With a few exceptions, only Robechek, Peters and a few other former Toledo Scale people in top management remained…largely those who implemented the MO/PO structure and the new culture. Most who left were replaced with outside hires. At the same time, many long-time vendors were replaced with new ones.

Veteran Toledo Scale employees probably wished they were valued as highly as old Toledo Scale products, which were commanding high prices in the antique market.

The original fan and cylinder mechanical retail scales bearing Toledo's name and the slogan "No Springs—Honest Weight" became prized possessions among collectors and antique dealers. They began to sell for as much as $800…three or four times as much as when they were new.

"The Toledos have become very popular in the last few years," said T. S. Carley, vice president of the International Society of Antique Scale Collectors. "Of course, no one is interested in the new ones, but the old ones that were made in Toledo have become very big, particularly on the West coast," he said.

John Hellman, a developer and dealer from Lakewood, Colorado, has accumulated over 2,500 scales. He said, "The large Toledo Scales for butcher shops have replaced antique slot machines as the rage among West coast collectors. I've sold them to restaurants seeking an old fashioned look. The smaller scales are popular with designers decorating kitchens. They go for as much as $150," he said.

By 1998, the antique scale marketplace had fragmented into two groups according to Len Nosal, an enthusiastic scale collector and restorer in White Lake, Michigan. Nosal is such an enthusiast that he chose the e-mail address, Scalefreak@aol.com.

"The first group is composed of hard-core scale collectors," Nosal said. "These people are more likely to be interested in the history of scales and scale companies. They appreciate scales as antiques…as artifacts of a bygone era. They take the position that whatever the condition of the scale, it ought to be left in that condition and not restored beyond cleaning it of grime and putting it in working condition." He reports that any further restoration is considered to be something akin to a sacrilege. "Yet this group will seldom pay more than $500 for an antique scale, no matter how good its condition," he said.

"The second group is attracted to certain types of scales for the way they look, primarily early computing scales. They especially admire the more ornate examples dating from the late 1800s to the early teens," Nosal said. "They consider these the 'golden age of computing scales' when they were embellished with ornate castings, fancy pinstriped decoration, colorful decals and varnish transfers."

He explained, "This camp pretty much feels that anything goes. They're likely to refinish every scale they get their hands on, using automotive lacquers in all colors of the rainbow. Pinstriping is applied, sometimes in a period style but often regrettably in the style usually seen on custom cars. Nickel plated trim is stripped to the underlying brass, polished and lacquered or even gold plated which requires no lacquer to resist tarnishing. When executed tastefully such restoration can produce scales of great beauty which are coveted by persons who may have no interest in collecting scales but who want an object of home decor," he said.

"At the extreme fringe of this group are professional scale dealers who do such restoration for profit," Nosal declared. "They tend also to be dealers in cash registers, slot machines and other coin-operated devices which get similar treatment. They often have many of the ornate parts reproduced to replace missing parts. But they also transform more common scale models into something they never were, basically creating fakes. That's why these scales are often seen at Coin-Op shows."

"At an auction," he continued, "when a desirable scale is up for bid, the hard-core purist is easily outbid by the advocate of restoration who has in mind the greater potential value of the scale after it's restored. Scale restorers have no trouble finding buyers willing to pay much more for their refinished scales than for the same scale in its original condition. Some of the rarer scales have been seen priced as high as $8,000!"

So Nosal sees the market for retail scales that have not been restored topping out at about $500 while restored scales—even if not authentically restored—going as high as $8,000.

CHAPTER 35

Moving On

The Paul Werth Corporate Image Study had stated, "There is no evidence to indicate that Mettler Toledo's single-brand strategy has taken hold." In spite of this report, it's likely that Spoerry will never abandon the strategy as unworkable in the American market.

By the time of the public offering, Mettler Toledo's name recognition had moved up in awareness studies, but was still way behind the name Toledo Scale. An unaided recall awareness study for "Scales & Weighing Systems" by *Purchasing* magazine in 1997 showed the name Toledo or Toledo Scale was mentioned by their readers more than three times as often as the name Mettler Toledo.

After having been dropped for more than five years, the Toledo Scale name remained the single most recognized scale brand name by far. Like ol' man river, the name just keeps rollin' along. The separate Toledo Scale identity kept hanging on with customers and the public...much to Spoerry's chagrin.

In the national television coverage of the 1997 World Series for example, sportscaster Bob Costas announced a Cleveland relief pitcher with the instinctive remark, "He's a big guy—he 'tips the Toledo' at 265 pounds!"

Before Ciba-Geigy acquired Toledo Scale, the U.S. lab business for Mettler had their headquarters in Hightstown, New Jersey. Hightstown is near Princeton where Mettler had located their first U.S. office because they believed that a Princeton address carried extra prestige.

Mettler balances and instruments are sold through catalog houses for the most part. Executives from the lab group had no experience marketing industrial scales to American industry. They didn't know the industrial scale products or the markets.

Once in Columbus, several complained about what the former industrial marketing group had been doing...and pushed marketing methods they had used for the lab group. A Swiss transplant assigned to head marketing services didn't know industrial scale products or the markets either, and had no experience with them.

As one transferred lab manager took control of his industrial scale group, his marketing observations to them sounded war-like and quite bloodthirsty. Speaking about small competitive scale companies he said, "I don't want to just chase all those little competitive dogs away from our food dish, I want to bite their heads off!"

He assigned his people to a Strike Force, then several sub-Task Forces. It gave the impression that he was organizing a blitzkrieg to attack customers.

The New Jersey people had hoped to be perceived in Columbus as representing the intellectual Swiss and sophisticated New York cultures. At first a few did see them that way. As time passed, perception changed. A number of people who had to work with them were heard to observe, "They're just typical New Yorkers...know-it-all, arrogant snobs."

They often gave the impression that they lacked respect for Midwesterners and anyone who chose to live in America's heartland, displaying disdain for most of their Columbus "street smart" associates...especially Toledo Scale people. Responding to a question about who should be invited to a briefing, one is reported to have said, "Don't involve him...he doesn't know what he's doing."

This executive—and a second transplant—lasted a little over a year. Sales were down in the industrial scale area.

The move to the new headquarters building at 1900 Polaris Parkway was made a week before Thanksgiving in 1998. Though the building is far enough north to be out of Franklin County in Delaware County, it still uses a Columbus address. Mettler Toledo leased the first, fifth and sixth floors in the new six-floor building. A consolidated training center is located on the first floor. The fifth and sixth floors contain all headquarters activities including the complete North American marketing organization.

The office arrangement is an "open environment" intended to encourage a team concept. There are no separate offices...or even any Dilbert-like cubicles. Everyone sits facing each other at an angle in individual, alternating pods each containing a computer. There are meeting areas scattered throughout each floor for when people need to talk face to face.

In early 1999, Tom Quertinmont accepted an early retirement offer. Except for a few specialized engineers, he was the last Toledo Scale employee who had moved from Toledo to Columbus in 1976. Tom's father, Ed Quertinmont, had joined the company 61 years previously in 1938. It was one of many families in which several generations served the company. It helped mark the end of the Toledo Scale era.

Then in March 1999, Spoerry announced another change. He consolidated the industrial and retail divisions for the Americas and Europe into one global division, naming Lucas Braunschweiler to head it. Braunschweiler had been head of the European operations but would now move to Columbus to head the global operation. Robechek now reported to him. Three months later, Robechek resigned.

Overall, the company was doing quite well. Mettler-Toledo International, Inc. reported net sales of over $935 million in their 1998 Annual Report with an 8% growth in local currencies from the previous year. Earnings-per-share were $1.19, a 45% increase. No dividends were paid. The Annual Report stated: "The company does not have a dividend policy. To date, the company has never paid any dividends on common stock. The company has used its cash flow to reduce debt and make acquisitions."

Many smaller companies had been acquired in the scientific instrument field to better serve the growing pharmaceutical market.

The laboratory market now represented 38% of net sales with the traditional industrial/retail market still providing the majority.

By 1998, Mettler-Toledo International was a totally different, truly global company. Europe provided 46% of the business, the Americas 43%, with Asia and other areas providing 11%. 1999 first-quarter results showed continued growth. In his April 30, 1999 memo to employees, Ken Peters reported that his marketing group had exceeded the bookings seasonal budget by over 40%, and the billings budget by more than 15%.

Every area did well…except for industrial business, which missed their budget by over 10%. He wrote: "The industrial business is the largest in the MO, and also has the highest profit margins. So when that business does not perform, it is quite difficult for the rest of the business areas to make up the margin difference. There are several actions underway to improve this segment of the business and we are confident that it will perform at a higher level in the second half of the year."

One long-time employee offered this possible explanation: "The Toledo Scale brand name remains strongest in American industry. When the Swiss management changed the name, I doubt they considered the long useful life of Toledo mechanical dial scales. Remember, many thousands of Toledo mechanical scales with the familiar large TOLEDO—HONEST WEIGHT dial remain in use in plants and factories all over the world. And person-weigher scales are still before the public in banks, health clubs and supermarkets everywhere. All these Toledo dial scales keep the name alive."

He said, "Even though these mechanical scales were largely made obsolete years ago by electronic scales, they're kept in use because they continue to weigh accurately year after year. And often an accurate weight is all they need. I still see many in use that even display NO SPRINGS as well as HONEST WEIGHT on the dial…which means these are probably more than 50 years old. They've become part of our industrial culture. So thousands of people still see the name shouted from the large, easily-recognized dial in plants and factories everywhere."

The electronic scales that replaced mechanical scales do not enjoy this quick recognition advantage. On electronic instruments, the brand name appears in small type on a comparatively small, box-like electronic indicator. No longer can anyone see the scale brand name on a large dial from 50 feet away.

On top of that, electronic indicators from all scale manufacturers look very much alike, making it more difficult to differentiate one brand from another. This makes it even harder to establish a unique, recognizable Mettler Toledo brand.

"After all," he concluded, "Toledo mechanical scales were built to last. They're rugged. They work reliably with minimum maintenance for decades. So the TOLEDO brand name will more than likely continue to live all by itself for years to come, whether they like it or not."

The 70-year-old oil paintings by Georges LaChance of Toledo craftsmen, Henry Theobald and Hugh Bennett had been hanging in the Worthington headquarters since the company relocated to Columbus. They were a constant reminder of Toledo Scale's heritage and Mettler Toledo didn't want to be connected to the Toledo Scale name. They didn't know what to do with the paintings.

Just prior to the Polaris move, the company made a decision to donate the paintings along with Toledo Scale's complete historical archives to the Lucas County/Maumee Valley Historical Society. Since Toledo Scale played a major part in 20th century Toledo history, the Society was glad to accept the donation.

The Historical Society is in the process of collecting material for a museum of 20th century Toledo area industrial developments. Since a home for the collection does not exist yet, a "virtual museum" has been created on the internet by the Society, the Toledo-Lucas County Public Library and the University of Toledo. Called "Toledo's Attic," the paintings may now be seen on www.history.utoledo.edu/attic.

With the donation of the complete archives and paintings, Mettler Toledo severed the last connection with the Toledo Scale name.

It's been over a century now since Allen DeVilbiss, Jr. invented the automatic computing pendulum scale device that became the first Toledo Scale.

For over nine-tenths of the 20th Century the brand name TOLEDO appeared alone on scales, weight printers and other related devices. And for the first two-thirds of the century, Toledo Scale Company was a force in its home town of Toledo, Ohio.

The company was one of Toledo's top ten employers, providing jobs to as many as 1,500 people in local manufacturing and thousands more indirectly all over the globe. Today, there is almost no evidence the company was ever in Toledo, Ohio.

Still, a group of former Toledo Scale employees led by Joe La Coney, Barb Siler, Dick Lause, Ray West and others organized an updated "Quarter Century Club" for anybody who ever worked at Toledo Scale. The group meets together several times a year to share reminiscences, entirely at their own expense.

More than a hundred ex-employees and their families get together every summer for a picnic with fellowship, fun and games. Several employees who transferred to Columbus in 1976 including Tom and Mary Jane Siegler still make the trek to Toledo to see old friends almost a quarter century after the move. The summer picnic and fall banquet are always well attended.

The original building that came with the DeVilbiss Computing Scale Company purchase on the corner of Albion and Bishop streets was torn down many years ago. The lot is now vacant. Theobald's large home on his estate at 422 West Woodruff has also been torn down. The land now contains a medical structure that's part of the nearby Mercy Hospital complex.

Hugh Bennett's home at 2247 Collingwood Boulevard was torn down and the land used as a parking lot for the Red Cross.

And of course the long dreamed of scale manufacturing plant build in 1939 at 5225 Telegraph Road was completely destroyed by fire in 1985.

Oddly enough, the only original structure that remains is the four-story building at the corner of Monroe and Albion Streets built in 1901 by Rakestraw for Theobald. This plant served as the main Toledo Scale factory until 1939.

Though intact, this structure is showing its age. All the signage is gone…there is no indication anywhere on the building that it was ever the factory and first home of Toledo Scale. Virtually everything that identified Toledo Scale with Toledo, Ohio has disappeared.

Everything, that is, except for the many thousands of retail and mechanical dial scales still in use just about everywhere on the face of the earth. Dials that read "TOLEDO—Peso Exacto, TO-LEDO—Poids Honnête, TOLEDO—Pesagens Exactas," and other translations.

For many years to come, they will display the proud heritage of "TOLEDO—HONEST WEIGHT" throughout the civilized world. Like General Douglas MacArthur—and Harris McIntosh—it seems that the Toledo Scale name will never die, but over time, just…fade away.